KIDD'S METHOD OF QUELLING A MUTINY

Moore, his gunner, accused Kidd of having ruined them all, when the pirate captain seized a bucket and with it broke the man's skull so that he died the next day.

The Romance of Piracy

THE STORY OF THE ADVENTURES, FIGHTS, AND DEEDS OF
DARING OF PIRATES, FILIBUSTERS, AND BUCCANEERS
FROM THE EARLIEST TIMES TO THE PRESENT DAY

BY
E. Keble Chatterton, B.A.Oxon.
Author of "The Romance of the Ship" "Fore and Aft, the
Story of the Fore and Aft Rig" "Through Holland in
the *Vivette*" "Sailing Ships and Their Story"
&c., &c.

WITH SIXTEEN ILLUSTRATIONS

HERITAGE BOOKS
2012

HERITAGE BOOKS
AN IMPRINT OF HERITAGE BOOKS, INC.

Books, CDs, and more—Worldwide

For our listing of thousands of titles see our website
at
www.HeritageBooks.com

A Facsimile Reprint
Published 2012 by
HERITAGE BOOKS, INC.
Publishing Division
100 Railroad Ave. #104
Westminster, Maryland 21157

Originally published: London
Seeley, Service & Co. Limited
38 Great Russell Street
1914

Copyright © 2003 Heritage Books, Inc.

— Publisher's Notice —
In reprints such as this, it is often not possible to remove blemishes from the original. We feel the contents of this book warrant its reissue despite these blemishes and hope you will agree and read it with pleasure.
This book starts on page 13; nothing is missing.

International Standard Book Numbers
Paperbound: 978-0-7884-2298-0
Clothbound: 978-0-7884-9420-8

CONTENTS

CHAP.		PAGE
I.	THE EARLIEST PIRATES	17
II.	THE NORTH SEA PIRATES	29
III.	PIRACY IN THE EARLY TUDOR TIMES	37
IV.	THE CORSAIRS OF THE SOUTH	48
V.	THE WASPS AT WORK	60
VI.	GALLEYS AND GALLANTRY	70
VII.	PIRACY IN ELIZABETHAN TIMES	79
VIII.	ELIZABETHAN SEAMEN AND TURKISH PIRATES	89
IX.	THE STUART NAVY GOES FORTH AGAINST THE "PYRATS"	101
X.	THE GOOD SHIP *EXCHANGE* OF BRISTOL	114
XI.	A WONDERFUL ACHIEVEMENT	126
XII.	THE GREAT SIR HENRY MORGAN	136
XIII.	"BLACK BEARD" TEACH	151
XIV.	THE STORY OF CAPTAIN KIDD	162
XV.	THE EXPLOITS OF CAPTAIN AVERY	172
XVI.	A "GENTLEMAN" OF FORTUNE	183
XVII.	PAUL JONES, PIRATE AND PRIVATEER	196

CONTENTS

CHAP.		PAGE
XVIII. A NOTORIOUS AMERICAN PIRATE		210
XIX. THE LAST OF THE ALGERINE CORSAIRS		217
XX. PIRATES OF THE PERSIAN GULF		224
XXI. THE STORY OF AARON SMITH		235
XXII. SMITH AND THE PIRATE SCHOONER		248
XXIII. PLOT AND COUNTER-PLOT		259
XXIV. CHANCE AND CIRCUMSTANCE		270
XXV. THE CRUISE OF THE *DEFENSOR DE PEDRO*		281
XXVI. THE PIRATES OF BORNEO		293
XXVII. CRUISING AMONG CHINESE PIRATES		304

LIST OF ILLUSTRATIONS

KIDD'S METHOD OF QUELLING A MUTINY	*Frontispiece*
	FACING PAGE
A NORTH SEA PIRATE	30
A VIKING'S FUNERAL	34
A DARING ATTACK	54
GALLEY SLAVES	76
SPANISH GALLEONS IN THE TIME OF ELIZABETH	80
GALLANTRY AGAINST ODDS	90
BLIGHTED HOPES	104
AMONG THE PIRATES OF ALGIERS	118
THE BITER BIT	148
A FIERCE DUEL	158
BOMBARDMENT OF ALGIERS	220
ATTACKING A PIRATE STRONGHOLD	232
A BRAVE MAN	250
THE FATE OF PIRATE MUTINEERS	256
ATTACK ON MALAY PIRATE PRAHUS	296

THE ROMANCE OF PIRACY

CHAPTER I

THE EARLIEST PIRATES

I SUPPOSE there are few words in use which at once suggest so much romantic adventure as the words pirate and piracy. You instantly conjure up in your mind a wealth of excitement, a clashing of lawless wills, and there pass before your eyes a number of desperate daredevils whose life and occupation are inseparably connected with the sea.

The very meaning of the word, as you will find on referring to a Greek dictionary, indicates one who *attempts to rob*. In classical times there was a species of Mediterranean craft which was a light, swift vessel called a *myoparo* because it was chiefly used by pirates. Since the Greek verb *peirao* means literally "to attempt," so it had the secondary meaning of "to try one's fortune in thieving on sea." Hence a *peirates* (in Greek) and *pirata* (in Latin) signified afloat the counterpart of a brigand or highwayman on land. To many minds piracy conjures up visions that go back no further than the seventeenth century: but though it is true that during that period piracy attained unheard-of heights in certain seas, yet the avocation of searobbery dates back very much further.

THE EARLIEST PIRATES

Robbery by sea is certainly one of the oldest professions in the world. I use the word profession advisedly, for the reason that in the earliest days to be a pirate was not the equivalent of being a pariah and an outcast. It was deemed just as honourable then to belong to a company of pirates as it is to-day to belong to the navy of any recognised power. It is an amusing fact that if in those days two strange ships met on the high seas, and one of them, hailing the other, inquired if she were a pirate or a trader, the inquiry was neither intended nor accepted as an insult, but a correct answer would follow. It is a little difficult in these modern days of regular steamship routes and powerful liners which have little to fear beyond fog and exceptionally heavy weather, to realise that every merchant ship sailed the seas with fear and trepidation. When she set forth from her port of lading there was little certainty that even if the ship herself reached the port of destination, her cargo would ever be delivered to the rightful receivers. The ship might be jogging along comfortably, heading well up towards her destined port, when out from the distance came a much faster and lighter vessel of smaller displacement and finer lines. In a few hours the latter would have overhauled the former, the scanty crew of the merchantman would have been thrown into the sea or pressed into the pirate's service, or else taken ashore to the pirate's haunt and sold as slaves. The rich cargo of merchandise could be sold or bartered when the land was reached, and the merchant ship sunk or left to wallow in the Mediterranean swell.

It is obvious that because the freight ship had to be big-bellied to carry the maximum cargo she was in most instances unable to run away from the swift-moving pirate except in heavy weather. But in order to possess some

THE EARLIEST PIRATES

means of defence it was not unusual for these peaceful craft to be provided with turrets of great height, from which heavy missiles could be dropped on to the attacking pirate. In the bows, in the stern and amidships these erections could easily be placed and as quickly removed. And as a further aid oars would be got out in an endeavour to accelerate the ship's speed. For whilst the pirate relied primarily on oars, the trader relied principally on sail power. Therefore in fine settled weather, with a smooth sea, the low-lying piratical craft was at its best. It could be manœuvred quickly, it could dart in and out of little bays, it could shelter close in to the shore under the lee of a friendly reef, and it was, because of its low freeboard, not easy to discern at any great distance, unless the sea was literally smooth. But all through history this type of vessel has been shown to be at a disadvantage as soon as it comes on to blow and the unruffled surface gives way to high crest and deep furrows.

It is as impossible to explain the growth of piracy as it is to define precisely the call of the sea. A man is born with a bias in favour of the sea or he is not: there is no possibility of putting that instinct into him if already he has not been endowed with that attitude. So also we know from our own personal experience, every one of us, that whilst some of our own friends fret and waste in sedentary pursuits, yet from the time they take to the sea or become explorers or colonisers they find their true *métier*. The call of the sea is the call of adventure in a specialised form. It has been said, with no little truth, that many of the yachtsmen of to-day, if they had been living in other ages, would have gone afloat as pirates or privateers. And so, if we want to find an explanation for the amazing historical fact that for century after century, in spite of all the efforts which many

THE EARLIEST PIRATES

a nation made to suppress piracy, it revived and prospered, we can only answer that, quite apart from the lust of wealth, there was at the back of it all that love of adventure, that desire for exciting incident, that hatred of monotonous security which one finds in so many natures. A distinguished British admiral remarked the other day that it was his experience that the best naval officers were usually those who as boys were most frequently getting into disfavour for their adventurous escapades. It is, at any rate, still true that unless the man or boy has in him the real spirit of adventure, the sea, whether as a sport or profession, can have but little fascination for him.

International law and the growth of navies have practically put an end to the profession of piracy, though privateering would doubtless reassert itself in the next great naval war. But if you look through history you will find that, certainly up to the nineteenth century, wherever there was a seafaring nation there too had flourished a band of pirates. Piracy went on for decade after decade in the Mediterranean till at length it became unbearable, and Rome had to take the most serious steps and use the most drastic measures to stamp out the nests of hornets. A little later you find another generation of sea-robbers growing up and acting precisely as their forefathers. Still further on in history you find the Barbarian corsairs and their descendants being an irrepressible menace to Mediterranean shipping. For four or five hundred years galleys waylaid ships of the great European nations, attacked them, murdered their crews and plundered the Levantine cargoes. Time after time were these corsairs punished: time after time they rose again. In vain did the fleets of southern Christian Europe or the ships of Elizabeth or the Jacobean navy go forth to quell them. Algiers and Tunis were veritable plague-spots in

THE EARLIEST PIRATES

regard to piracy. Right on through time the northern coast of Africa was the hotbed of pirates. Not till Admiral Lord Exmouth, in the year 1816, was sent to quell Algiers did Mediterranean piracy receive its death-blow, though it lingered on for some little time later.

But piracy is not confined to any particular nation nor to any particular sea, any more than the spirit of adventure is the exclusive endowment of any particular race. There have been notorious pirates in the North Sea as in the Mediterranean, there have been European pirates in the Orient just as there have been Moorish pirates in the English Channel. There have been British pirates on the waters of the West Indies as there have been of Madagascar. There have flourished pirates in the North, in the South, in the East and the West—in China, Japan, off the coast of Malabar, Borneo, America and so on. The species of ships are often different, the racial characteristics of the sea-rovers are equally distinct, yet there is still the same determined clashing of wills, the same desperate nature of the contests, the same exciting adventure; and in the following pages it will be manifest that in spite of differences of time and place the romance of piratical incident lives on for the reason that human nature, at its basis, is very much alike the whole world over.

But we must make a distinction between isolated and collected pirates. There is a great dissimilarity, for instance, between a pickpocket and a band of brigands. The latter work on a grander, bolder system. So it has always been with the robbers of the sea. Some have been brigands, some have been mere pickpockets. The "grand" pirates set to work on a big scale. It was not enough to lie in wait for single merchant ships: they swooped down on to seaside towns and villages, carried off by sheer force

THE EARLIEST PIRATES

the inhabitants and sold them into slavery. Whatever else of value might attract their fancy they also took away. If any important force were sent against them, the contest resolved itself not so much into a punitive expedition as a piratical war. There was nothing petty in piracy on these lines. It had its proper rules, its own grades of officers and drill. *Lestarches* was the Greek name for the captain of a band of pirates, and it was their splendid organisation, their consummate skill as fighters, that made them so difficult to quell.

I have said that piracy was regarded as an honourable profession. In the earliest times this is true. The occupation of a pirate was deemed no less worthy than a man who gained his living by fishing on the sea or hunting on land. Just as in the Elizabethan age we find the sons of some of the best English families going to sea on a roving expedition to capture Spanish treasure ships, so in classical times the Mediterranean pirates attracted to their ships adventurous spirits from all classes of society, from the most patrician to the most plebeian : the summons of the sea was as irresistible then as later on. But there were definite arrangements made for the purpose of sharing in any piratical success, so there was an incentive other than that of mere adventure which prompted men to become pirates.

To-day, if the navies of the great nations were to be withdrawn, and the policing of the seas to cease, it is pretty certain that those so disposed would presently revive piracy. Nothing is so inimical to piracy as settled peace and good government. But nothing is so encouraging to piracy as prolonged unsettlement in international affairs and weak administration. So it was that the incessant Mediterranean wars acted as a keen incentive to piracy. War breeds war, and the spirit of unrest on

THE EARLIEST PIRATES

sea affected the pirate no less than the regular fighting man. Sea-brigandage was rampant. These daring robbers went roving over the sea wherever they wished, they waxed strong, they defied opposition.

And there were special territories which these pirates preferred to others. The Liparian Isles—from about 580 B.C. to the time of the Roman Conquest—were practically a republic of Greek corsairs. Similarly the Ionians and the Lycians were notorious for piratical activities. After the period of Thucydides, Corinth endeavoured to put down piracy, but in vain. The irregularity went on until the conquest of Asia by the Romans, in spite of all the precautions that were taken. The Ægean Sea, the Pontus, the Adriatic were the happy cruising-grounds for the corsairs. The pirate-admiral or, as he was designated, *archipeirates*, with his organised fleet of assorted craft, was a deadly foe to encounter. Under his command were the myoparones, already mentioned—light and swift they darted across the sea; then there were, too, the hemiolia, which were so called because they were rowed with one and a half banks of oars; next came the two-banked biremes and the three-banked triremes, and with these four classes of ships the admiral was ready for any craft that might cross his wake. Merchantmen fled before him, warships by him were sent to the bottom: wherever he coasted there spread panic through the sea-girt towns. Even Athens itself felt the thrill of fear.

Notorious, too, were the Cretan pirates, and for a long time the Etruscan corsairs were a great worry to the Greeks of Sicily. The inhabitants of the Balearic Islands were especially famous for their piratical depredations and for their skilful methods of fighting. Wherever a fleet was sent to attack them they were able to inflict great

THE EARLIEST PIRATES

slaughter by hurling vast quantities of stones with their slings. It was only when they came to close quarters with their aggressors the Romans, and the latter's sharp javelins began to take effect, that these islanders met their match and were compelled to flee in haste to the shelter of their coves. At the period which preceded the subversion of the Roman commonwealth by Julius Cæsar, there was an exceedingly strong community of pirates at the extreme eastern end of the Mediterranean. They hailed from that territory which is just in the bend of Asia Minor and designated Cilicia. Here lived—when ashore—one of the most dangerous body of sea-rovers recorded in the pages of history. It is amazing to find how powerful these Cilicians became, and as they prospered in piracy so their numbers were increased by fellow-corsairs from their neighbours the Syrians and Pamphylians, as well as by many who came down from the shores of the Black Sea and from Cyprus. So powerful indeed became these rovers that they controlled practically the whole of the Mediterranean from east to west. They made it impossible for peaceful trading craft to venture forth, and they even defeated several Roman officers who had been sent with ships against them.

And so it went on until Rome realised that piracy had long since ceased to be anything else but a most serious evil that needed firm and instant suppression. It was the ruin of overseas trade and a terrible menace to her own territory. But the matter was at last taken in hand. M. Antonius, proprætor, was sent with a powerful fleet against these Cilician pirates; they were crushed thoroughly, and the importance of this may be gathered from the fact that on his return to Rome the conqueror was given an ovation.

In the wars between Rome and Mithradates the

THE EARLIEST PIRATES

Cilician pirates rendered the latter excellent service. The long continuance of these wars and the civil war between Marius and Sylla afforded the Cilicians a fine opportunity to increase both in numbers and strength. To give some idea of their power it is only necessary to state that not only did they take and rob all the Roman ships which they encountered, but they also voyaged among the islands and maritime provinces and plundered no fewer than 400 cities. They carried their depredations even to the mouth of the Tiber and actually took away from thence several vessels laden with corn. Bear in mind, too, that the Cilician piratical fleet was no scratch squadron of a few antique ships. It consisted of a thousand vessels, which were of great speed and very light. They were well manned by most able seamen, and fought by trained soldiers, and commanded by expert officers. They carried an abundance of arms, and neither men nor officers were lacking in daring and prowess. When again it became expedient that these Cilicians should be dealt with, it took no less a person than Pompey, assisted by fifteen admirals, to tackle them; but finally, after a few months, he was able to have the sea once more cleared of these rovers.

We can well sympathise with the merchant seamen of those days. The perils of wind and wave were as nothing compared with the fear of falling into the hands of powerful desperadoes, who not merely were all-powerful afloat but in their strong fortresses on shore were most difficult to deal with. With the Balearic Islanders in the west, the Cilicians in the east, the Carthaginians in the south, the Illyrians along the Adriatic in their low, handy liburnian galleys, there were pirates ready to encircle the whole of the Mediterranean Sea. It is worth noting—for he who reads naval history must often be struck with the fact that an

THE EARLIEST PIRATES

existing navy prevents war, but the absence of a navy brings war about—that as long as Rome maintained a strong navy piracy died down: but so soon as she neglected her sea-service piracy grew up again, commerce was interrupted both east and west, numerous illustrious Romans were captured and either ransomed or put to death, though some others were pressed into the service of the pirates themselves. By means of prisoners to work at the oars, by the addition of piratical neighbours and by mercenaries as well, a huge piratical community with a strong military and political organisation continued to prevent the development of overseas trade. This piracy was only thwarted by keeping permanent Roman squadrons always ready.

Of course there were pirates in these early times in waters other than the Mediterranean. On the west coast of Gaul the Veneti had become very powerful pirates, and you will recollect how severely they tried Cæsar, giving him more trouble than all the rest of Gaul put together. They owned such stalwart ships and were such able seamen that they proved most able enemies. During the time of the Roman Empire piracy continued also on the Black Sea and North Sea, though the Mediterranean was now for the most part safe for merchant ships. But when the power of Rome declined, so proportionately did the pirates reappear in their new strength. There was no fearful navy to oppose them, and so once more they were able to do pretty much as they liked. But we must not forget that long before this they had ceased to be regarded as the equivalent of hunters and fishermen. They were, by common agreement, what Cicero had designated "enemies of the human race": and so they continued till the nineteenth century, with only temporary intervals of inactivity.

The thousand ships which the Cilician pirates employed

THE EARLIEST PIRATES

were disposed in separate squadrons. In different places they had their own naval magazines located, and during that period already mentioned, when they were driven off the sea, they resisted capture by retreating ashore to their mountain fastnesses until such time as it was safe for them to renew their ventures afloat. When Pompey defeated them he had under him a fleet of 270 ships. As the inscription, carried in the celebration of his triumph on his return to Rome, narrated, he cleared the maritime coasts of pirates and restored the dominion of the sea to the Roman people. But the pirates could always boast of having captured two Roman prætors, and Julius Cæsar, when a youth on his way to Rhodes to pursue his studies, also fell into their hands. However, he was more lucky than many another Roman who, when captured, was hung up to the yard-arm, and the pirate ship went proudly on her way.

In the declining years of the Roman Empire the Goths came down from the north to the Mediterranean, where they got together fleets, became very powerful and crossed to Africa, made piratical raids on the coast and carried on long wars with the Romans. Presently the Saxons in the northern waters of Europe made piratical descents on to the coasts of France, Flanders and Britain. Meanwhile, in the south, the Saracens descended upon Cyprus and Rhodes, which they took, seized many islands in the Archipelago, and thence proceeded to Sicily to capture Syracuse, and finally overran the whole of Barbary from Egypt in the east to the Straits of Gibraltar in the west. From there they crossed to Spain and reduced the greater part thereof, until under Ferdinand and Isabella these Moors were driven out of Spain and compelled to settle once more on the north coast of Africa. They established themselves notably at Algiers, took to the sea, built themselves galleys and, after

THE EARLIEST PIRATES

living a civilised life in Spain for seven hundred years, became for the next three centuries a scourge of the Mediterranean, a terror to ships and men, inflicted all the cruelties which the fanaticism of the Moslem race is capable of, and cast thousands of Christians into the bonds of slavery. In many ways these terrifying Moorish pirates—of which to this day some still go afloat in their craft off the north coast of Africa—became the successors of those Cilician and other corsairs of the classical age. In due course we shall return to note the kind of piratical warfare which these expatriated Moors waged for most of three hundred years. But before we come to that period let us examine into an epoch that preceded this.

CHAPTER II

THE NORTH SEA PIRATES

I AM anxious to emphasise the fact that piracy is nearly as old as the ship herself. It is extremely improbable that the Egyptians were ever pirates, for the reason that, excepting the expedition to Punt, they confined their navigation practically to the Nile only. But as soon as men built sea-going vessels, then the instinct to rob and pillage on sea became as irresistible as on land. Might was right, and the weakest went to the bottom.

Bearing this in mind, and remembering that there was always a good deal of trade from the Continent up the Thames to London, especially in corn, and that there was considerable traffic between Gaul and Britain across the English Channel, it was but natural that the sea-rovers of the north should exist no less than in the south. After Rome had occupied Britain she established a navy which she called the " Classis Britannica," and it cannot have failed to be effective in policing the narrow seas and protecting commerce from wandering corsairs. We know very well that after Rome had evacuated Britain, and there was no navy to protect our shores, came the Angles and Saxons and Jutes. We may permissibly regard these Northmen, who pillaged and plundered till the time of William the Conqueror and after, as pirates. In the sense that a pirate

THE NORTH SEA PIRATES

is one who not merely commits robbery on the high seas but also makes descents on the coast for the purpose of pillage, we may call the Viking seamen pirates. But, strictly speaking, they were a great deal more than this, and the object of this book is concerned rather with the incidents of the sea than the incursions into the land. Although the Vikings did certainly commit piracy both in their own waters and off the coasts of Britain, yet their depredations in this respect, even if we could obtain adequate information thereof, would sink into insignificance before their greater conquests. For a race of men who first swoop down on to a strange coast, vanquish the inhabitants and then settle down to live among them, are rather different from a body of men who lie in wait to capture ships as they proceed on their voyages.

The growth of piracy in English waters certainly owed much to the Cinque Ports. In these havens dwelt a privileged class of seamen, who certainly for centuries were a very much favoured community. It was their privilege to do that which in the Mediterranean Cicero had regarded with so much disfavour. These men of the Cinque Ports, according to Matthew of Paris, were commissioned to plunder as they pleased all the merchant ships as they passed up and down the English Channel. This was to be without any regard to nationality, with the exception that English ships were not to be molested. But French, Genoese, Venetian, Spanish or any others could be attacked at the will of the Cinque Port seamen. Some persons might call this sort of thing by the title of privateering, yet it was really piracy and nothing else. You can readily imagine that with this impetus thus given to a class of men who were not particularly prone to lawfulness, the practice of piracy on the waters that wash Great Britain grew at a

A North Sea Pirate

The sails of Viking ships were frequently gaily coloured and decorated with quaint devices. Notice the dragon's head at the forward end of the ship, and the shields arranged along the bulwarks.

THE NORTH SEA PIRATES

great rate. Thus in the thirteenth century the French, the Scotch, Irish and Welsh fitted out ships, hung about the narrow seas till they were able to capture a well-laden merchantman as their fat reward. So, before long, the English Channel was swarming with pirates, and during the reign of Henry III. their numbers grew to an alarming extent. The net result was that it was a grave risk for commodities to be brought across the Channel, and so, therefore, the price of these goods rose. The only means of remedy was to increase the English fleet, and this at length was done in order to cope with the evil.

But matters were scarcely better in the North Sea, and English merchant ships sailed in perpetual fear of capture. During the Middle Ages pirates were always hovering about for any likely ship, and the wool trade especially was interfered with. Matters became somewhat complicated when, as happened in the reign of Edward II., peaceable English ships were arrested by Norway for having been suspected—erroneously—of slaughtering a Norwegian knight, whereas the latter had been actually put to death by pirates. "We marvell not a little," wrote Edward II. in complaint to Haquinus, King of Norway, "and are much disquieted in our cogitations, considering the greevances and oppressions, which (as wee have beene informed by pitifull complaints) are at this present, more than in times past, without any reasonable cause inflicted upon our subjects, which doe usually resort unto your kingdome for traffiques sake." For the fact was that one nation was as bad as the other, but that whenever the one had suffered then the other would lay violent hands on a ship that was merely suspected of having [acted piratically. Angered at the loss to their own countrymen they were prompted by revenge on alien seamen found in their own waters and even

THE NORTH SEA PIRATES

lying quietly in their own havens with their cargoes of herrings.

As an attempt to make the North Sea more possible for the innocent trading ships, the kings of England at different dates came to treaties with those in authority on the other side. Richard II., for example, made an agreement with the King of Prussia. In 1403 " full restitution and recompense " were demanded by the Chancellor of England from the Master-General of Prussia for the " sundry piracies and molestations offered of late upon the sea." Henry IV., writing to the Prussian Master-General, admitted that " as well our as your marchants . . . have, by occasion of pirates, roving up and downe the sea " sustained grievous loss. Finally it was agreed that all English merchant ships should be allowed liberty to enter Prussian ports without molestation. But it was further decided that if in the future any Prussian cargoes should be captured on the North Sea by English pirates, and this merchandise taken into an English port, then the harbour-master or " governour " was, if he suspected piracy, to have these goods promptly taken out of the English ship and placed in safe keeping. Between Henry IV. and the Hanseatic towns a similar agreement was also made which bound the cities of Lubec, Bremen, Hamburg, Sund and Gripeswold " that convenient, just and reasonable satisfaction and recompense " might be made " unto the injured and endamaged parties " " for all injuries, damages, grievances, and drownings or manslaughters done and committed " by the pirates in the narrow seas.

It would be futile to weary the reader with a complete list of all these piratical attacks, but a few of them may here be instanced. About Easter-time in the year 1394 a Hanseatic ship was hovering about the North Sea when she

THE NORTH SEA PIRATES

fell in with an English merchantman from Newcastle-on-Tyne. The latter's name was the *Godezere* and belonged to a quartette of owners. She was, for those days, quite a big craft, having a burden of 200 tons. Her value, together with that of her sails and tackle, amounted to the sum of £400. She was loaded with a cargo of woollen cloth and red wine, being bound for Prussia. The value of this cargo, plus some gold and certain sums of money found aboard, aggregated 200 marks. The Hanseatic ship was able to overpower the *Godezere*, slew two of her crew, captured ship and contents and imprisoned the rest of the crew for the space of three whole years.

A Hull craft belonging to one Richard Horuse, and named the *Shipper Berline of Prussia*, was in the same year also attacked and robbed by Hanseatic pirates, goods to the value of 160 nobles being taken away. The following year a ship named the *John Tutteburie* was attacked by Hanseatics when off the coast of Norway, and goods consisting of wax and other commodities to the value of 476 nobles were captured. A year later and pirates of the same federation captured a ship belonging to William Terry of Hull called the *Cogge*, with thirty woollen broad cloths and a thousand narrow cloths, to the value of £200. In 1398 the *Trinity* of Hull, laden with wax, oil and other goods, was captured by the same class of men off Norway. Dutch ships, merchant craft from the port of London, fishing vessels, Prussian traders, Zealand, Yarmouth and other ships were constantly being attacked, pillaged and captured.

In the month of September, of the year 1398, a number of Hanseatic pirates waylaid a Prussian ship whose skipper was named Rorebek. She carried a valuable cargo of woollen cloth which was the property of various merchants in Colchester. This the pirates took away with them,

THE NORTH SEA PIRATES

together with five Englishmen, whom they found on board. The latter they thrust into prison as soon as they got them ashore, and of these two were ransomed subsequently for the sum of 20 English nobles, while another became blind owing to the rigours of his imprisonment. In 1394 another Prussian ship, containing a number of merchants from Yarmouth and Norwich, was also captured off the Norwegian coast with a cargo of woollen goods and taken off by the Hanseatic pirates. The merchants were cast into prison and not allowed their liberty until the sum of 100 marks had been paid for their ransom. Another vessel, laden with the hides of oxen and sheep, with butter, masts and spars and other commodities to the value of 100 marks, was taken in Longsound, Norway.

In June 1395 another English ship, laden with salt fish, was taken off the coast of Denmark, the value of her hull, inventory and cargo amounting to £170. The crew consisted of a master and twenty-five mariners, whom the pirates slew. There was also a lad found on board, and him they carried into Wismar with them. The most notorious of these Hanseatic pirates were two men, named respectively Godekins and Stertebeker, whose efforts were as untiring as they were successful. There is scarcely an instance of North Sea piracy at this time in which these two men or their accomplices do not figure. And it was these same men who attacked a ship named the *Dogger*. The latter was skippered by a man named Gervase Cat, and she was lying at anchor while her crew were engaged fishing. The Hanseatic pirates, however, swept down on them, took away with them a valuable cargo of fish, beat and wounded the master and crew of the *Dogger* and caused the latter to lose their fishing for that year, "being endamaged thereby to the summe of 200 nobles."

A VIKING'S FUNERAL

A Viking's burial was a fitting end to a life of adventure and piracy. The ship on which he had sailed was filled with inflammable material, on which he was laid in full panoply. Around him lay the corpses of his slaves, whose souls would serve him in the next world; while his favourite charger lay at his feet. The material was then set on fire, the sails hoisted, and the ship floated out to sea.

THE NORTH SEA PIRATES

In the year 1402 other Hanseatic corsairs, while cruising about near Plymouth, captured a Yarmouth barge named the *Michael*, the master of which was one Robert Rigweys. She had a cargo of salt and a thousand canvas cloths. The ship and goods being captured, the owner, a man named Hugh ap Fen, complained that he was the loser to the extent of 800 nobles: and the master and mariners assessed the loss of wages, canvas and "armour" at 200 nobles. But there was no end to the daring of these corsairs of the North. In the spring of 1394 they proceeded with a large fleet of ships to the town of Norbern in Norway, and having taken the place by assault, they captured all the merchants therein, together with their "goods and cattels," burnt their houses and put their persons up to ransom. Twenty-one houses, to the value of 440 nobles, were destroyed, and goods to the value of £1815 were taken from the merchants. With all this lawlessness on the sea and the consequent injury to overseas commerce, it was none too soon that Henry IV. took steps to put down a most serious evil.

We cannot but feel sorry for the long-suffering North Sea fishermen, who, in addition to having to ride out bad weather in clumsy leaky craft, and having to work very hard for their living, were liable at any time to see a pirate ship approaching them over the top of the waves. You remember the famous Dogger Bank incident a few years ago when one night the North Sea trawlers found themselves being shelled by the Russian Baltic fleet. Well, in much the same way were the mediæval ancestors of these hardy fishermen surprised by pirates when least expecting them and when most busily occupied in pursuing their legitimate calling. The fisherman was like a magnet to the pirates, because his catch of fish had only to be taken

THE NORTH SEA PIRATES

to the nearest port and sold. That was the reason why, in 1295, Edward had been induced to send three ships of Yarmouth across the North Sea to protect the herring-ships of Holland and Zealand.

The following incident well illustrates the statement that, in spite of all the efforts which were made to repress piracy, yet it was almost impossible to attain such an object. The month is July, and the year 1327, the scene being the English Channel. Picture to your mind a beamy, big-bellied, clumsy ship with one mast and one great square sail. She has come from Waterford in Ireland, where she has taken on board a rich cargo, consisting of wool, hides and general merchandise. She has safely crossed the turbulent Irish Sea, she has wallowed her way through the Atlantic swell round Land's End and found herself making good headway up the English Channel in the summer breeze. Her port of destination is Bruges, but she will never get there. For from the eastward have come the famous pirates of the Cinque Ports, and off the Isle of Wight they fall in with the merchant ship. The rovers soon sight her, come up alongside, board her and relieve her of forty-two sacks of wool, twelve dickers of hides, three pipes of salmon, two pipes of cheese, one bale of cloth, to say nothing of such valuable articles as silver plate, mazer cups, jewels, sparrow-hawks and other goods of the total value of £600. Presently the pirates bring their spoil into the Downs below Sandwich and dispose of it as they prefer.

CHAPTER III

PIRACY IN THE EARLY TUDOR TIMES

THE kind of man who devotes his life to robbery at sea is not the species of humanity who readily subjects himself to laws and ordinances. You may threaten him with terrible punishments, but it is not by these means that you will break his spirit. He is like the gipsy or the vagrant: he has in him an overwhelming longing for wandering and adventure. It is not so much the greed for gain which prompts the pirate, any more than the land tramp finds his long marches inspired by wealth. But some impelling blind force is at work within, and so not all the treaties and agreements, not all the menaces of death could avail to keep these men from pursuing the occupation which their fathers and grandfathers had for many years been employed in.

Therefore piracy was quite as bad in the sixteenth century as it had been in the Middle Ages. The dwellers on either side of the English Channel were ever ready to pillage each other's ships and property. About the first and second decade of the sixteenth century the Scots rose to some importance in the art of sea-robbery, and some were promptly taken and executed. In vain did Henry VIII. write to Francis I. saying that complaints had been made by English merchants that their ships had been pirated by

PIRACY IN THE EARLY TUDOR TIMES

Frenchmen pretending to be Scots, for which redress could not be obtained in France. In 1531 matters had become so bad, and piracy was so prevalent, that commissioners were appointed to make inquisitions concerning this illegal warfare round our coasts. Viscount Lisle, Vice-Admiral of England, and others were appointed to see to the problem. So cunning had these rovers become that it was no easy affair to capture them. But in this same year a notorious pirate named Kellwanton was taken in the Isle of Man; while another, De Melton by name, who was one of his accomplices, fled with the rest of the crew in the ship to Grimsby.

Sometimes the very ships which had been sent by the king against the pirates actually engaged in pillage themselves. There was at least one instance about this time of some royal ships being unable to resist the temptation to plunder the richly laden Flemish ships. But after complaint was made the royal reply came that the Flemings should be compensated and the plunderers punished. It was all very well to set a thief to catch a thief, but there were few English seamen of any experience who had not done some piracy at some time of their career, and when they at last formed the crews of preventive ships and got wearied of waiting for pirate craft to come along, it was too much to expect them to remain idle on the seas when a rich merchantman went sailing past.

Sometimes the pirates would waylay a whole merchant fleet, and if the latter were sailing light, would relieve the fleet of their victuals, their clothes, their anchors and cables and sails. But it was not merely to the North Sea nor to the English Channel that the English pirates confined themselves. In October 1533 they captured a Biscayan ship off the coast of Ireland. And during the reign of Henry VIII. there was an interesting incident connected with

PIRACY IN THE EARLY TUDOR TIMES

a ship named the *Santa Maria Desaie*. This craft belonged to one Peter Alves, a Portingale, who hired a mariner, William Phelipp, to pilot his ship from Tenby to Bastabill Haven. But whilst off the Welsh coast a piratical bark named the *Furtuskewys*, containing thirty-five desperate corsairs, attacked the *Santa Maria* and completely overpowered her. Alves they promptly got rid of by putting him ashore somewhere on the Welsh coast, and they then proceeded to sail the ship to Cork, where they sold her to the mayor and others, the value of the captured craft and goods being 1524 crowns. Alves did not take this assault with any resignation, but naturally used his best endeavours to have the matter set right. From the King's Council he obtained a command to the Mayor of Cork for restitution, but such was the lawlessness of the time that this was of no avail. The mayor, whose name was Richard Gowllys, protested that the pirates told him they had captured the ship from the Scots and not from the Portingale, and he added that he would spend £100 rather than make restitution.

But stricter vigilance caused the arrest of some of these pirates. Six of them were sentenced to death in the Admiralty Court at Boulogne, eleven others were condemned to death in the Guildhall, London: and in 1537 a ship was lying at Winchelsea "in gage to Bell the mayor" for £35 for the piracies committed in her, for she had been captured after having robbed a Gascon merchantman of a cargo of wines.

The finest of the French sailors for many a century until even the present day have ever been the Bretons. And just as in the eighteenth century the most expert sailormen on our coasts were the greatest smugglers, so in Tudor times the pick of all seamen were sea-rovers. About the time of Lent, 1537, a couple of Breton pirate ships caused a great deal of anxiety to our west-country men. One of the

PIRACY IN THE EARLY TUDOR TIMES

two had robbed an English ship off the Cornish coast and pillaged his cargo of wine. From Easter-time till August these rovers hung about the Welsh coast, sometimes coming ashore for provisions and most probably also to sell their ill-gotten cargoes, but for the most part remaining at sea. It would seem from the historical records that originally there had been only one Breton ship that had sailed from St. Malo; but having the good fortune to capture a fishing craft belonging to Milford Haven, the crew had been split up into two. Presently the numbers of these French pirates increased till there was quite a fleet of them cruising about the Welsh coast. A merchant ship that had loaded a fine cargo at Bristol, bound across the Bay of Biscay, had been boarded before the voyage had been little more than begun. For week after week these men robbed every ship that came past them. But especially were they biding their time waiting for the English, Irish and Welsh ships who were wont about this period of the year to come to St. James's Fair at Bristol.

However, in the meanwhile, the men of the west were becoming much more alert, and were ready for any chance that might occur. And a Bristol man named Bowen, after fourteen Breton pirates had come ashore near Tenby to obtain victuals, acted with such smartness that he was able to have the whole lot captured and put into prison. And John Wynter, another Bristolian, knowing that the pirates were hovering about for those ships bound for the fair, promptly manned a ship, embarked fifty soldiers, as well as the able seamen, and cruised about ready to swoop down on the first pirate ship which showed up on the horizon. The full details of these men and what they did would make interesting reading if they were obtainable; but we know that of the above-mentioned fourteen, one, John du

PIRACY IN THE EARLY TUDOR TIMES

Laerquerac, was captain of the Breton craft. On being arrested he stoutly denied that he had ever "spoiled" English ships. That was most certainly a bare-faced lie, and presently Peter Dromyowe, one of his own mariners, confessed that he himself had robbed one Englishman; whereupon Laerquerac made a confession that, as a matter of fact, he had taken ships' ropes, sailors' wearing apparel, five pieces of wine, a quantity of fish, a gold crown in money and eleven silver halfpence or pence, as well as four daggers and a "couverture"!

It was because the English merchants complained that they lost so much of their imports and exports by depredations from the ships of war belonging to Biscay, Spain, the Low Countries, Normandy, Brittany and elsewhere, that Henry VIII. had been prevailed upon to send Sir John Dudley, his Vice-Admiral, to sea with a small fleet of good ships. Dudley's orders were to cruise between the Downs on the east and St. Michael's Mount on the west—in other words, the whole length of the English Channel—according as the wind should serve. In addition, he was to stand off and on between Ushant and Scilly and so guard the entrance to the Channel. Furthermore, he was to look in at the Isle of Lundy in the Bristol Channel—for both Lundy and the Scillies were famous pirate haunts—and after having so done he was to return and keep the narrow seas. Dudley was especially admonished to be on the look out to succour any English merchant ships, and should he meet with any foreign merchant craft which, under the pretence of trading, were actually robbing the King's subjects, he was to have these foreigners treated as absolute pirates and punished accordingly.

For the state of piracy had become so bad that the King "can no longer suffer it." So also Sir Thomas Dudley, as

PIRACY IN THE EARLY TUDOR TIMES

well as Sir John, was busily employed in the same preventive work. On the 10th of August of that same year, 1537, he wrote to Cromwell that he had at Harwich arrested a couple of Frenchmen who two years previously had robbed a poor English skipper's craft off the coast of Normandy, and this Englishman had in vain sued in France for a remedy, since the pirates could never be captured. But there were so many of these corsairs being now taken that it was a grave problem as to how they should be dealt with. "If they were all committed to ward," wrote Sir Thomas, "as your letters direct, they would fill the gaol." Then he adds: "They would fain go and leave the ship behind them, which only contains ordnance, and no goods or victuals to find themselves with. If they go to gaol, they are like to perish of hunger, for Englishmen will do no charity to them. They are as proud naves as I have talked with."

Eleven days later came the report from Sir John Dudley of his experiences in the Channel. He stated that while on his way home he encountered a couple of Breton ships in the vicinity of St. Helen's, Isle of Wight, where he believed they were lying in wait for two Cornish ships "that were within Porchemouthe haven, laden with tin to the value of £3000." Portsmouth is, of course, just opposite St. Helen's, and on more than one occasion in naval history was the latter found a convenient anchorage by hostile ships waiting for English craft to issue forth from the mainland. But when these Breton pirates espied Dudley's ships coming along under sail, they "made in with Porchemouthe," where Dudley's men promptly boarded them and placed them under arrest, with the intention of bringing them presently to the Thames. Dudley had no doubt whatever that these were pirates, but at a later date the French ambassador endeavoured to show that there was no foundation for such

PIRACY IN THE EARLY TUDOR TIMES

a suspicion. These two French crafts, he sought to persuade, were genuine merchantmen who had discharged their cargo at "St. Wallerie's" (that is to say, St. Valery-sur-Somme), but had been driven to the Isle of Wight by bad weather, adding, doubtless as a subtle hint, that they had actually rescued an Englishman chased by a Spaniard. It is possible that the Frenchmen were telling the truth, though unless the wind had come southerly and so made it impossible for these bluff-bowed craft to beat into their port, it is difficult to believe that they could not have run into one of their own havens. At any rate, it was a yarn which Dudley's sailors found not easy to accept.

This was no isolated instance of the capture of Breton craft. In the year 1532 a Breton ship named the *Mychell*, whose owner was one Hayman Gillard, her master being Nicholas Barbe of St. Malo, was encountered by a crew of English seamen who entertained no doubts whatsoever as to her being anything else than a pirate. Their suspicions were made doubly sure when they found her company to consist of nine Bretons and five Scots. They arrested her at sea, and when examined she was found well laden with wool, cloth and salt hides. Some French pirate ships even went so far as to wear the English flag of St. George, with the red cross on a white ground. This not unnaturally infuriated English seamen, especially when it was discovered that the Bretons had also carried Englishmen as their pilots and chief mariners, and were training them to become experts in piracy.

But there were times when English seamen and merchants were able to " get their own back " with interest, as the following incident will show. At the beginning of June, in the year 1538, an English merchant, Henry Davy, freighted a London ship named the *Clement*, which was

PIRACY IN THE EARLY TUDOR TIMES

owned by one Grenebury, who lived in Thames Street, and dispatched her with orders to proceed to the "Bay in Breteyne." She set forth under the command of a man named Lyllyk, the ship's purser being William Scarlet, a London clothworker. Seven men formed her crew, but when off Margate they took on board nine more. They then proceeded down Channel and took on board another four from the shore, but espying a Flemish ship of war they deemed it prudent to get hold of the coast of Normandy as soon as possible. In the "mayne" sea—by which I understand the English Channel near the mainland of the Continent—they descried coming over the waves three ships, and these were found to be Breton merchantmen.

This caused some discussion on board the *Clement*, and Davy, the charterer, who had come with the ship, remarked to the skipper Lyllyk that they had lost as much as £60 in goods, which had been captured by Breton pirates at an earlier date, and had never been able to obtain compensation in France in spite of all their endeavours. Any one who has any imagination and a knowledge of seafaring human nature, can easily picture Lyllyk and his crew cordially agreeing with Davy's point of view, and showing more than a mere passive sympathy. The upshot of the discussion was that they resolved to take the law into their own hands and capture one of these three ships.

The resolution was put into effect, so that before long they had become possessed of the craft. The Breton crew were rowed ashore in a boat and left there, and after collecting the goods left behind, the Englishmen stowed them in the hold of the *Clement*. A prize crew, consisting of a man whose name was Cornelys, and four seamen, were placed in charge of the captured ship, which now got under way. The *Clement*, too, resumed her voyage, and made for

PIRACY IN THE EARLY TUDOR TIMES

Peryn in Cornwall, where she was able to sell, at a good price, the goods taken out of the Breton. The gross amount obtained was divided up among the captors, and though the figures may not seem very large, yet the sum represented the equivalent of what would be to-day about ten times that amount of money. Henry Davy, being the charterer, received £17; the master, the mate, the quartermaster and the purser received each thirty shillings, while the mariners got twenty shillings apiece. Lyllyk and nine of the crew then departed, while Davy, Scarlet, Leveret the carpenter and two others got the ship under way, sailed up Channel and brought the *Clement* back to the Thames, where they delivered her to the wife of the owner.

But Englishmen were not always so fortunate, and the North Sea pirates were still active, in spite of the efforts which had been made by English kings in previous centuries. In 1538 the cargo ship *George Modye* put to sea with goods belonging to a company of English merchant adventurers, consisting of Sir Ralph Waryn, "good Mr. Lock and Rowland Hyll" and others. She never reached her port of destination, however, for the Norwegian pirates pillaged her and caused a loss to the adventurers of £10,000, whereupon, after complaint had been made, Cromwell was invoked to obtain letters from Henry VIII. to the kings of Denmark, France and Scotland that search might be duly made. There was, in fact, a good deal of luck, even yet, as to whether a ship would ever get to the harbour whither she was sent. In September 1538 we find Walter Herbart complaining that twice since Candlemas he had been robbed by Breton pirates. But, a week later, it is recorded that some pirates, who had robbed peaceable ships bound from Iceland, had been chased by John Chaderton and others of Portsmouth and captured about this time.

PIRACY IN THE EARLY TUDOR TIMES

And it was not always that Englishmen dealt with these foreigners in any merciful manner, regardless of right or wrong. I have already emphasised the fact that, as regards the question of legality, there was little to choose between the seamen of any maritime nation. Rather it was a question of opportunity, and the very men who to-day complained bitterly of the robbery of their ships and cargoes might to-morrow be found performing piracy themselves. A kind of sea-vendetta went on, and in the minds of the mariners the only sin was that of being found out. So we notice that, in the spring of 1539, an instance of a Breton ship being captured by English corsairs who, according to the recognised custom of the sea, forthwith threw overboard the French sailors. These were all drowned except one who, " as if by a miracle, swam six miles to shore." So says the ancient record, though it is difficult to believe that even a strong swimmer could last out so long after being badly knocked about. The Bretons had their revenge this time, for complaint was made to the chief justices, who within fifteen days had the culprits arrested and condemned, and six of them were executed on the 19th of May. Before the end of the month Francis I. wrote to thank the English king for so promptly dealing with the culprits.

Bearing in mind the interest which Henry VIII. took in nautical matters and in the welfare of his country generally; recollecting, too, the determination with which he pursued any project to the end when once his mind had been made up, we need not be surprised to find that a few months later in that year this resolute monarch again sent ships—this time a couple of barks of 120 and 90 tons respectively —" well manned and ordnanced " to scour the seas for these pirate pests that inflicted so many serious losses on the Tudor merchants.

PIRACY IN THE EARLY TUDOR TIMES

A little earlier in that year Vaughan had written to Cromwell that he had spoken with one who lately had been a " common passenger " in hoys between London and Antwerp and knew of certain pirates who intended to capture the merchant ships plying between those two ports. Valuable warning was given concerning one of these roving craft. She belonged to Hans van Meghlyn, who had fitted out a ship of the " portage " of 20 lasts and 45ᵉ tons burthen. She was manned by a crew of thirty, her hull was painted black with pitch, she had no " foresprit," and her foremast leaned forward like a " lodeman's " boat. (" Lodeman " was the olden word for pilot—the man who hove the lead.) Cromwell was advised that this craft would proceed first to Orfordness (the natural landfall for a vessel to make when bound across the North Sea from the Schelde), and thence she would proceed south and lie in wait for ships at the mouth of the Thames. In order to be ready to pillage either the inward or outward bound craft which traded with London, this pirate would hover about off White Staple (Whitstable). Vaughan's informant thought that sometimes, however, she would change her locality to the Melton shore in order to avoid suspicion, and he advised that it would be best to capture her by means of three or four well-manned oyster boats. There was also another " Easterling " (that is, one from the east of Germany or the the Baltic) pirate who had received his commission from the Grave of Odenburg. This rover was named Francis Beme and was now at Canfyre with his ship, waiting for the Grave of Odenburg's return from Brussels with money. But the warning news came in time, and in order to prevent the English merchant ships from falling into the sea-rovers' hands, the former were ordered by proclamation to remain in Antwerp from Ash Wednesday till Easter.

CHAPTER IV

THE CORSAIRS OF THE SOUTH

WHEN, in the year 1516, Hadrian, Cardinal St. Chryogon, wrote to Wolsey bitterly lamenting that from Taracina right away to Pisa pirates, consisting of Turks and African Moors, were swarming the sea, he was scarcely guilty of any exaggeration. Multifarious and murderous though the pirates of Northern Europe had long since shown themselves, yet it is the Mediterranean which, throughout history, and more especially during the sixteenth century, has earned the distinction of being the favourite and most eventful sphere of robbery by sea.

You may ask how this came about. It was no longer the case of the old Cilicians or the Balearic Islanders coming into activity once more. On the contrary, the last-mentioned people, far from being pirates in the sixteenth century, were actually pillaged than pillagers. A new element had now been introduced, and we enter upon a totally different sphere of the piratical history. Before we seek to inquire into the origin and development of this new force which comes across the pages of history, let us bear in mind the change which had come over the Mediterranean. During the classical times piracy was indeed bad enough, because, among other things, it interfered so seriously with the corn ships which carried the means of sustenance. But in those days the

THE CORSAIRS OF THE SOUTH

number of freight ships of any kind was infinitesimal compared with the enormous number of fighting craft that were built by the Mediterranean nations. And however much Greece and Rome laboured to develop the warlike galley, yet the evolution of the merchant ship was sadly neglected, partly, no doubt, because of the risks which a merchant ship ran and partly because the centuries of fighting evoked little encouragement for a ship of commerce.

During the centuries which followed the downfall of the Roman Empire it must not be supposed that the sea was bereft of pirates. As we have already seen, the decay of Rome was commensurate with the revival of piracy. But with the gradual spread of southern civilisation the importance of and the demand for commercial ships, as differentiated from fighting craft, increased to an unheard-of extent. No one requires to be reminded of the rise to great power of Venice and Genoa and Spain. They became great overseas traders within limits, and this postulated the ships in which goods could be carried. So it came to this that crossing and recrossing the Mediterranean there were more big-bellied ships full of richer cargoes and traversing the sea with greater regularity than ever had been in the history of the world. And as there will always be robbers when given the opportunity, either by sea or by land, irrespective of race or time, so when this amount of wealth was now afloat the sea-robber had every incentive to get rich quickly by a means that appealed in the strongest terms to an adventurous temperament.

In Italy the purely warlike ship had become so obsolete that, in the opinion of some authorities, it was not till about the middle of the ninth century that these began to be built, at any rate as regards that great maritime power, Venice. She had been too concerned with the production and

THE CORSAIRS OF THE SOUTH

exchange of wealth to centre her attention on any species of ship other than those which would carry freights. But so many defeats had she endured at the hands of the Saracens and pirates that ships specially suitable for combat had, from the year 841, to be built. The Saracens hailed from Arabia, and it is notable that at that time the Arabian sailors who used to sail across the Indian Ocean were far and away the most scientific navigators in the whole world, many of their Arabic terms still surviving in nautical terminology to this day. Indeed, the modern mariner who relies so much on nautical instruments scarcely realises how much he owes to these early seamen. Just as the Cilicians and others had in olden times harassed the shores of the Mediterranean, so now the Saracens made frequent incursions into Sardinia, Corsica, Sicily, as well as intercepting the ships of the Adriatic.

Let us remember that both in the north and south of Europe the sailing seasons for century after century were limited to that period which is roughly indicated between the months of April and the end of September. Therefore the pirate knew that if he confined his attentions to that period and within certain sea-areas, he would be able to encompass practically the whole of the world's sea-borne trade. These sailing periods were no arbitrary arrangement: they were part of the maritime legislation, and only the most daring and, at the same time, most lawless merchant skippers ventured forth in the off-season.

Realising that the mariner had in any lengthy voyage to contend not merely with bad weather but probably with pirates, the merchant pilots were instructed to know how to avoid them. For instance, their main object should be to make the merchant ship as little conspicuous on the horizon as possible. Thus, after getting clear of the land, the white sail should be lowered and a black one hoisted instead.

THE CORSAIRS OF THE SOUTH

They were warned that it was especially risky to change sail at break of day when the rising sun might make this action easily observable. A man was to be sent aloft to scan the sea, looking for these rovers and keep a good look out. That black sail was called the "wolf," because it had the colour and cunning of such an animal. At night, too, similar precautions were employed against any danger of piratical attack, strict silence being absolutely enforced, so that the boatswain was not even allowed to use his whistle, nor the ship's bell to be sounded. Every one knows how easily a sound carries on the sea, especially by night, so the utmost care was to be exercised lest a pirate hovering about might have the rich merchant ship's presence betrayed to her avaricious ears.

But the Saracens, whose origin I have just mentioned, must not be confused with the Barbarian corsairs. It is with the latter—the grand pirates of the South—that I pass on now to deal. So powerful did they become that it took the efforts of the great maritime powers of Europe till the first quarter of the nineteenth century before they could exterminate this scourge: and even to-day, in this highly civilised century, if you were to be becalmed off the coast of North Africa in a sailing yacht, you would soon find some of the descendants of these Barbarian corsairs coming out with their historic tendency to kill you and pillage your ship. If this statement should seem to any reader somewhat incredible, I would refer him to the captain of any modern steamship who habitually passes that coast: and I would beg also to call to his attention the incident a few years ago that occurred to the famous English racing yacht *Ailsa*, which was lying becalmed somewhere between Spain and Africa. But for a lucky breeze springing up, her would-be assailants might have captured a very fine prize.

THE CORSAIRS OF THE SOUTH

I shall use the word Moslem to mean Mussulman, or Mohammedan, or Moor, and I shall ask the reader to carry his mind back to the time when Ferdinand and Isabella turned the Moors out from Spain, and sent them across the straits of Gibraltar back to Africa. For seven hundred years these Moors had lived in the Iberian peninsula. It must be admitted in fairness that these Moors were exceedingly gifted intellectually, and there are ample evidences in Spain to this day of their accomplishments. On the other hand, it is perfectly easy to appreciate the desire of a Christian Government to banish these Mohammedans from a Catholic country. Equally comprehensible is the bitter hatred which these Moors for ever after manifested against all Christians of any nation, but against the Spanish more especially.

What were these Spanish Moors, now expatriated, to do? They spread themselves along the North African coast, but it was not immediately that they took to the sea; when, however, they did so accustom themselves it was not as traders but as pirates of the worst and most cruel kind. The date of their expulsion from Granada was 1492, and within a few years of this they had set to work to become avenged. The type of craft which they favoured was of the galley species, a vessel that was of great length, in proportion to her extreme shallowness, and was manned by a considerable number of oarsmen. Sail power was employed but only as auxiliary rather than of main reliance. Such a craft was light, easily and quickly manœuvred, could float in creeks and bays close in to the shore, or could be drawn up the beach if necessary. In all essential respects she was the direct lineal descendant of the old fighting galleys of Greece and Rome. From about the beginning of the sixteenth century till the battle of Lepanto in 1571 the Moslem

THE CORSAIRS OF THE SOUTH

corsair was at his best as a sea-rover and a powerful racial force. And if he was still a pest to shipping after that date, yet his activities were more of a desultory nature. Along the Barbarian coast at different dates he made himself strong, though of these strongholds Algiers remained for the longest time the most notorious.

In considering these Moslem corsairs one must think of men who were as brutal as they were clever, who became the greatest galley-tacticians which the world has ever seen. Their greed and lust for power and property were commensurate with their ability to obtain these. Let it not be supposed for one moment that during the grand period these Moorish pirate leaders were a mere ignorant and uncultured number of men. On the contrary, they possessed all the instincts of a clever diplomatist, united to the ability of a great admiral and an autocratic monarch. Dominating their very existence was their bitter hatred of Christians either individually or as nations. And though a careful distinction must be made between these Barbarian corsairs and the Turks, who were often confused in the sixteenth-century accounts of these rovers, yet from a very early stage the Moorish pirates and the Turks assisted each other. You have only to remember that they were both Moslems; to remind yourself that the downfall of Constantinople in 1453 gave an even keener incentive to harass Christians; and to recollect that though the Turks were great fighters by land yet they were not seamen. They had an almost illimitable quantity of men to draw upon, and for this as well as other reasons it was to the Moors' interests that there should be a close association with them.

During the fifteenth and especially the sixteenth centuries there was in general European use a particular word which instantly suggested a certain character that

THE CORSAIRS OF THE SOUTH

would stink in the nostrils of any Christian, be he under the domination of Elizabeth or Charles v. This word was "renegade," which, of course, is derived from the Latin *nego*, I deny. "Renegade," or, as the Elizabethan sailors often used it, "renegado" signifies an apostate from the faith—a deserter or turncoat. But it was applied in those days almost exclusively to the Christian who had so far betrayed his religion as to become a Moslem. In the fifteenth century a certain Balkan renegade was exiled from Constantinople by the Grand Turk. From there he proceeded to the south-west, took up his habitation in the island of Lesbos in the Ægean Sea, married a Christian widow and became the father of two sons, named respectively Uruj and Kheyr-ed-din. The renegade, being a seaman, it was but natural that the two sons should be brought up to the same avocation.

Having regard to the ancestry of these two men, and bearing in mind that Lesbos had long been notorious for its piratical inhabitants, the reader will in no wise be surprised to learn that these two sons resolved to become pirates too. They were presently to reach a state of notoriety which time can never expunge from the pages of historical criminals. For the present let us devote our attention to the elder brother, Uruj. We have little space to deal with the events of his full life, but this brief sketch may suffice. The connection of these two brothers with the banished Moors is that of organisers and leaders of a potential force of pirates. Uruj, having heard of the successes which the Moorish galleys were now attaining, of the wonderful prizes which they had carried off from the face of the sea, felt the impulse of ambition and responded to the call of the wild. So we come to the year 1504, and we find him in the Mediterranean longing for a suitable base whence he could

A Daring Attack

Uruj with his one craft attacked the two galleys of Pope Julius II laden with goods from Genoa. His officers remonstrated with Uruj on the desperate venture, but to enforce his commands and prevent any chance of flight he had the oars thrown overboard. He then attacked and overcame the galleys.

THE CORSAIRS OF THE SOUTH

operate; where, too, he could haul his galleys ashore during the winter and refit.

For a time Tunis seemed to be the most alluring spot in every way: and strategically it was ideal for the purpose of rushing out and intercepting the traffic passing between Italy and Africa. He came to terms with the Sultan of Tunis, and, in return for one-fifth of the booty obtained, Uruj was permitted to use this as his headquarters, and from here he began with great success to capture Italian galleys, bringing back to Tunis both booty and aristocratic prisoners for perpetual exile. The women were cast into the Sultan's harem, the men were chained to the benches of the galleys.

One incident alone would well illustrate the daring of Uruj, who had now been joined by his brother. The story is told by Mr. Stanley Lane Poole in his history of the Barbarian corsairs, that one day, when off Elba, two galleys belonging to Pope Julius II. were coming along laden with goods from Genoa for Civita Vecchia. The disparity and the daring may be realised when we state that each of these galleys was twice the size of Uruj's craft. The Papal galleys had become separated, and this made matters easier for the corsair. In spite of the difference in size, he was determined to attack. His Turkish crew, however, remonstrated and thought it madness, but Uruj answered this protestation by hurling most of the oars overboard, thus making escape impossible: they had to fight or die.

This was the first time that Turkish corsairs had been seen off Elba, and as the Papal galley came on and saw the turbaned heads, a spirit of consternation spread throughout the ship. The corsair galley came alongside, there was a volley of firing, the Turkish men leapt aboard, and before long the ship and the Christians were captured. The

THE CORSAIRS OF THE SOUTH

Christians were sent below, and the Papal ship was now manned by Turks who disguised themselves in the Christians' clothes. And now they were off to pursue the second galley. As they came up to her the latter had no suspicion, but a shower of arrows and shot, followed by another short, sharp attack, made her also a captive. Into Tunis came the ships, and the capture amazed both Barbarian corsair and the whole of Christendom alike. The fame of Uruj spread, and along the whole coast of North Africa he was regarded with a wonder mingled with the utmost admiration. He became known by the name Barbarossa, owing to his own physical appearance, the Italian word *rossa* signifying red, and *barba* meaning a beard. He followed up this success by capturing next year a Spanish ship with 500 soldiers. And there were other successes, so that in five years he had eight vessels. But Tunis now became too small for him, so for a time he moved to the island of Jerba, on the east coast of Tunis, and from there he again harassed Italy.

Such was the fame of Barbarossa that he was invited to help the Moors. It chanced that the Moslem king of Bujeya had been driven out of his city by the Spaniards, and the exile appealed to Barbarossa to assist him in regaining his own. The reward offered to the Turk was that, in the event of victory, Barbarossa should henceforth be allowed the free use of Bujeya, the strategic advantage of this port being that it commanded the Spanish sea. The Turk accepted the invitation on these terms, and having now a dozen galleys, with ample armament, in addition to 1000 Turkish soldiers, as well as a number of renegades and Moors, he landed before the town in August of 1512. Here he found the King ready with his 3000 troops, and they proceeded to storm the bastion, in which an all too

THE CORSAIRS OF THE SOUTH

weak Spanish garrison had been left. Still, for eight days the Spaniards held out, and then when a breach was made and a fierce assault was being carried out, Barbarossa had the misfortune to have his left arm amputated, so, Bujeya being now left alone, Barbarossa and his brother put to sea again. They had not won the victory, but they had captured a rich Genoese galley full of merchandise. Barbarossa took her back with him to his headquarters, and while he recovered from his wounds his brother Kheyr-ed-din acted in his stead.

Not unnaturally the Genoese were angered at the loss of their fine galliot and sent forth Andrea Doria, the greatest Christian admiral, with a dozen galleys to punish the Turks. The Christians landed before Tunis, drove Kheyr-ed-din back into Tunis, and took away to Genoa one-half of Barbarossa's ships. Kheyr-ed-din now proceeded to Jerba to build other ships as fast as possible, and as soon as his wounds allowed him, Barbarossa here joined him. Meanwhile the Moors were still chafing at their inability to get even with the Spaniards, and once more an attempt was made to take Bujeya, though unsuccessfully, and the corsair's ships were burnt lest they might fall into the hands of the enemy.

At length the Barbarossas resolved to quit Tunis and Jerba, for they had now chosen to settle at Jijil, sixty miles to the east of Bujeya. Their fame had come before them; the inhabitants were proud to welcome the brother corsairs who had done many wonderful things by land and sea, and before long the elder Barbarossa was chosen as their Sultan. In 1516 died Ferdinand, and about this time the Algerine Moors declined any longer to pay tribute to Spain. To Barbarossa came an invitation to aid these inhabitants of Algiers in driving the Spanish garrison from their fort.

THE CORSAIRS OF THE SOUTH

The invitation was accepted, 6000 men and sixteen galliots were got together. Arrived before the fortress of Algiers, Barbarossa offered a safe conduct to the garrison if they would surrender, but the latter's reply was merely to remind the corsair of Bujeya. Then for twenty days Barbarossa battered away at the fortress, but without making a breach, and meanwhile the Moors began to regret that they had asked the red beard to aid them. But it would be less easy to turn them out now that once these daredevils had set foot on their territory. Barbarossa knew this and waxed insolent. The Algerines made common cause with the soldiers in the fortress, and a general rising against the red beard was planned. But they had reckoned without their guest. For Barbarossa had spies at work and became informed of this plot.

Whilst at prayers one Friday in the mosque, Barbarossa had the gates closed, the conspirators brought before him one by one, and then after twenty-two of them had been put to death there was an end to this plotting against the corsair of Lesbos. Barbarossa increased in power, in the number of his galleys, in the extent of his territory and in the number of his subjects, so that by now he had become Sultan of Middle Barbary. Practically the whole of that territory marked on our modern maps of Algeria was under his sway. Step by step, leaping from one success to another, ignoring his occasional reverses, he had risen from a mere common pirate to the rank of a powerful Sultan. So potent had he become, in fact, that he was able to make treaties with other Barbarian Sultans, and all the summer season his galleys were scouring the seas bringing back increased wealth and more unfortunate Christian prisoners. Richly laden merchant ships from Genoa, from Naples, from Venice, from Spain set forth from home, and neither the ships nor their

THE CORSAIRS OF THE SOUTH

contents were ever permitted to return or to reach their ports of destination.

However, the time came when the Christian States could no longer endure this terrible condition of affairs. And Charles v. was moved to send a strong force to deal with the evil. Ten thousand seasoned troops were sent in a large fleet of galleys to Northern Africa, and at last the wasp was killed. For Barbarossa, with his 1500 men, was defeated, and he himself was slain while fighting boldly. Unfortunately the matter ended there, and the troops, instead of pressing home their victory and wiping the Barbarian coast clean of this Moorish dirt, left Algiers severely alone and returned to their homes. Had they, instead, ruthlessly sought out this lawless piratical brood, the troublesome scourge of the next three centuries would probably never have caused so many European ships and so many English and foreign sailors and others to end their days under the lash of tyrannical monsters.

CHAPTER V

THE WASPS AT WORK

BUT if Barbarossa was dead, his sagacious brother Kheyr-ed-din was ready to take up his work, and he proceeded on more scientific principles. He began by sending an ambassador to Constantinople, and begged protection for the province of Algiers. This, having been granted, he was appointed officially, in 1519, Governor of Algiers. His next step was to reinforce his garrisons at different parts of the coast and so secure his territory from attacks by sea. And in order to make for safety on the southern or landward side, he entered into alliances with the leading Arabian tribes up-country.

He was thus about as secure as it was possible for human diplomacy and organisation to achieve. His ships could still go on their piratical cruises and return with little enough risk. In vain did the Spaniards send an Armada against him. The men indeed landed, but they were driven back, and a storm springing up did the rest. Gradually more and more seaports fell into the net of this corsair, so there were plenty of harbours to run for, plenty of safe shelters whither to bring the valuable prizes. It was not merely the middle or the eastern end of the Mediterranean which was now harassed, but the west end. Those were the days, you will remember, when Spain was developing the

THE WASPS AT WORK

rich resources of the New World, so there was a great opportunity for the Barbarian pirates to go out some little distance into the Atlantic and capture the West Indiamen homeward bound for Cadiz with gold and other treasures. And in addition to these prizes, no less than the merchantmen of Italy, Kheyr-ed-din occasionally made raids on the Spanish coast or even carried off slaves from the Balearic Islands. From end to end these Algerine corsairs were thus masters of the Mediterranean. No commercial ship could pass on her voyages in any safety—even Spanish flagships found themselves being brought captive into Algiers.

True, the small Spanish garrison still remained in Algiers, and because it was immured within a very strong fortress it held out. The time now came for this to be attacked with great vigour. For a period of fifteen days it was bombarded, and at length, after a most stubborn resistance, it was overcome. The stronghold was then pulled down, and Christian prisoners who in the summer season had rowed chained to their seats in the corsair galleys, were in the off-season employed to build with these stones the great mole to protect the harbour of Algiers from the western side. It was a stupendous undertaking, and seven thousand of these unhappy creatures accomplished the work in most of two years.

Nothing succeeds like success, and the corsair prospered in power and possession to such an extent that he was pre-eminent. This naturally attracted to his dominion many thousands of other followers, and there was thus established not a mere small colony of pirates, but a grand corsair kingdom where the industry of sea-robbery was well organised with its foundries and dockyards, and with every assistance to agriculture, and a firm, hard government to keep the land in fit and proper cultivation.

THE WASPS AT WORK

And now yet another invitation came to Kheyr-ed-din. Andrea Doria had defeated the Turks at Patras and in the Dardanelles. Like the policy of the corsairs, after each victory the Christian admiral employed the infidel captives to work at the oars of his galleys. Thus it was that the Sultan of Turkey—Solyman the Magnificent—realising that the Christian admiral was draining the best Turkish seafaring men, determined to invite Kheyr-ed-din to help him against Andrea Doria. So one of the Sultan's personal guard was dispatched to Algiers requesting Barbarossa to come to Constantinople and place himself at the head of the Ottoman navy. Barbarossa accepted this as he had accepted other invitations, seeing that it was to his own interest, and in August 1533 left Algiers with seven galleys and eleven other craft. On the way he was joined by sixteen more craft belonging to a pirate named Delizuff, but before they had got to the end of the voyage Delizuff was killed in an attack on a small island named Biba. There followed some friction between the men of the deceased pirate and those of Barbarossa, and finally one dark night the ships of Delizuff stole away from Barbarossa's fleet.

Eventually this Sultan of Algiers, with his ships, arrived at Constantinople. The case stood thus. The Ottoman subject was an excellent man to fight battles by land, but not by sea. Barbarossa was a true fighting seaman: therefore let him do for us that which we ourselves cannot do. He was only three years short of becoming an octogenarian, yet this veteran corsair was as able as he was wicked, and so, after the Ottoman dockyards in the following year had provided him with additional ships, Barbarossa set forth from Constantinople and began by sacking Reggio, burning Christian ships and carrying off their crews. Thence he laid waste the coast until he came to Naples, and altogether

THE WASPS AT WORK

made 11,000 Christians prisoners, and returned to the Bosphorus with an abundance of spoil and slaves. Sardinia, too, was depleted of wealth and humanity till it was almost bereft of both, and at last the fleet arrived before Tunis, to the amazement of the inhabitants. To condense a long story it may be said at once that, after some fighting, Tunis found itself now in submission to him who was also Sultan of Algiers and commander-in-chief of the Ottoman fleet. But trouble was brewing.

Again Christendom was moved to action. The successes of this all-conquering King of Corsairs were endangering the world, so the great Charles v. set on foot most elaborate preparations to cope with the evil. The preparations were indeed slow, but they were sure and they were extensive. But there was just one disappointing fact. When Francis the First, King of France, was invited to take his share in this great Christian expedition it is as true as it is regrettable to have to record the fact, that not only did he decline, but he actually betrayed the news of these impending activities to Barbarossa. This news was not welcome even to such a hardened old pirate, but he set to work in order to be ready for the foe, employed the Christian prisoners in repairing the fortifications of Tunis, summoned help to his standard from all sides, all united in the one desire to defeat and crush utterly any Christian force that might be sent against the followers of Mahomet. Spies kept him informed of the latest developments, and from Algiers came all the men that could possibly be spared. And finally, when all preparations had been made, there was on the one side the mightiest Christian expedition about to meet the greatest aggregation of Moslems. By the middle of June the invaders reached the African coast and found themselves before Tunis. It was to be a contest of Christian forces

THE WASPS AT WORK

against infidels: it was to represent an attempt once and for all to settle with the greatest pirate even the Mediterranean had ever witnessed. It was, if possible, to set free the hordes of brother-Christians from the tyrannous cruelty of a despotic corsair. Of those who now came over the sea, many had lost wife, or sister, or father, or son, or brother at the hands of these heathens. For once, at last, this great Christian Armada had the sea to itself: the wasps had retreated into their nest.

So the attack began simultaneously from the land and from the sea. The men on shore and those in the galleys realised they were battling in no ordinary contest but in a veritable crusade. Twenty-five thousand infantry and six hundred lancers, with their horses, had been brought across the sea in sixty-two galleys, a hundred and fifty transports, as well as a large number of other craft.[1] The Moslems had received assistance from along the African coast and from the inland tribes. Twenty thousand horsemen, as well as a large quantity of infantry, were ready to meet the Christians. The Emperor Charles v. was himself present, and Andrea Doria, the greatest Christian admiral, was there opposed to the greatest admiral of the Moslems.

Needless to say the fight was fierce, but at last the Christians were able to make a breach in the walls not once but in several places, and the fortress had to be vacated. Tunis was destined to fall into Christian hands. Barbarossa realised this now full well. What hurt him most was that he was beaten at his own game: his own beloved galleys were to fall into the enemies' hands. Pres-

---

[1] See *Sea-Wolves of the Mediterranean*, by Commander E. Hamilton Currey, R.N., to which I am indebted for certain information regarding these corsairs and their Christian foes.

THE WASPS AT WORK

ently the corsairs were routed utterly, and Barbarossa with only about three thousand of his followers escaped by land. Now inside Tunis were no fewer than 20,000 Christian prisoners. These now succeeded in freeing themselves of their fetters, opened the gates to the victorious army, and the latter, unable to be controlled, massacred the people they had been sent against right and left. The 20,000 Christians were rescued, the victory had been won, the corsair had been put to flight, and Muley Hassan, a mere puppet, was restored to his kingdom of Tunis by Charles v. on conditions, amongst which it was stipulated that Muley Hassan should liberate all Christian captives who might be in his realm, give them a free passage to their homes, and no corsair should be allowed again to use his ports for any purpose whatsoever.

This was the biggest blow which Barbarossa had ever received. But brute though he was, cruel tyrant that he had shown himself, enemy of the human race though he undoubtedly must be reckoned, yet his was a great mind, his was a spirit which was only impelled and not depressed by disasters. At the end of a pitiful flight, he arrived farther along the African coast at the port of Bona, where there remained just fifteen galleys which he had kept in reserve. All else that was his had gone—ships, arsenal, men. But the sea being his natural element, and piracy his natural profession, he began at once to embark. But just then there arrived fifteen of the Christian galleys, so Barbarossa, not caring for conflict, drew up his galleys under the fort of Bona, and the enemy deemed it prudent to let the corsair alone, and withdrew. Soon after Barbarossa put to sea and disappeared, when Andrea Doria with forty galleys arrived on the scene too late.

THE WASPS AT WORK

Just as on an earlier occasion already narrated, the Christian expedition made the mistake of not pressing home their victory and so settling matters with the pirates for good and all. Algiers had been drained so thoroughly of men that it was really too weak to resist an attack. But no; the Christians left that alone, although they took Bona. About the middle of August Charles re-embarked his men and, satisfied with the thrashing he had given these pirates, returned home. But Barbarossa proceeded to Algiers, where he got together a number of galleys and waited till his former followers—or as many as had survived battle and the African desert—returned to him. If Moslem piracy had been severely crushed, it was not unable to revive, and, before long, Barbarossa with his veterans was afloat again, looting ships at sea, and carrying off more prisoners to Algiers. For this piracy was like a highly infectious disease. You might think for a time that it was stamped out, that the world had been cleansed of it, but in a short time it would be manifest that the evil was as prevalent as ever.

Once more he was summoned to visit Soliman the Magnificent; once more the arch-corsair sped to Constantinople to receive instructions to deal with the conquering Christians. Andrea Doria was at sea, burning Turkish ships, and only this Sultan of Algiers could deal with him. So away Barbarossa went in his customary fashion, raiding the Adriatic towns, sweeping the islands of the Archipelago, and soon he returned to Constantinople with 18,000 slaves, to say nothing of material prizes. Money was obtained as easily as human lives, and the world marvelled that this corsair admiral, this scourge of the sea, this enemy of the Christian race, should, after a crushing defeat, be able to go about his dastardly work,

THE WASPS AT WORK

terrifying towns and ships as though the expedition of Charles v. had never been sent forth.

But matters were again working up to a crisis. If the corsair admiral was still afloat, so was Andrea Doria, the great Christian admiral. At the extreme south-west corner of the Epirus, on the Balkan side of the Adriatic, and almost opposite the heel of Italy, lies Prevesa. Hither in 1569 came the fleets of the Cross and the Crescent respectively. The Christian ships had been gathered together at the Island of Corfu, which is thirty or forty miles to the north-west of Prevesa. Barbarossa came, assisted by all the great pirate captains of the day, and among them must be mentioned Dragut, about whom we shall have more to say later.

But Prevesa, from a spectacular standpoint, was disappointing. It was too scientific, too clearly marked by strategy and too little distinguished by fighting. If the reader has ever been present at any athletic contest where there has been more skill than sport, he will know just what I mean. It is the spirit of the crowd at a cricket match when the batsman is all on the defensive and no runs are being scored. It is manifested in the spectators' indignation at a boxing match when neither party gets in a good blow, when there is an excess of science, when both contestants, fairly matched and perhaps overtrained and nervous of the other's prowess, hesitate to go in for hardhitting, so that in the end the match ends in a draw.

It was exactly on this wise at Prevesa. Andrea Doria and Barbarossa were the two great champions of the ring. Neither was young; both had been trained by years of long fighting. They were as fairly matched as it was possible to find a couple of great admirals. Each realised the other's value; both knew that for spectators they had the whole of Europe—both Christian and Moslem.

THE WASPS AT WORK

Victory to the one would mean downfall to the other, and unless a lucky escape intervened, one of the two great admirals would spend the rest of his life rowing his heart out as a galley-slave. Certainly it was enough to make the boxers nervous and hesitating. They were a long time getting to blows, and there was but little actually accomplished. There was an unlucky calm on the sea, and the *Galleon of Venice* was the centre of the fighting which took place. It was the splendid discipline on board this big craft, it was the excellence of her commander and the unique character of her great guns which made such an impression on Barbarossa's fleet that although the *Galleon* was severely damaged, yet at the critical time when the corsairs might have rushed on board and stormed her as night was approaching, for once in his life the great nerve of the corsair king deserted him. No one was more surprised than the Venetians when they found the pirate not pressing home his attack. True, the latter had captured a few of the Christian ships, but these were a mere handful and out of all proportion to the importance of the battle. He had been sent forth to crush Andrea Doria and the Christian fleet; he had failed so to do.

Next day, with a fair wind, Andrea Doria made away. The honour of the battle belonged to the *Galleon of Venice*, but for Barbarossa it was a triumph because, with an inferior force, he had put the Christian admiral to flight. Doria's ship had not been so much as touched, and yet Barbarossa had not been taken prisoner. That was the last great event in the career of Kheyr-ed-din, and he died in 1548 at Constantinople as one of the wickedest and cruellest murderers of history, the greatest pirate that has ever lived, and one of the cleverest tacticians and strategists the Mediterranean ever bore on its waters. There has rarely

THE WASPS AT WORK

lived a human being so bereft of the quality of mercy, and his death was received by Christian Europe with a sigh of the greatest relief.

In the whole history of piracy there figure some remarkably clever and consummate seamen. Like many another criminal they had such tremendous natural endowments that one cannot but regret that they began badly and continued. The bitterest critic of this Moslem monster cannot but admire his abnormal courage, resource; his powers of organisation and his untameable determination. The pity of it all is that all this should have been wasted in bringing misery to tens of thousands, in dealing death and robbery and pillage.

CHAPTER VI

GALLEYS AND GALLANTRY

BUT there was a third great Barbarian corsair to complete this terrible trio. Uruj and Kheyr-ed-din we have known. There is yet to be mentioned Dragut, who succeeded to the latter. He too was a Moslem who had been born in a coast village of Asia Minor, opposite the island of Rhodes. His early life is that of most pirates. He went to sea when quite young, was devoted to his profession, was filled with ambition, became an expert pilot and later became a skipper of his own craft. Then, feeling the call of the wild, he devoted himself to piracy and rose to notoriety.

But the turning-point in his career came when he joined himself to the service of Kheyr-ed-din, who appointed Dragut to the entire command of a dozen of the corsair king's galleys. Henceforward his life was that of his master, ravaging the Italian coasts, pillaging Mediterranean ships and dragging thousands of lives away into slavery. Two years after the battle of Prevesa, Dragut was in fame second only to Kheyr-ed-din, and another Doria — the nephew of Andrea—was sent forth to capture this new wasp of the sea. Doria succeeded in throwing his net so well that off the Corsican coast he was able to bring back Dragut as prisoner, and for the next four years the ex-

GALLEYS AND GALLANTRY

corsair was condemned to row as a slave in a Christian galley, until on a day his late master Kheyr-ed-din came sailing into Genoa. During his active, pillaging life he had obtained plenty of riches, so it was nothing for him to pay 3000 ducats and thus redeem from slavery a man who had been particularly useful to his own schemes.

And from this day until Dragut fell fighting in 1565, he followed in the footsteps of the man who brought him his release. When Kheyr-ed-din died, the Turkish Sultan appointed Dragut as admiral of the Ottoman fleet. Like Barbarossa, Dragut's first object was to obtain a base in Northern Africa, and eventually he was able to capture the town of "Africa" or Mehedia, to the east of Tunis. His next proceeding was to fortify this place. The news came to the ears of Charles v. that this had happened. The two Barbarossas were dead, but there was another almost as pernicious. Was this pestilence of piracy never to cease? Andrea Doria was an old man now, but he was bidden by Charles to go after Dragut, and he went. Nor was he sorry for an opportunity of wiping out his own undistinguished action at Prevesa. Dragut was away harrying the coasts of Spain, and his nephew Aisa was left in charge of "Africa." Meanwhile Doria searched for him along the African coast, came to "Africa," but after losing some men and with great damage to his own ship, Doria, as the season was getting late, returned home.

But the following June, Doria with his fleet arrived off Mehedia, besieged the city, and, after an expenditure of great effort, took it, capturing Aisa.

Mehedia was lost, but Dragut was still at large. He repaired to Constantinople and thence to Jerbah, the island off the east coast of Tunis. Hither also came Andrea Doria and hemmed the corsair in. At last the pirate was

GALLEYS AND GALLANTRY

in a trap, but like many another clever rascal he found a way out with consummate cleverness. What he did may briefly be summed up as follows: Outside were the waiting Christian fleet, which was merely amused by the sight of a new fort becoming daily greater. But these earthworks were just so much bluff. For Dragut, by means of these, was able to conceal what was being done on the other side. With marvellous ingenuity he had caused a road to be made across the island to the sea on the other side; he had laid down a surface of well-greased planks, and under the further cover of darkness had made his men drag his galleys across till they were launched into the sea on the opposite coast. The rest was easy, and the corsair fleet once more escaped, having fooled Dorea in a manner that amazed him. To add impudence to insult, Dragut at once captured a Sicilian galley on its way to Dorea, containing Muley Hassan, Sultan of Tunis. The latter was promptly sent as a present to the Sultan of Turkey, who allowed him to end his days in prison.

Of the rest of the acts of this corsair we have but little space to speak. It is sufficient if we say that he well bore the mantle which had fallen to him from the shoulders of Barbarossa. He continued his scourging of the seas, he fought gallantly, he laid waste and he captured prisoners for slavery. Power and dominion came to him as to his predecessors, and before long he was the ruler of Tripoli and more than ever the enemy of the Christian race. Finally he died at the siege of Malta, but he in turn was succeeded by Ali Basha of Algiers, who conquered the kingdom of Tunis, captured Maltese galleys, and showed that the old corsair spirit was still alive.

But the day of reckoning was at hand, and there was to be settled in one of the most momentous events of history

GALLEYS AND GALLANTRY

a debt that had long been owing to the Christians. Of all the decisive battles of the world few stand out more conspicuously than the battle of Lepanto. In spite of all the great maritime expeditions which had been sent to put down piracy in the Mediterranean, the evil had recurred again and again. There were two reasons why Christian Europe was determined to beat these corsairs: firstly, the latter were natural enemies because they were Moslems; but, secondly, they were the worst type of pirates. All the losses of Christian lives, goods and ships merely increased the natural hatred of these Mohammedans. And in Lepanto we see the last great contest in which these truculent corsairs fought as a mighty force. Thereafter there were repeated piratical attacks by these men, but they of a more individualistic nature than proceeding from an enormous organisation.

Lepanto was fought sixteen years before the Elizabethans defeated the Armada. Before we say anything of the contest itself it is necessary to remind the reader that whereas in the contest which took place in the waters that wash England, the bulk of the ships were sail-propelled and had high freeboard (with some exceptions), yet at Lepanto it was the reverse. The fighting ship of the Mediterranean from the very earliest times had always been of the galley type, even though it contained variations of species. And never was this characteristic more clearly manifested than at the battle of which we are now to speak. There were galleys and galleasses, but though the former were certainly somewhat big craft, yet the latter were practically only big editions of the galley.

The value of Lepanto is twofold. It proved to the world that the great Ottoman Empire was not invincible on sea. It showed also that in spite of all that the cleverest

GALLEYS AND GALLANTRY

corsair seamen could do, there were sufficient unity and seamanlike ability in Christian Europe to defeat the combined efforts of organised piracy and Mohammedanism. No one can deny that Ali Basha distinguished himself as a fine admiral at this battle, yet he was not on the side of victory. When he found himself defeated there fell simultaneously the greatest blow which organised piracy had received since it established itself along the southern shores of the Mediterranean. Lepanto was no mere isolated event; it was the logical outcome of the conflict between Christianity on the one hand and Mohammedanism with piracy on the other. It is as unfair to omit the consideration of Moslemism from the cause of this battle as it were to leave out the fact of piracy.

The solidarity of the Christian expedition was formed by what was called the Holy League, embracing the ships of the Papal States, Spain and Venice. The unity of the opposing side was ensured by the fidelity of the Barbarian corsairs to the Sultan of Turkey. In supreme command of the former was Don John of Austria, son of that Charles v. who had done so much to oust these corsair wasps. The Christian fleet numbered about three hundred, of which two-thirds were galleys, and they collected at Messina. The scene where the battle was to take place was already historic. It was practically identical with that of Prevesa, of which we have already spoken, and with that of the classical Actium in 31 B.C., though exactly it was a little to the south of where Prevesa had been fought. Just as in the latter Kheyr-ed-din had fought against Andrea Doria, so now Dragut was to fight against John Andrea Doria. The Moslem strength may be gauged from the statement that it contained 250 galleys plus a number of smaller ships. But just as Prevesa had been marked

GALLEYS AND GALLANTRY

by little fighting but much manœuvring, so Lepanto was distinguished by an absence of strategy and a prevalence of desperate, hard hitting. Whatever strategy was displayed belonged to Ali Basha. The galleasses of the Christian side dealt wholesale death into the Moslems, though Andrea's own flagship suffered severely in the fight. Spanish, Venetian and Maltese galleys fought most gallantly, but Ali Basha, after capturing the chief of the Maltese craft, was obliged to relinquish towing her, and himself compelled to escape from the battle. At least 5000 Christians perished at Lepanto, but six times that amount were slaughtered of the Moslems, together with 200 of the latter's ships. The corsairs had rendered the finest assistance, but they had failed with distinction.

Christian craft had won the great day, and never since that autumn day in 1571 have the pirates of Barbary attained to their previous dominion and organised power. Ali returned to Constantinople, and even the next year was again anxious to fight his late enemies, though no actual fighting took place. Still another year later Tunis was taken from the Turks by Don John of Austria. For nine years after the event of Lepanto, Ali Basha lived on, and, like his predecessors, spent much of his time harrying the Christian coastline of southern Italy. There were many pirates for long years after his death, but with the decease of Ali Basha closed the grand period of the Moslem corsairs. It had been a century marked by the most amazing impudence on the part of self-made kings and tyrants. But if it showed nothing else, it made perfectly clear what enormous possibilities the sea offered to any man who had enough daring and self-confidence in addition to that essential quality of sea-sense. From mere common sailormen these four great corsairs—the two Barbarossas, Dragut

GALLEYS AND GALLANTRY

and Ali Basha—rose to the position of autocrats and admirals. Mere robbers and bandits though they were, yet the very mention of their names sent a shudder through Christendom. And it was only the repeated and supreme efforts of the great European powers which could reduce these pirate kings into such a condition that honest ships could pursue their voyages with any hope of reaching their destined ports. Surely, in the whole history of lawlessness, there never were malefactors that prospered for so long and to such an extent!

We have spoken in this chapter of galleys and galleasses. Before we close, let us add a few words of explanation to facilitate the reader's vision. Bearing in mind the interesting survival of the galley type throughout Mediterranean warfare, it must not be forgotten that in detail this type of craft varied in subsequent centuries. There remained, however, the prevailing fact that she relied primarily on oars, and that she drew comparatively little water and had but little freeboard in proportion to the caravels, caracks and ocean-going ships of war and commerce. The great virtue of the galley consisted in her mobility. Her greatest defect lay in her lack of sea-keeping qualities. For the galley's work was concerned with operations within a limited sphere with the land not far away; in other words, she was suited for conditions the exact opposite of that kind of craft which could sail to the West Indies or go round Cape Horn.

The amazing feature of these galleys was the large number of oarsmen required; but this was an age when human life was regarded more cheaply than to-day. Slaves could be had by raiding towns or capturing ships. The work of pulling at the oar was healthy if terribly hard. A minimum of food and the stern lash of the boatswain as he

GALLEY SLAVES

The life of a galley slave was one of dreadful hardship. They were chained five or six to an oar, fed on the scantiest of food, and a boatswain walked up and down a gangway in the centre wielding his terrible lash on those who incurred his anger.

GALLEYS AND GALLANTRY

walked up and down the gangway that ran fore-and-aft down the centre of the ship kept the men at their duty, and their shackles prevented them from deserting. But when their poor, wearied bodies became weak, they were thrown overboard before their last breath had left them. The prints, which are still in existence, show that the number of oarsmen in a sixteenth-century galley ran into hundreds—two or three hundred of these galley-slaves would be no rare occurrence in one craft. They retained the beak and the arrangement of the yards from the time of the Romans. At the stern sat the commander with his officers. When these craft carried cannon the armament was placed in the bows. By the sixteenth, or at any rate the seventeenth, century, the galley had reached her climax, and it was not thought remarkable that her length should be about 170 feet and her breadth only about 20 feet. She may be easily studied by the reader on referring to an accompanying illustration. Whether used by Christian or corsair, by Maltese knights or Moslem Turks, they were not very different from the picture which is here presented. With five men to each heavy oar, with seamen to handle the sails when employed, with soldiers to fight the ship, she was practically a curious kind of raft or floating platform. Irrespective of religion or race, it was customary for the sixteenth-century nations to condemn their prisoners to row chained to these benches. Thus, for example, when the Spaniards captured Elizabethan seamen, the latter were thus employed, just as Venetian prisoners were made to row in Moslem galleys. Convicted criminals were also punished by this means.

The difference between the old and new was never better seen than in the late sixteenth century, when the big-bellied man-of-war with sails and guns were beginning to discard

GALLEYS AND GALLANTRY

the old boarding tactics. It was the gun and not the sword on which they were now relying. But the galley was dependent less on her gunnery than on boarding. It was her aim to fight not at a distance but at close quarters—to get right close alongside and then pour her soldiers on to the other ship and obtain possession. The galeass of the Mediterranean, although the word was somewhat largely used, signified an attempt to combine the sea-qualities of the big-bellied ship with the mobility of the galley. Compromises are, however, but rarely successful, and though the galleass was a much more potent fighting unit, yet she was less mobile, if a better sea craft. She began by being practically a big galley with forecastle and sterncastle and another deck; she ended in being little less clumsy than the contemporary ship of the line which relied on sails and guns. Anyone who cares to examine the contemporary pictures of the Spanish galleasses used by the Armada against England in the reign of Elizabeth can see this for himself. It is true that even as far north as Amsterdam in the seventeenth century the galley was employed, and there are many instances when she fought English ships in the Channel, off Portsmouth and elsewhere. For a time some lingered on in the British Navy, but they were totally unsuited for the waters of the North Sea and English Channel, and gave way to the sail-propelled ships of larger displacement.

CHAPTER VII

PIRACY IN ELIZABETHAN TIMES

BUT although the Mediterranean was the sphere of the Barbarian corsairs, yet this sea lawlessness was not confided to that area. The Narrow Seas were just about as bad as they had been in the Middle Ages. And Elizabeth, with the determination for which she was famous, took the matter in hand.

As early as the year 1564 she commanded Sir Peter Carew to fit out an expedition to clear the seas of any pirates and rovers that haunted the coasts of Devonshire and Cornwall; yet it was an almost impossible task. For the men of these parts especially had gotten the sea-fever. Fishing was less profitable than it might be, but to capture ships instead of fish was a very paying industry and had just that amount of adventure which appealed to the Elizabethans. And bear in mind that, as in the case of the later smugglers, these men had at their backs for financial support the rich land-owners, who found the investment tempting.

It was because the colonies in the New World were yielding such wondrous treasure that the English pirates found the Spanish ships so well worth waiting for and pillaging. Again and again did Philip make demands to Elizabeth that this nuisance should be stopped, insisting

PIRACY IN ELIZABETHAN TIMES

that in no case should a convicted English pirate be pardoned. He requested that Her Majesty's officers in the west of England ports should cease from allowing these marauders to take stores aboard or even frequent these harbours. Rewards, he begged, should even be offered for their capture, and all persons on shore who aided these miscreants should be punished severely.

It was because of Philip's complaint, no less than of the complaint of her own merchants, that the Queen was compelled to adopt severe measures. She despatched more ships to police the seas, but with what advantage? Up came a ship bound from Flanders to Spain with a cargo of tapestry, clocks and various other articles for Philip. The English pirates could not let such a prize go past, so they stopped the ship and plundered her. The Queen's next effort was to cause strict inquiries to be made along the coast in order to discover the haunts of these Northern corsairs. Harbour commissioners were appointed, says Lindsay, to inquire and report on all vessels leaving or entering port, and all landed proprietors who had encouraged the pirates were threatened with penalties. But it was an impossible task, as I will explain. First of all, consider the fact that after centuries of this free sea-roving, no government, no amount of threats, could possibly transform the character of the English seaman. If, for instance, to-morrow, Parliament were to make it law forbidding the North Sea fishermen to proceed in their industry, nothing but shells from men-of-war would prevent the men putting to sea. Years of occupation would be too strong to resist.

So it was with the seamen in the Elizabethan age. It began by that hatred of their French neighbours; it was encouraged by the privileges which the Cinque Ports enjoyed, though it was in the blood of the English seamen

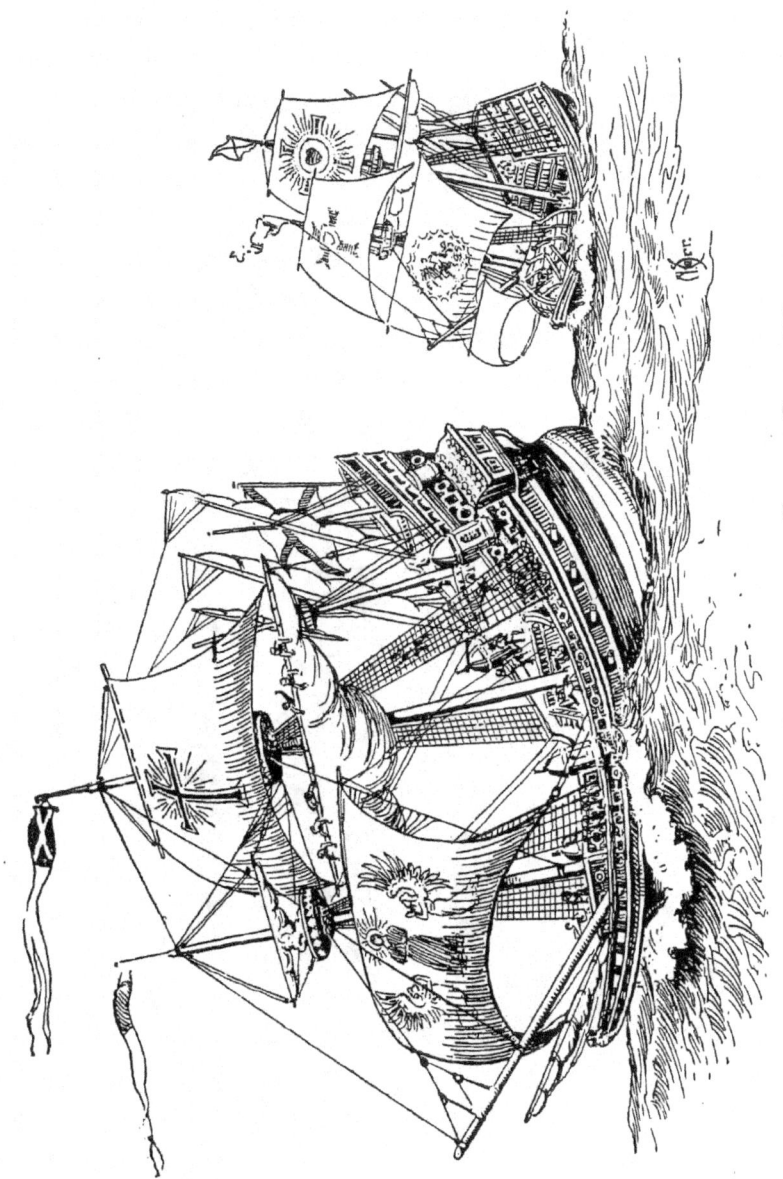

SPANISH GALLEONS IN THE TIME OF ELIZABETH

At the time when the colonies in the New World were yielding such wondrous treasures these ships were the object of many an attack by English pirates, greatly to the indignation of King Philip.

PIRACY IN ELIZABETHAN TIMES

quite apart from any royal permission. But there was in the time of Elizabeth still a further difficulty. Those privateers whom the law had permitted to go forth sea-roving had become too strong to be suppressed. Privateering strictly consists of a private ship or ships having a commission to seize or plunder the ships of an enemy; in effect it amounts to legalised piracy, and any one can realise that in a none too law-abiding age, such as the sixteenth century, the dividing line between piracy and privateering was so very fine that it was almost impossible to say which pillaging was legal and which was unjustifiable. That alone was sufficient reason for the frequent releases of alleged pirates at this time.

True, the Crown allowed privateering, though the commissions were limited only to the attacks on our acknowledged enemies, yet it was futile to expect that these rude Devonshire seamen would have any respect to legal *finesse*. To control these men adequately was too much to expect. French and Spanish and Flemish merchantmen, regardless of nationality, were alike liable to fall into the English pirates' hands. Some of the backers were making quite a handsome income, and who shall say that some of those fine Elizabethan mansions in our country were not built out of such illegal proceeds? The Mayor of Dover, for instance, with some of the leading inhabitants of that port, had captured over 600 prizes from the French, to say nothing of the number of neutrals which he had pillaged. This was in the year 1563, and already he had plundered sixty-one Spanish ships. And there was the valuable trade passing to and from Antwerp and London, which was a steady source of revenue for the pirates of this time. You cannot be surprised, then, at that important incident in 1564, that did so much to enrage the English seamen and

PIRACY IN ELIZABETHAN TIMES

help matters forward to the climax in the form of the Spanish Armada; for what happened? Philip, seeing how little Elizabeth was doing to put down this series of attacks on his treasure ships, had, in the year mentioned, suddenly issued an order arresting every English ship and all the English crews that happened to be found within his own harbours. It was a drastic measure, but we can quite understand the impetuous and furious Spaniard acting on this wise.

During Elizabeth's reign there were of course some pirates who had the bad fortune to be arrested. One little batch suspected included a Captain Heidon, Richard Deigle and a man named Corbet. Included in the same gang were Robert Hitchins, Philip Readhead, Roger Shaster and others. The first three mentioned succeeded in fleeing away beyond capture, but the remainder admitted their guilt. Hitchins was a man about fifty years old and a native of Devonshire, but both he and his companions protested that they had been deceived by Heidon and Deigle; they had undertaken a voyage to Rochelle presumably in a merchant ship, whereas the trip turned out to be nothing else than a piratical expedition.

Their version of the incident was that in June 1564 they captured a Flemish ship, and to her were transferred thirteen Scots who were forming part of this supposedly merchant ship. The Flemish ship with the Scots on board now sailed away, as there was some disagreement with the rest of the party. They proceeded to Ireland, where their skipper joined them, and they also committed robberies on the coast of Spain. Having captured a ship with a cargo of wine they proceeded to that extreme south-west corner of Ireland which, even in this twentieth century, is still a wild, lonely spot and rarely visited by any craft excepting

PIRACY IN ELIZABETHAN TIMES

the British Navy, an occasional cable-laying ship and sometimes a coaster or two. Berehaven is a mighty fjord which goes out of Bantry Bay. On the one side rise high, rocky hills; on the other lies the island of Bere. It is a safe, clear anchorage and a wild, inaccessible spot.

Here the captured ship was taken and the wines sold. An arrangement was made with the Lord O'Sullivan by which the pirates could rely on his assistance. For Corbet with one ship, and a man named Lusingham, who had charge of another ship, were prevented by O'Sullivan from falling into the hands of Elizabeth's ships that had been sent to capture them. Lusingham, however, had been slain by "a piece of ordnance," as he was in the act of waving his cap towards the Queen's ships at Berehaven, but Corbet was yet alive. It was alleged that Heidon and Corbet had agreed jointly to fit out the *John of Sandwich*, giving her all the necessary guns with the hope of being able to capture a good ship wherewith to provide Corbet. But whilst in the English Channel a storm had sprung up and the ship had sprung a leak. They were therefore forced into Alderney, where the vessel became a wreck, and Heidon, Corbet, Deigle, as well as fourteen others, made their escape in a small pinnace.

It was discovered that Robert Hitchins had been all his life given to piracy, so, after having been arrested in the Channel Isles, he was executed at low-water mark near St. Martin's Point, Guernsey, and there his body was left in chains as a warning to others. The rest of the prisoners were afterwards ordered by Elizabeth to be set free, " after a good and sharp admonition to beware hereafter to fall again into the damage of our laws." They were bidden to return to their native places and to get their living by honest labour. It is a proof that the Crown really valued her sea-

PIRACY IN ELIZABETHAN TIMES

men by an interesting proclamation that was made in 1572 when there was a likeliness of war. The Queen went so far as to promise pardon for all piracies hitherto committed by any mariners who should now put their ships into her naval service, and we must not forget that, at a later date, the first tidings of the Armada's advent were brought into Plymouth by a patriotic English pirate named Fleming. "Fleming," wrote John Smith, the great Elizabethan traveller and founder of the English colony of Virginia, "was as expert and as much sought for" as any other pirates of the Queen's reign, "yet such a friend to his Country, that discovering the Spanish Armado, he voluntarily came to Plymouth, yeelded himselfe freely to my Lord Admirall, and gave him notice of the Spaniards comming; which good warning came so happily and unexpectedly, that he had his pardon, and a good reward."

"As in all lands," writes this delightful Elizabethan, "where there are many people, there are some theeves, so in all seas much frequented, there are some pirates; the most ancient within the memory of threescore yeares was one Callis, who most refreshed himselfe upon the Coast of Wales; Clinton and Pursser his companions, who grew famous, till Queene Elizabeth of blessed memory, hanged them at Wapping." Now this John Callis or Calles, after his arrest, wrote a letter of repentance to Walsyngham saying: "I bewail my former wicked life, and beseech God and Her Majesty to forgive me. If she will spare my life and use me in her service by sea, with those she can trust best, either to clear the coasts of other wicked pirates or otherwise, as I know their haunts, roads, creeks, and maintainers so well, I can do more therein than if she sent ships abroad and spent £20,000."

Thinking thereby to obtain pardon, Calles accordingly

PIRACY IN ELIZABETHAN TIMES

forwarded particulars of his fellow pirates, their "maintainers and victuallers of me and my companies." This list contained the names and addresses of the purchasers and receivers of goods which had been pillaged from two Portuguese, one French, a Spanish and a Scotch ship, which Calles and a Captain Sturges of Rochelle had pirated. If he were given his liberty, this loquacious corsair further promised that he would also bring in a Danish ship, which he had pirated. He promised also to warn Walsyngham to take care that Sulivan Bere of Berehaven "does not practise any treason" towards Her Majesty there, as he alleged that Sulivan had told Calles in the former's castle at Berehaven that James Fitzmorris and a number of Frenchmen were determined to land there if they could obtain pilots to guide them thither. The old pirate further alleged that they had tried to persuade himself to join them and become their guide, promising him "large gifts." "But I would not join any rebel of Her Majesty," he wrote grandiloquently, "hoping her mercy in time to come."

Last March, he went on, while he was riding at anchor at Torbay, he met a Frenchman, commanded by Captain Molloner, who came aboard Calles's ship and sought information regarding the Irish coast and the best harbours. Calles informed him the best were Cork and Kinsale. His inquirers then asked whether Berehaven and Dingell were not good places where to land. "They told me if I would go over with them to France, I need not fear the Queen for any offence I had done." The French King would pardon him for anything Calles had done against His Majesty's subjects, and would give him 3000 crowns to become his subject and be sworn his man, as well as a yearly fee during life. "I asked him why his master wanted to use me, and he said his master shortly meant to do some

PIRACY IN ELIZABETHAN TIMES

service on the coast of Ireland, and wanted pilots." Calles protested that he had declined this invitation, to which the other man was reported to have replied that he would never have such a chance of preferment offered him in England. But though this made a very fine yarn, the authorities were too well aware of Calles's past history to give it too much credence.

"The misery of a Pirate (although many are as sufficient Seamen as any) yet in regard of his superfluity," wrote the founder of Virginia, "you shall finde it such, that any wise man would rather live amongst wilde beasts than them: therefore let all unadvised persons take heed, how they entertaine that quality: and I could wish Merchants, Gentlemen, and all setters forth of ships, not to bee sparing of a competent pay, nor true payment, for neither Souldiers nor Seamen can live without meanes, but necessity will force them to steale: and when they are once entered into that trade, they are hardly reclaimed."

Poverty as well as the love of adventure and the lust for gain had certainly to be reckoned among the incentives to this life. So steadily had the evil grown that on 7th August 1579, Yorke complained to Lord Burghley that the sea had never been so full of pirates, and a Plymouth ship which had set out from St. Malo bound for Dartmouth had been robbed and chased on to the rocks. None the less, the "persons of credit" who had been appointed in every haven, creek or other landing-place round the coast, in order to deal with the evil, were doing their best, and three notable pirates had some time before been arrested and placed in York Castle together with other pirates.

But the practice of piracy, as we have seen, was the peculiar failing of no country exclusively, though in certain parts of the world and in certain centuries pirates were more

PIRACY IN ELIZABETHAN TIMES

prevalent than elsewhere. The very men who in the English Channel might have attained disgrace and wealth as sea-robbers might, also, when he went into the Mediterranean, be himself pillaged by those Barbarian corsairs of whom we spoke just now. Many an exciting brush did the mariners of England encounter with these men, and many were the sad tales which reached England of the cruelties of these Moslem tyrants. An interesting account of such an adventure is related by Master Roger Bodenham. The incident really happened seven years before Elizabeth came to the throne, but it may not be out of place here to deal with it.

After having set forth from Gravesend in the "great barke *Aucher*" bound for the islands of Candia and Chio in the Levant, the ship arrived at Messina in Sicily. But it was made known that a good many Moslem galleys were in the Levant and the rest of the voyage would be more than risky. The *Aucher's* crew got to know of this, so that Bodenham was not likely to get farther on his way and deliver his cargo at Chio. "Then," he writes, "I had no small businesse to cause my mariners to venture with the ship in such a manifest danger. Neverthelesse I wan them to goe with me, except three which I set on land." But these presently begged to come aboard again and were taken, and the ship got under way. A Greek pilot was taken on board, and when off Chio three Turkish pirates were suddenly espied. These were giving chase to a number of small boats which were sailing rigged with a lateen-sail. It happened that in one of the latter was the son of the pilot, and at this Greek's request Bodenham steered towards the Turks and caused the *Aucher's* gunner to fire a demi-culverin at the chaser that was just about to board one of the boats. This was such a good shot that the Turk

PIRACY IN ELIZABETHAN TIMES

dropped astern. Presently all the little boats came and begged that they might be allowed to hang on to the *Aucher's* stern till daylight. After clearing from Chio, Bodenham took his ship to Candia and Messina. But whilst on the way thither and in the very waters where the battle of Lepanto was presently to be fought, he found some of the Turkish galleots pirating some Venetian ships laden with muscatels, and, good Samaritan that he was, Bodenham succeeded in driving off the Moslem aggressors and rescuing the merchantmen. "I rescued them," he writes briefly, "and had but a barrell of wine for my powder and shot."

CHAPTER VIII

ELIZABETHAN SEAMEN AND TURKISH PIRATES

BUT a much more adventurous voyage was that of a ship called *The Three Half Moones*, which, with a crew of thirty-eight men and well found in arms— "the better to encounter their enemies withall"—set out from Portsmouth in the year 1563.

In some ways the story reads like mere romance, but it has been so thoroughly well-vouched for that there is not a particle of suspicion connected with it. Having set forth bound for the south of Spain they arrived near the Straits of Gibraltar, when they found themselves surrounded by eight Turkish galleys. (It should be mentioned that the Elizabethans used the word Turk somewhat loosely to mean Moslems.) It was rapidly made clear that only two alternatives were possible. Flight was out of the question, and either the *Aucher* must fight to a finish or she must be sunk. But being English and a gallant crew, they decided to fight. Now, amongst those on board were the owner, the master, the master's mate, the boatswain, the purser and the gunner as officers.

When their desperate situation was realised, the owner exhorted his men to behave valiantly, to be brave, and to bear a reverse with resignation. Then, falling on their

ELIZABETHAN SEAMEN AND

knees, they all commended themselves to God and prepared for the fight. "Then stood up one Grove, the master, being a comely man, with his sword and target, holding them up in defiance against his enemies. So likewise stood up the Owner, the Master's mate, Boatswaine, Purser, and every man well appointed. Nowe likewise sounded up the drums, trumpets and flutes, which would have encouraged any man, had he never so litle heart or courage in him." But next let us introduce to the reader John Foxe, the ship's gunner, a man of marvellous resource, as we will see presently. Foxe saw that the guns were arranged to the best effect and that the Turks were receiving a hot fire. But three times as fast as the English shot came the infidel's fire, and the fight raged furiously with eight galleys to one big ship. The Turks advanced, and then came the time for the English bowmen to let fly their arrows, which fell thickly among the rowers. Simultaneously the English poured out from their guns a hotter fire than ever, and the Turks fell like ninepins. But meanwhile the *Aucher* was receiving serious damage below her waterline, and this the Turks seeing, the infidels endeavoured now to board the ship. As they leapt on board many of them fell never again to rise, the others engaging in a tremendous conflict on the *Aucher's* deck. "For the Englishmen," writes the narrator in fine, robustous Elizabethan language, "shewed themselves men in deed, in working manfully with their browne bills and halbardes: where the owner, master, boateswaine, and their company stoode to it lustily, that the Turkes were halfe dismaied. But chiefly the boateswaine shewed himself valiant above the rest: for he fared amongst the Turkes like a wood Lion: for there was none of them that either could or durst stand in his face, till at the last there came a shot from the Turkes, which brake his whistle asunder, and

GALLANTRY AGAINST ODDS

The Englishmen showed themselves men indeed against the Moors, especially the boatswain, who was brought down by a bullet in his chest. But overcome by numbers the brave crew were overwhelmed, and the survivors condemned to the oars.

TURKISH PIRATES

smote him on the brest, so that he fell downe, bidding them farewell, and to be of good comfort, encouraging them likewise to winne praise by death, rather than to live captives in misery and shame."

Such was the fine gallantry of these brave men, but they were fighting against heavy odds. The Turks pressed them sorely, and not one of the company but behaved as a man, except the master's mate "who shrunke from the skirmish, like a notable coward, esteeming neither the valure of his name, nor accounting of the present example of his fellowes, nor having respect to the miseries, whereunto he should be put." The rest of the crew covered themselves with glory, but at length it was of no avail, for the Turks won the day. Then, in accordance with the historic custom of the sea, the crew of the *Aucher* were placed in the galleys, set to row at the oars "and they were no sooner in them, but their garments were pulled over their eares, and torne from their backes," for the galley slave was always condemned to row stark naked.

At length the galleys reached their stronghold at the port of Alexandria, which was well protected in those days by means of fortifications. The reader will recollect that it was stated some time back that the sailing season was confined only to the late spring and summer, and that in the winter the ships were laid up. The close time now approaching, the Christian prisoners were brought ashore at Alexandria and cast into prison until the time came round again for the season of piracy. At this port, says the Elizabethan chronicler, "the Turkes doe customably bring their gallies on shoare every yeere, in the winter season, and there doe trimme them, and lay them up against the spring time. In which road there is a prison, wherein the captives and such prisoners as serve in the gallies, are put for all that time, untill the seas be calme and passable for the gallies, every prisoner being most grievously laden with irons on their legges, to their great paine."

So the voyage of the *Aucher* had come to a tragic ending. But after a time the news of this incident evidently reached England, for both the master and the owner were ransomed by their friends from their prison. The rest had to bear their ill-treatment and semi-starvation as best they would. But he who bore it all with wonderful endurance was the gunner John Foxe and "being somewhat skilfull in the craft of a Barbour, by reason thereof made great shift in helping his fare now and then with a good meale." In the course of time the keeper of the prison became rather fond of him and allowed him special privileges, so that he could walk as far as the sea and back when he liked, but he was warned always to return by night, and he was never allowed to go about without his shackles on his legs. Later on, six more of the prisoners were allowed a like privilege.

The life sped wearily on, and now, for fourteen sorry years, this durance vile had continued. It was the year 1577, and the winter season had come round again and the galleys drawn up the beach. The masts and sails thereof were brought ashore and properly housed till once more the spring should return, and the Turkish masters and mariners were now "nested in their own homes," as the narrative quaintly words it. The galley-slaves had again resumed their long bondage ashore, and now there were no fewer than 268 wretched Christians there, languishing in captivity, having been captured from sixteen different nations. It was then that John Foxe, man of resource that he was, resolved that escape must be made and his fellow-prisoners also released. If you consider such a project as the release

TURKISH PIRATES

of nearly 300 prisoners from the hands of these Turkish pirates, the idea seems entirely impracticable and utterly visionary.

To John Foxe, however, it seemed otherwise, and this is how he set to work. After pondering over a method for a very long time and saying many prayers that his scheme might be successful, he betook himself to a fellow-prisoner —a Spanish Christian—named Peter Unticaro, who had been in captivity no less than thirty years. This man was lodged in "a certaine victualling house" near the roadstead. He had never attempted escape during all those years, so was treated with less suspicion and trusted. Foxe and Unticaro had often discussed their bondage, however, and at last the Englishman took the risk of making him his confidant, and also one other fellow-prisoner. These three men put their heads together, and Foxe unfolded a method of escape. Their chances of meeting were but few and short, but at the end of seven weeks they had been able to agree on a definite plan. Five more prisoners were now taken into their confidence whom they thought they could safely trust.

The last day of the old year came round, and these eight men agreed to meet in the prison and inform the rest of the prisoners of the plan. On the 31st of December, then, this was done. It needed but little persuasion to cause these two hundred odd to join in the scheme, and Foxe having "delivered unto them a sort of files, which he had gathered together for this purpose, by the meanes of Peter Unticaro," admonished them to be ready at eight o'clock the next night with their fetters filed through. So on the next day Foxe, with his six companions, resorted to the house of Peter Unticaro. In order to prevent any suspicions of a dark deed, they spent the time in mirth till

ELIZABETHAN SEAMEN AND

the night came on and the hour of eight drew nigh. Foxe then sent Unticaro to the keeper of the road, pretending that he had been sent by one of the Turkish officials, ordering him to come at once. The keeper promptly came, and before doing so, told the warders not to bar the gate as he should not be long away.

In the meantime the other seven prisoners had been able to arm themselves with the best weapons they could find in the house of the Spaniard, and John Foxe was able to lay his hands on a rusty old sword blade " without either hilt or pomell," but he managed to make it effective. By now the keeper had arrived, but as soon as he came to the house and saw it silent and in darkness he began to be suspicious. John Foxe was ready for him, and before the keeper had retraced his steps more than a few yards, the Englishman sprang out, and, calling him a villain and " a bloodsucker of many a Christian's blood, lift up his bright shining sword of tenne yeeres rust " and killed him on the spot. They then marched quietly in the direction of the warders of the road and quickly dispatched these six officials. Foxe then barred the gate and put a cannon against it to prevent pursuit. So far all had worked with remarkable smoothness. They next proceeded to the gaoler's lodge, where they found the keys of the fortress and prison by his bedside. They also found some better weapons than the arms they were using. But there was also a chest full of ducats. To three of the party this wonderful sight proved irresistible. Foxe would not have anything to do with the money for " that it was his and their libertie which he sought for, to the honour of his God, and not to make a marte of the wicked treasure of the Infidels." But Unticaro and two others helped themselves liberally, and concealed the money between their skin and their shirt.

TURKISH PIRATES

These eight men, armed with the keys, now came to the prison, whose doors they opened. The captives were ready and waiting. Foxe called on them to do their share, and the whole band—between two and three hundred—poured forth. To each section did Foxe bestow some duty. The eight prison warders were put to death, but some of the prisoners Foxe had wisely sent down to the water, where they got ready for sea the best galley, called the *Captain of Alexandria*. Whilst some were getting her launched, others were rushing about bringing her masts and sails and oars and the rest of her inventory from the winter quarters. The whole place was seething with suppressed excitement. Meanwhile there was a warm contest going on at the prison before all the warders were slain. The latter had fled to the top of the prison, and Foxe with his companions went after them with ladders. Blood and slaughter were all round them. Three times was Foxe shot, but by a miracle the shot only passed through his clothing on each occasion. But, as if by way of punishment for their greed, Unticaro and his two companions who had taken the ducats were killed outright, b ing "not able to weild themselves, being so pestered with the weight and uneasie carrying of the wicked and prophane treasure."

In this conflict one of the Turks was run through with a sword and, not yet dead, fell from the top of the prison wall to the ground. Such a noise did he then begin to make that the alarm was raised, and the authorities were amazed to find the Christian prisoners were "paying their ransoms" by dealing death to their late masters. Alexandria was now roused, and both a certain castle as well as a strong fortress were bestirring themselves to action. It seemed as if the prisoners, after all their years of suffering, after having brought about so gallant an escape, were now to fail just as

ELIZABETHAN SEAMEN AND

victory was well in sight. It was a saddening thought. But there was one road of escape and one only. Whilst some of the prisoners were still running down to the sea carrying munitions, some additional oars, victuals and whatever else were required for the galleys, others were getting ready for pushing off. The last of the Christians leapt aboard, the final touch was given to the gear, and up went the yards and the sails were unloosed. There was a good breeze and this, the swiftest and best of all Alexandria's ships, was speeding on at a good pace. But ashore the Turks have already got to their guns, and the roar of cannon is heard from both the castle and fortress. The sea is splashing everywhere with Turkish ball and the smoke is swept by the breeze off the shore. Five and forty times did these guns fire and never once did a shot so much as graze the galley, although she could see the splashes all around her.

On and still on sailed this long, lean galley, increasing her speed all the time, till at length, by God's mercy, she, with her long-suffering crew, who by years of involuntary training had learnt to handle her to perfection, were at last out of range of any Turkish cannon. In the distance they could see their late masters coming down to the beach "like unto a swarme of bees," and bustling about in a futile endeavour to get their other galleys ready for the sea. But it was of little avail. The Christians had long been preparing for flight in the *Captain*, so the Turks found it took an unbearable time in seeing out the oars and masts, and cables and everything else necessary to a galley's inventory lying hidden away in winter quarters. They had never suspected such a well-planned escape as this. Nothing was ready; all was confusion. And even when the galleys were at last launched and rigged, the weather was so boisterous, there was such a strong wind that no man cared about

TURKISH PIRATES

taking charge of these fine-weather craft just at that time.

So the escaping galley got right away, and then, as soon as they were a safe distance away, Foxe summoned his men to do what Nelson was to perform less than three centuries later at almost this very spot. You remember how, after the glorious battle of the Nile, when the British fleet had obtained such a grand victory over the French, Nelson sent orders through the fleet to return thanksgiving to Almighty God for the result of the battle. All work was stopped, and men who had spent the whole night risking death and fighting for their lives, dishevelled and dirty with sweat and grime, now stood bareheaded and rendered their thanks. So it was now on the galley *Captain.* Foxe " called to them all, willing them to be thankfull unto Almighty God for their deliverie, and most humbly to fall downe upon their knees, beseeching Him to aide them unto their friends' land, and not to bring them into an other daunger, sith Hee had most mightily delivered them from so great a thraldome and bondage." It must have been a momentous occasion. Men who, after being prisoners for thirty years and less, men who had just come through a night of wild excitement, men who had fought with their arms and sweated hard to get their galley ready for sea, men who even at the last minute had barely escaped being blown into eternity by the Turkish cannon, now halted in their work and made their thanksgiving, whilst most of them hardly could realise that at length they were free men and the time of their tribulation was at an end.

And then they resumed their rowing, and instead of working till they dropped for faintness, each man helped his neighbour when weariness was stealing over the oarsmen. Never did a more united ship's company put to sea. One

ELIZABETHAN SEAMEN AND

object alone did they all possess—to come to some Christian land with the least possible delay. They had no charts, but Foxe and his English fellow-seamen knew something about astronomy, and by studying the stars in the heavens they roughly guessed the direction in which they ought to steer.

With such haphazard navigation, however, they soon lost their position when variable winds sprang up. Those light-draught ships made a good deal of leeway, and as the wind had been from so many points of the compass " they were now in a new maze." But troubles do not come singly : they were further troubled by their victuals giving out, so that it seemed as if they had escaped from one form of punishment only to fall into a worse kind of hardship. As many as eight died of starvation, but at last, on the twenty-ninth day after leaving Alexandria, the others picked up the land again and found it was the island of Candia. Their distance made good had thus been about 350 miles north-west, which works out at about twelve miles a day. But though this is ridiculously small it must be borne in mind that their courses were many and devious, that to row for twenty-nine consecutive days was a terrible trial for human endurance, and latterly they were rowing with empty stomachs. They came at length to Gallipoli in Candia and landed. Here the good abbot and monks of the Convent of Amerciates received them with welcome and treated them with every Christian hospitality. They refreshed these poor voyagers and attended to their wants until well enough to resume their travels. Two hundred and fifty-eight had survived, and good nourishment, with kindly treatment on land, restored their health and vigour.

We need not attempt to suggest the warmth of the welcome which these poor prisoners received and the congratula-

TURKISH PIRATES

tions which were showered upon them in having escaped from the hands of the Turks. It was in itself a remarkable achievement that so many had come out alive. As a token and remembrance of this miraculous escape Foxe left behind as a present to the monks the sword with which the Englishman had slain the keeper of the prison. Esteeming it a precious jewel it remained hanging up in a place of honour in the monastery. When the time came for the *Captain* to get under way again, she coasted till she arrived at Tarento (in the heel of Italy) and so concluded their voyage. They were once again in a Christian land and away from their oppressors. The galley they sold at this port and immediately started to walk on foot to Naples. Yes, they had escaped, but by how little may be gathered from the fact that the Christians having started their long walk in the morning, there arrived that self-same night seven Turkish galleys. But the latter were too late: their captives were now inland.

Having reached Naples without further adventure, the Christians separated and, according to his nationality, made for their distant homes. But Foxe proceeded first to Rome, arriving there one Easter Eve, where he was well entertained by an Englishman who brought the news of this wonderful escape to the notice of the Pope. Foxe was without any means of livelihood, and it was a long way to walk to the English Channel, so he determined to try his luck in Spain. The Pope treated the poor man with every consideration, and sent him on his journey with a letter to the King of Spain. "We, in his behalf, do in the bowels of Christ desire you," wrote His Holiness, "that, taking compassion of his former captivity and present penury, you do not only suffer him freely to pass throughout your cities and towns, but also succour him with your charitable alms,

ELIZABETHAN SEAMEN

the reward whereof you shall hereafter most assuredly receive."

Leaving Rome in April 1577, Foxe arrived in Spain apparently the following August. The Spanish king appointed him to the office of gunner in the royal galleys at a salary of eight ducats a month. Here he remained for about two years, and then, feeling homesick, returned to England in 1579. "Who being come into England," as we read in Hakluyt, "went unto the Court, and shewed all his travell unto the Councell: who, considering of the state of this man, in that hee had spent and lost a great part of his youth in thraldome and bondage, extended to him their liberalitie, to helpe to maintaine him now in age, to their right honour, and to the incouragement of all true heartied Christians."

Such, then, was the happy ending to Foxe's travels sixteen years after his ship had set forth from Portsmouth. He had shown himself not merely to be a man of exceptional physical endurance, but a man of considerable resource and a born leader of men in times of crisis and despair. We may well relish the memory of such a fine character.

CHAPTER IX

THE STUART NAVY GOES FORTH AGAINST THE "PYRATS"

AFTER the death of Queen Elizabeth and the respite from the Anglo-Spanish naval fighting there was little employment for those hundreds of our countrymen who had taken to the sea during the time of Drake. Fighting the Spaniards or lying in wait for treasure ships bound from the West Indies to Cadiz was just the life that appealed to them. But now that these hostilities had passed, they felt that their means of livelihood were gone. After the exciting sea life with Drake and others, after the prolonged Armada-fighting, it would be too tame for them to settle down to life ashore. Fishing was not very profitable, and there was not sufficient demand for all the men to ship on board merchant ships.

So numbers of these English seamen unfortunately took to piracy. Some of them, it would be more truthful to say, *resumed* piracy and found their occupation haunting the English Channel, the Scillies being a notorious nest for pirates. Notwithstanding the number of these robbers of the sea who were always on the look out, yet, says our friend Smith of Virginia, "it is incredible how many great and rich prizes the little barques of the West Country daily brought home, in regard of their small charge."

But the strenuous measures which were being now taken

THE STUART NAVY GOES FORTH

in the narrow seas by the North European governments made piracy in this district less remunerative than hitherto. In the Mediterranean these unemployed seamen knew that piracy was a much better paid industry. They knew that the Moors would be glad to avail themselves of the services of such experienced seamen, so they betook themselves to Barbary. At first, be it remembered, these Englishmen had established themselves as North African pirates " on their own " without any connection with the Moors. Smith mentions that Ward, " a poore English sailor," and Dansker, a Dutchman, here began some time before the Moors scarcely knew how to sail a ship. An Englishman named Easton made such a profit that he became, says Smith, a " Marquesse in Savoy," and Ward " lived like a Bashaw in Barbary." From these men the Moors learnt how to become good sea-fighters. Besides Englishmen there came also French and Dutch adventurers to join them, attracted by this mode of life, but very few Spaniards or Italians ever joined their throng. After a time, however, disagreements arose and the inevitable dissensions followed.

They then became so split up and disunited that the Moors and Turks began to obtain the upper hand over them and to compel them to be their slaves. Furthermore, they made these expert European sailors teach themselves how to become distinguished in the nautical arts. This " many an accursed runnagado, or Christian turned Turke, did, till they have made those Sally men, or Moores of Barbary, so powerfull as they be, to the terror of all the Straights." Other English pirates hovered about off the Irish coasts, and three men, named respectively Gennings, Harris and Thompson, in addition to some others, were captured and hanged at Wapping. A number of others were captured and pardoned by James I.

AGAINST THE "PYRATS"

A contemporary account of rowing in a Barbarian galley in the time of Elizabeth has been preserved to us, written by one Thomas Sanders. "I and sixe more of my fellowes," he writes, "together with fourescore Italians and Spaniards were sent foorth in a Galeot to take a Greekish Carmosell, which came into Africa to steale Negroes, and went out of Tripolis unto that place, which was two hundred and fourtie leagues thence, but wee were chained three and three to an oare, and wee rowed naked above the girdle, and the Boteswaine of the Galley walked abaft the maste, and his Mate afore the maste . . . and when their develish choller rose, they would strike the Christians for no cause. And they allowed us but halfe a pound of bread a man in a day without any other kinde of sustenance, water excepted . . . we were then also cruelly manackled in such sort, that we could not put our hands the length of one foote asunder the one from the other, and every night they searched our chaines three times, to see if they were fast riveted."

And the same man related the unhappy experience of a Venetian and seventeen captives who, after enduring slavery for some time at the hands of the Sultan of Tripoli, succeeded in getting a boat and got right away to sea. Away they sped to the northward, and at length they sighted Malta. Their hopes ran high: their confidence was now undoubted. On they came, nearer and nearer to the land, and now they were within only a mile of the shore. It was beautifully fine weather, and one of them remarked, "*In dispetto de Dio adesso venio a pilliar terra*"—"In the despite of God I shall now fetch the shoare." But the man had spoken with an excess of confidence. For presently a violent storm sprang up, so that they were forced to up-helm and to run right before the gale, which was now blowing right on to the Tripolitan coast. Arrived off there

THE STUART NAVY GOES FORTH

they were heart-broken to find that they were compelled to row up and down the very coast-line which they had imagined they had escaped from. For three weeks they held out as best they could, but the weather being absolutely against them, and their slender victuals being at length exhausted, they were compelled to come ashore, hoping to be able to steal some sheep. The Barbarian Moores, however, were on the watch and knew that these unlucky men would be bound to land for supplies. Therefore a band of sixty horsemen were dispatched who secreted themselves behind a sandhill near the sea. There they waited till the Christians had got well inland a good half mile. Then, by a smart movement, the horsemen cut off all retreat to the sea, whilst others pursued the starving voyagers and soon came back with them. They were brought back to the place whence they had so recently escaped. The Sultan ordered that the fugitives should, some of them, have their ears cut off, whilst others were most cruelly thrashed.

The enterprising voyages of the English ships to the Levant in the sixteenth century had been grievously interfered with by the Algerine galleys roving about the Mediterranean, especially in proximity to the Straits of Gibraltar. They would set out from England with goods to deliver and then return with Mediterranean fruits and other commodities. But so often were these valuable ships and cargoes captured by the hateful infidels that the English merchants who had dispatched the goods became seriously at a loss and were compelled to invoke the aid of Elizabeth, who endeavoured, by means of diplomacy, to obtain the release of these ships and to prevent such awkward incidents recurring. To give the names of a few such ships, and to indicate the loss in regard to ships'

BLIGHTED HOPES

The seamen had escaped from Tripoli and were within sight of Malta when a violent storm drove them back to the Moorish coast. Compelled by hunger to land, they were cut off by a party of horsemen, and again thrown into captivity to be most barbarously treated.

AGAINST THE "PYRATS"

freights and of men held captive in slavery we have only to mention the following: The *Salomon* of Plymouth had been captured with a load of salt and a crew of thirty-six men. The *Elizabeth* of Guernsey was seized with ten Englishmen and a number of Bretons, her value being 2000 florins. The *Maria Martin*, under the command of Thomas More, with a crew of thirty-five, had been taken while returning from Patrasso in Morea. Her value was 1400 florins. The *Elizabeth Stokes* of London, under the command of David Fillie of London, whilst bound for Patrasso, had been also captured, but her value was 20,000 or 30,000 florins. The *Nicolas* of London, under the command of Thomas Foster, had also been seized, at a loss of about 5000 florins. So also in like manner could be mentioned the *Judith* of London, the *Jesus* of London, the *Swallow* of London.

But England, of course, was not the only country which suffered by these piratical acts. In 1617 France was moved to take serious action, and sent a fleet of fifty ships against these Barbarian corsairs. Off St. Tropez they captured one of these roving craft, and later on met another which was captured by a French renegado of Rochelle. The latter defended himself fiercely for some time, but at length, seeing that the day was going against him, he sunk his ship and was drowned, together with the whole of his crew, rather than be captured by the Christians. And from now onwards, right up to the nineteenth century, there were at different dates successive expeditions sent against these rovers by the chief European powers.

Many of these expeditions were of little value, some were practically useless, while others did only ephemeral good. Thus, you will remember, the only active service which the navy of our James I. ever saw was in 1620, when

THE STUART NAVY GOES FORTH

it was sent against the pirates of Algiers. But they had become so successful and so daring that they were not easily to be tackled. Not content now with roving over the Mediterranean, not satisfied with those occasional voyages out through the Gibraltar Straits into the Atlantic, they now, if you please, had the temerity to cross the Bay of Biscay and to cruise about the approaches of the English Channel. These Algerine pirates actually sailed as far north as the south of Ireland, where they acted just as they had for generations along the Mediterranean: that is to say, they landed on the Munster shore, committed frightful atrocities and carried away men, women and children into the harsh slavery which was so brutally enforced in their Barbarian territory. What good did the Jacobean expedition which we sent out, you may naturally ask? The answer may be given in the fewest words. Although the fleet contained six of our royal ships and a dozen merchantmen, yet it returned home with no practical benefit, the whole affair having been a hopeless muddle.

In 1655, Blake, the great admiral of Cromwell's time, was sent to tackle these pirate pests. It was a big job, but there was no one at that time better suited for an occasion that required determination. Tunis was a very plague-spot by its piratical colony and its captives made slaves. It had to be humbled to the dust, and Blake, with all the austerity and thoroughness of a Puritan officer, was resolved to do his duty to Christendom. But Tunis was invulnerable, so it was a most difficult undertaking. He spent the early spring of this year cruising about the neighbourhood, biding his time and being put to great inconvenience by foul winds and tempestuous weather. He found that these Tunis pirates were obstinate and wilful: they were unprepared to listen to any reason. Intractable and insolent,

AGAINST THE "PYRATS"

it was impossible to treat with them: force was the only word to which they could be made to hearken. "These barbarous provocations," wrote Blake in giving an account of his activities here, "did so far work upon our spirits that we judged it necessary, for the honour of the fleet, our nation and religion, seeing they would not deal with us as friends, to make them feel us as enemies"; and it was thereupon resolved, at a council of war, to endeavour the firing their ships in Porto Farina.

Tunis, itself, being invulnerable, Blake entered the neighbouring harbour, this Porto Farina, very early in the morning. The singular thing was that he was favoured with amazingly good luck—a fair wind in and a fair wind out. But let me tell the story in the Admiral's own words: "Accordingly, the next morning very early, we entered with the fleet into the harbour, and anchored before their castles, the Lord being pleased to favour us with a gentle gale off the sea, which cast all the smoke upon them, and made our work the more easy. After some hours' dispute we set on fire all their ships, which were in number nine; and, the same favourable gale still continuing, we retreated out again into the road. We had twenty-five men slain, and about forty besides hurt, with very little other loss. It was also remarkable by us that, shortly after our getting forth, the wind and weather changed, and continued very stormy for many days, so that we could not have effected the business, had not the Lord afforded that nick of time in which it was done."

But these attacks by the powers were regarded by the pirates as mere pin-pricks. For it was nothing to them that even all their galleys should be burnt. Such craft were easily built again, and there was an overwhelming amount of slave-labour and plenty of captive seamen to rig these

THE STUART NAVY GOES FORTH

ships as soon as finished. So the evil continued and the epidemic spread as before. In 1658, these Barbarian corsairs attacked a ship called the *Diamond*, homeward bound from Lisbon to Venice. She was laden with a valuable cargo, and her captain saw that he would not be able to defend his ship against three galleys, so, rather than let her fall into piratical hands, he determined to destroy her. He placed an adequate quantity of powder, and then laying a match to the same, he jumped into his long-boat, from which presently he had the pleasure of seeing his enemies blown into space by the terrific explosion just as these infidels were in the act of boarding the *Diamond*.

Ten years later Sir Thomas Allen was sent during the summer with a squadron once more to repress Algerine piracy. He arrived before Algiers, and was so successful that he compelled the release of all the English captives which had been accumulating there. Indeed, it is amazing to count up so many of these expeditions from England alone. Thus, in the early spring of 1671, we find Sir Edward Spragge sent out to the Mediterranean for the same purpose. The following account is condensed from his own dispatch and is of no ordinary interest. On the 20th of April, Spragge was cruising in his flagship the *Revenge*, about fifteen or twenty miles off Algiers, when he met his other ships, the *Mary*, *Hampshire*, *Portsmouth* and the *Advice*, which were all frigates. These informed him that several Algerine war-craft were at Bougie. He called a council of war, at which it was agreed that Spragge should make the best of his way there with the *Mary*, the *Portsmouth* pink and his fireships, and he should endeavour to destroy these corsairs in their own lair. The *Hampshire* and the *Portsmouth* were left to cruise off Algiers till further orders should reach them.

AGAINST THE "PYRATS"

The wind was now easterly, and one of his ships, named the *Dragon*, had been gone five days, as she was busy chasing a couple of Algerine corsair craft: but as the wind for some days had been from the south-west, Spragge was in hopes that the chase would have carried the ships to the eastward and thus force the Algerines into Bougie. And so, on the 23rd of April, the *Dragon* returned to Spragge, having been engaged for two days in fighting the two Algerine craft. Unfortunately her commander, Captain Herbert (whom the reader will remember by his later title when he became the Earl of Torrington), had been shot in the face by a musket shot, and nine of his men had also been wounded with small shot. The wind continued easterly until 28th April, but at eight o'clock that night it flew round to south-west and the weather became very gusty and rainy. This caused Spragge's *Little Eagle* fireship to become disabled, and she was dismasted by the wind. But, on the last day of April, Spragge got her fitted with masts again and re-rigged, for luckily he had with him a corn ship captured from the corsairs, and her spars, together with some topmasts and other spars, caused the fireship to be ready again for service. Unfortunately the same bad weather caused the *Warwick* to spring her mast—an accident that frequently befell the ships of the sixteenth and seventeenth centuries—so she " bore away to the Christian shore: my Brigantine at the same time bore away, and as yet I have no news of her."

The same day this admiral arrived in Bougie Bay, but here again he had bad luck. Just as he was within half a shot of the enemy's castles and forts the wind dropped and it fell a flat calm. Then the breeze sprang up, but it blew off shore. So the time passed. On the 2nd of May the winds were still very fluky, and after twice in vain attempting to do anything with these varied puffs, Spragge resolved

THE STUART NAVY GOES FORTH

to attack by night with his ships' boats and his smallest fireship. The water close to the forts was very shallow, and the English fireship could be rowed almost as well as a ship's long-boat. So about midnight he dispatched all the boats he could, as well as the *Eagle* fireship, under the command of "my eldest Lieutenant, Master Nugent." It was a dark night, and the high land was very useful for its obscuring effects.

Nugent, leaving one of the long-boats with the fireship, in addition to the fireship's own boat, now rowed off to reconnoitre the enemy, having first given the fireship's captain orders to continue approaching until he should find himself in shoal water: he was then immediately to anchor. Nugent had then rowed off and had scarcely left the fireship one minute when, after proceeding but a little way over the leaden waters, he found himself quite close to where the English squadron was anchored. He had thus lost his bearings in the dark and at once steered off again to find the fireship, when, to his great amazement, he suddenly saw the latter burst out into a sheet of flame. That, of course, was another piece of ill-luck, for it entirely upset all the carefully laid plans and instantly alarmed the enemy. It would have been useless to have attempted a boat attack that night, so the effort was postponed. What had happened was this: the little fireship had been all ready when, by an accident, the gunner had fired off his pistol. This had caused the ignition, and so the ship had been lost without any good being done. It was a thousand pities as, owing to her shallow draught, she had been relied upon for getting right close in.

With this warning the enemy the next day unrigged their ships, which lay in their harbour, then gathered together all the yards, the topmasts and spars generally off

AGAINST THE "PYRATS"

these ships, together with their cables. All this they made into a boom, which was buoyed up by means of casks. Spragge and his fleet watched this being done, for there was no wind, or, as he expressed it, we had "no opportunity of wind to do anything upon them." On the 8th of May they noticed that the corsairs ashore were reinforced by the arrival of horse- as well as foot-soldiers, which the Englishmen suspected rightly had come from Algiers. The Bougie corsairs greeted this arrival with wild cheering and by firing of the guns in their ships and castles, as well as by the display of colours.

About noon, just as Spragge was anxious to reopen operations, he was harassed by a flat calm. Luckily, however, at 2 p.m. a nice breeze sprang up, and the *Revenge*, *Dragon*, *Advice* and *Mary* advanced and let go in $3\frac{1}{2}$ fathoms nearer in, mooring stem and stern so that their broadsides might face Bougie's fortifications. The position was roughly thus. Looking towards Bougie, Spragge's six ships were moored roughly in a half-circle in the following order from left to right. First came the *Portsmouth*, then the *Garland*, the *Dragon*, the *Mary*, the *Advice* and finally the *Revenge* flagship. These were all, so to speak, in the foreground of the picture. In the background were the enemy's ships on the left, whilst on the right were the castles and fortifications. In the middle distance on the left was the boom defence already noted. The *Revenge* was in 4 fathoms, being close up to the castles and walls, and the fight began. For two hours these ships bombarded Bougie's ships and fortresses.

Spragge then decided to make a boat attack, his ships still remaining at anchor. He therefore sent away his pinnace, under the command of a man named Harman, " a Reformado seaman of mine." A "reformado," by the way,

THE STUART NAVY GOES FORTH

was a volunteer serving with the fleet without a commission yet with the rank of an officer. Harman was sent because Spragge's second lieutenant had been hurt by a splinter in the leg. Lieutenant Pin was sent in command of the *Mary's* boat, and Lieutenant Pierce had charge of the *Dragon's* boat. The project was to cut the boom, and this was bravely done by these three boats, though not without some casualties. Eight of the *Mary's* boat's crew and her lieutenant were wounded with small shot. In the Admiral's pinnace seven were killed outright, and all the rest were wounded excepting Harman. Of the *Dragon's* boat's crew ten were wounded as well as her lieutenant, and one was killed.

But the boom had been cut, and that was the essential point. That being done, the Admiral then signalled to his one remaining fireship, the little *Victory*, to do her work. She obeyed and got in so well through the boom that she brought up athwart the enemy's " bolt-sprits, their ships being aground and fast to the castles." The *Victory* burnt very well indeed, and destroyed all the enemy's shipping, ten in all. Of these ten, seven were the best ships of the Algerine fleet, and of the three others one was a Genoese prize and the other had been a ship the pirates had captured from an English crew. The commander, the master's mate, the gunner and one seaman of the fireship had been wounded badly in the fight, but the victory was complete and undoubted. On the 10th of May a Dutchman who had been captive with the corsairs for three years escaped by swimming off to the *Revenge*, and Spragge had him taken on board. The Dutchman informed the English Admiral that the enemy admitted that at least 360 Turkish soldiers had lost their lives in this engagement by fire and gunshot, as they could not get ashore from the ships. There were in

AGAINST THE "PYRATS"

all about 1900 men in addition to those 300 who came that morning from Algiers. The Dutchman, for himself, thought the losses far exceeded the number assessed by the enemy.

He stated that the castles and the town itself had been badly damaged, and as all their medicine-chests were on the ships and so burnt, it was impossible for the enemy to dress the wounds of their injured. " Old Treky, their Admiral, is likewise wounded," wrote Spragge. Among the enemy's killed was Dansker, a renegado, and our losses consisted only of 17 killed and 41 wounded.

CHAPTER X

THE GOOD SHIP *EXCHANGE* OF BRISTOL

A SATIRICAL English gentleman who lived in the reign of Charles II. and described himself as formerly "a servant in England's Navie," published a pamphlet in 1648 in which he complained bitterly of the inability of "the present Government," even in spite of the expense of vast quantities of money, "to clear England's seas of Ireland's Pyrates." The latter belonged at this time especially to Waterford and Wexford. A large amount of money, he bewailed, had been and was still being spent "to reduce half a dozen inconsiderable Pyrates," but yet the "pyrates are not reduced, neither are the seas guarded." One of these "pyrates" had in February 1647 in one day taken three small ships and one pinnace of a total value of £9000. One of these ships, whilst defending herself, had lost her master and one of her mates, as well as five mariners, besides other members of her crew wounded. And this author of *A Cordiall for the Calenture* asks if the present Government, with such an expenditure, cannot reduce half a dozen pirates, "how will England's Commonwealth be wasted if the French, the Danes, the Dutch, or all of them shall infest England's Seas."

Well, we know now that in time England's navy did actually defeat each of these—the Dutch, French and

THE *EXCHANGE* OF BRISTOL

Danes. And although the pirates were a real and lasting trouble, both in the narrow seas and in the Mediterranean, yet, as the reader has now seen, it was no easy matter to crush them more than for a short period. In 1675 we find Sir John Narborough with a squadron sent to chastise the pirates of Tripoli which were interrupting our overseas trade. At dead of night he arrived before Tripoli, manned his ships' boats and sent them into the port under his lieutenant, Mr. Cloudesly Shovell, who in later times was to achieve such naval fame. The latter in the present instance seized the enemy's guard-boat, and so was able to get right in undiscovered. He then surprised four Tripolitan ships, which were all that happened to be in port, and having burnt these, he returned to Narborough's squadron, having successfully accomplished that which he was sent to perform without the loss of a man.

France, too, at this time having risen to the status of a great naval power, was performing her share in putting down this perpetual nuisance. In 1681, as the Barbarian corsairs had for some time interrupted the French trade across the Mediterranean, Du Quesne was sent with a fleet against them. He was able to destroy eight galleys in the Port of Scio in the Archipelago, and threw in so many bombs that at length he subjected the corsairs to terms. Finally, in 1684, he had obtained from them all the French captives and had caused the pirates to pay 500,000 crowns for the prizes they had taken. And in 1682 Admiral Herbert had again been sent out by England against the Algerine pirates.

And now, before we leave this period, I want to put before the reader the interesting story which centres round the Bristol ship named the *Exchange*, which was so happily rescued from the Algerine pirates.

THE GOOD SHIP

The story begins on the 1st of November 1621, when two ships were sent on their voyage from Plymouth. The larger of these was the *George Bonaventure*, about 70 tons burthen. The smaller of the two was the *Nicholas*, of 40 tons burthen, and her skipper's name was John Rawlins, of whom we shall have much to say. These two vessels, after being freighted by Plymouth merchants, proceeded down Channel, past Ushant and, after a fair passage, found themselves across the Bay, round the Spanish coast and off Trafalgar by the 18th of November. But the next morning, just as they were getting into the Straits of Gibraltar, the watch descried five ships under sail coming towards them as fast as they could.

In a moment the English ships rightly guessed these were pirate craft, and immediately began to escape. But in spite of all their efforts, the pirates came the more quickly. There were five of them in all, and the first came right to windward of the English craft, the second came " up on our luff," and presently the remainder also came along. Their Admiral was one Callfater, whose ship was described as " having upon her main topsail two topgallant sails, one above another." For of these five ships two were prizes, one being a small London ship, and the other a west-country ship which, homeward bound with a cargo of figs and other goods, had had the misfortune to fall into the hands of these rovers.

So the *George Bonaventure* was taken and the Turkish Vice-Admiral, whose name was Villa Rise, now called upon the *Nicholas* to strike sail also, and Rawlins, seeing it was useless to do otherwise, obeyed. The same day, before nightfall, the Turkish Admiral sent twelve of the *George Bonaventure's* crew ashore, together with some other Englishmen whom he had taken prisoners from another previous

EXCHANGE OF BRISTOL

ship. The Admiral was doubtless nervous lest with so many English seamen a mutiny might break out. So some were set upon a strange land to fare as best they might. Villa Rise, the Vice-Admiral, ordered Rawlins and five of his company to go aboard Villa Rise's ship, leaving three men and a boy on the *Nicholas*. To the latter were sent thirteen Turks and Moors—a right proportion to overmaster the other four, in case mutiny should be meditated. The ships then set a course for Algiers.

But the next night a heavy gale sprang up, so that they lost sight of the *Nicholas*, and the pirates were afraid their own ships would likewise perish. On the 22nd of November Rawlins arrived at Algiers, but the *Nicholas* had not yet come into port. In this piratical stronghold he found numerous Englishmen now as slaves, and there were a hundred "handsome English youths" who had been compelled to turn Turks. For these inhuman Moslems, these vipers of Africa, these monsters of the sea, having caught a Christian in their net would next set about trying to make him change his Christianity for Mohammedanism. If he refused, he would be tortured without mercy, until some of them, unable to endure these terrible sufferings any longer, yielded and declared they would become Turks, being yet Christians at heart. These poor, ill-treated English slaves, though bowed down with their own troubles, welcomed this latest batch and, says the contemporary narrator, "like good Christians, they bade us 'Be of good cheer! and comfort ourselves in this! That God's trials were gentle purgations; and these crosses were but to cleanse the dross from the gold, and bring us out of the fire again more clear and lovely.'"

But if these Algerine pirates and taskmasters were ordinarily cruel towards English seamen they were now the

THE GOOD SHIP

more embittered than ever, for they were still smarting from the injury they had received in May of that year when Sir Robert Mansell's fleet had attempted to fire their ships in the Mole. Tortures and all manner of cruelties were dealt out to them by the infuriated Moslems, and there was but little respect for the dignity of humanity. Some of these men from the *George Bonaventure* and the *Nicholas* were sold by auction to the highest bidder, and the bargainers would assemble and look the sailormen over critically as if they were at a horse fair, for the *Nicholas* had arrived safely on the 26th of November. The Bashaw was allowed to take one of these prisoners for himself, the rest being sold. Rawlins was the last to be put up for sale, as he had "a lame hand." He was eventually bought by Villa Rise for the sum which in the equivalent of English money amounted to £7, 10s. The *Nicholas*' carpenter was also bought at the same time.

These and other slaves were then sent into Villa Rise's ship to do the work of shipwrights and to start rigging her. But some of these Algerines became exceedingly angry when they found Rawlins, because of his "lame" hand, could not do as much work as the other slaves. There was a loud complaint, and they threatened to send him up-country far into Africa, where "he should never see Christendom again" and be banished for life. In the meanwhile there lay at Algiers a ship called the *Exchange* of Bristol, which had some time previously been seized by the pirates. Here she "lay unrigged in the harbour, till, at last, one John Goodale, an English Turk, with his confederates (understanding she was a good sailer, and might be made a proper man-of-war) bought her from the Turks that took her" and got her ready for sea. Now the overseer happened be an English renegado named

AMONG THE PIRATES OF ALGIERS

Christian prisoners who in the summer season had rowed chained to their seats in the corsair galleys, were in the off-season employed to build the great mole to protect the harbour of Algiers from the western side.

EXCHANGE OF BRISTOL

Rammetham Rise, but his real name was Henry Chandler, and it was through him that Goodale became master of the *Nicholas*. They resolved that as there were so many English prisoners they should have only English slaves for their crew and only English and Dutch renegadoes as their gunners, but for soldiers they took also Moslems on board.

One of the saddest aspects of this Turkish piracy is the not infrequent mention of men who either from fear or from love of adventure had denied their religion and nationality to become renegades. It is easy enough to criticise those who were made so to act by compulsion and heartrending tortures, such as placing a man flat on the ground and then piling weights on to the top of his body till life's breath was almost crushed out of him: or thrashing him without mercy till he would consent to become a Moslem. The ideal man, of course, will in every instance prefer martyrdom to saving his life by the sacrifice of principles. But when the matter is pressed home to us as individuals we may well begin to wonder whether we should have played the man, as some of our ancestors did, or whether we should, after much torturing, have succumbed to the temptation of clinging to life at the critical moment. Of those renegades some were undoubtedly thorough-paced rascals, who were no credit to any community, but mere worthless men without a spark of honour. Such as these would as soon become Moslems as Christians, provided it suited their mode of life. But it was the knowledge of the sufferings of the other English prisoners which, with the loss of ships and merchandise, caused the Government repeatedly to send out those punitive expeditions. One would have thought that the only effective remedy would have been to have left a permanent Mediterranean squadron

THE GOOD SHIP

to patrol the North African coast and to chase the corsairs throughout at least the entire summer season. But there were many reasons which prevented this. The ships could not be spared; there were the long-drawn-out Anglo-Dutch wars, and it was not English ships and seamen exclusively that were the objects of these attacks. But, if by any means some continuous arrangement between the Christian powers had been possible whereby the North African coast could have been systematically patrolled, there is little doubt but that endless effort, time, money, lives, ships, commerce and human suffering might have been saved. To-day, for instance, if piracy along that shore were ever to break out again in a serious manner with ships such as might harass the great European liners trading to the Mediterranean, the matter would speedily be settled, if not by the British Mediterranean squadron, at least by some international naval force, as the Boxer troubles in China were dealt with.

Nine English slaves and one Frenchman worked away refitting the *Exchange*, and in this they were assisted by two of Rawlins' own seamen, named respectively Roe and Davies. The former hailed from Plymouth, the latter from Foy (or, as we spell it nowadays, Fowey). Now both Rammetham Rise (*alias* Chandler), the captain, and Goodale, the master, were both west-country men, so they were naturally somewhat favourably disposed to Roe and Davies, and promised them "good usage" if they did their duty efficiently. For these men were to go in the *Exchange* as soon as she was ready for sea-roving. Let us remind the reader that the position of the captain in those days was not quite analogous to what we are accustomed to-day. Rather he was the supreme authority aboard for keeping discipline. He was a soldier rather than a sailor, and

EXCHANGE OF BRISTOL

usually was ignorant of seamanship and navigation. He told the master where he wished the ship to go, and the latter saw that the sailors did their work in trimming sheets, steering the ship and so on. But the navigator was known as the pilot. So, too, the master gunner was responsible for all the guns, shot, powder, matches and the like.

Rammetham Rise (the captain) and Goodale (the master), now busying themselves getting together a crew for this square-rigged *Exchange*, had to find the right kind of men to handle her. What they needed most was a good pilot or navigator who was also an expert seaman, for neither Rammetham Rise nor Goodale were fit to be entrusted with such a task as soon as the ship should get beyond the Straits of Gibraltar and out of sight of land. They therefore asked Davies if he knew among these hundreds of prisoners of any Englishman who could be purchased to serve in the capacity of pilot. Davies naturally thought of his former skipper, and after searching for him some time found him, and informed his two new taskmasters that he understood that Villa Rise would be glad to sell Rawlins, "and for all he had a lame hand," continued Davies, "yet had he a sound heart and noble courage for any attempt or adventure." So at last Rawlins was bought for the sum of £10, and he was sent to supervise the fitting out of the *Exchange*, especially to look after the sails.

By the 7th of January 1622, the *Exchange*, with her twelve good cannon, her munitions and provisions, was ready for sea, and the same day she was hauled out of the Mole. In her went a full ship's company, consisting of sixty-three Turks and Moors as soldiers, nine English slaves, one Frenchman, four Hollanders and two English soldiers as

THE GOOD SHIP

gunners, as well as one English and one Dutch renegado. The good ship, with this miscellaneous crew, put to sea. It was better than slaving away ashore, but it was galling to John Rawlins, a fine specimen of an English sailor, to have to serve under these dogs. Rawlins, you must understand, was one of those hot-tempered, blunt and daring seamen such as had made England what she was in the time of Elizabeth. Forceful, direct, a man of simple piety, of great national pride, he was also a sailor possessing considerable powers of resource and organisation, as we shall presently see.

The *Exchange* was as fine and handsome a ship as England had built during the Elizabethan or early Stuart period. As she began to curtsey to the swell of the Mediterranean Sea, the slaves were at work looking after the guns and so on. Rawlins, in his brusque, fierce manner which is so typical of Drake and many another sailor of the late sixteenth or early seventeenth century, was working and raging at the same time. While he was busying himself among his fellow-countrymen, pulling ropes and looking after the cannon, he complained in no measured terms of the indignity of having to work merely to keep these Moslem brutes in a life of wickedness. He broke out into a torrent of complaint, as the other slaves besought him to be quiet "least they should all fare the worse for his distemperature." However, he had firmly resolved to effect an escape from all this, and after mentioning the matter cautiously to his fellow-slaves he found they were similarly minded.

From now onwards there follows one of the best yarns in the history of piracy, and the story is as true as it is exciting. On the 15th of January the morning tide had brought the *Exchange* near to Cape de Gatte, and

EXCHANGE OF BRISTOL

they were joined by a small Moslem ship which had followed them out of Algiers the day after. This craft now gave information that she had sighted seven small vessels in the distance, six of them being sattees. (A sattee was a very fast, decked species of galley, with a long, sharp prow and two or three masts, each setting a lateen sail.) The seventh craft was a polacca, a three-masted type of Mediterranean ship which usually carried square sails on her mainmast, but lateen sails on her fore and mizzen, though some of these vessels had square sails on all three masts.

Before long the *Exchange* also sighted these seven and made towards them. But when she had separated the polacca from the rest, this craft, rather than surrender to the infidels, ran herself ashore and split herself on the rocks, and her crew made their way inland. As near as she dare go the *Exchange* followed inshore and let go anchor when in the shallows. Both she and the other Moslem ship sent out boats with many musketeers and some English and Dutch renegades who, rowing off to the stranded polacca, boarded her without opposition. Seven guns were found on board, but after these had been hurled into the sea the polacca was so lightened that she was floated safely off. She was found to have a good cargo of hides and logwood, the latter to be used for dyeing purposes.

In the pillaging of this craft there arose a certain amount of dissension among the pirates, and eventually it was decided to send her and the Moslem ship which had joined them back to Algiers. Nine Turks and one English slave were accordingly taken out of the *Exchange* and six out of the Moslem craft to man the polacca till she reached Algiers. The *Exchange*, now alone, with a fair wind proceeded through the Straits into the Atlantic, which the Turks were wont to speak of as the "Marr Granada."

THE GOOD SHIP

Notwithstanding anything which has been said in this book so far, it must be borne in mind that the Turk was essentially not a seaman: he had no bias that way. He was certainly a most expert fighter, however. It was not till the renegade English, Dutch and other sailors settled among them—notably those Barbarossas and other Levantine sailors—that the Moslems learnt how to use the sea. Had it not been for these teachers they would have continued like the Ottomans, strong as land-fighters but disappointing afloat. These Algerine corsairs in the *Exchange* had no sea-sense and they did not relish going beyond the Gibraltar Straits. So long as they were within sight of land and in their oared galleys they were—given such able seamanlike leaders as the Barbarossas—able to acquit themselves well in any fighting. But to embark in an ocean-going, full-rigged ship, such as the *Exchange*, and to voyage therein beyond their familiar landmarks was to place them in a state of grave concern.

These Moslems never went to sea without their Hoshea or wizard, and this person would, by his charlatanism, persuade these incapable mariners what to do and how to act. Every second or third night, after arriving at the open sea, this wizard would go through various ceremonies, consult his book of wizardry, and from this he would advise the captain as to what sails ought to be taken in, or what sail to be set. The whole idea was thoroughly ludicrous to the rude, common-sense Devonshire seamen, who marvelled that these infidels could be so foolish.

The *Exchange* was wallowing on her way when there suddenly went up the cry, "A sail! A sail!" Presently, however, it was found only to be another of these Moslem corsairs making towards the *Exchange*. After speaking each other the ships parted, the *Exchange* now going

EXCHANGE OF BRISTOL

north, past Cape St. Vincent, on the look out for the well-laden ships which passed between the English Channel and the Straits of Gibraltar. All this time the English slaves were being subjected to the usual insults and maltreatment. The desire to capture the *Exchange* positively obsessed John Rawlins, and his active brain was busy devising some practical scheme. He resolved to provide ropes with "broad specks of iron" so that he might be able to close up the hatchways, gratings and cabins. Roughly his plan was to shut up the captain and his colleagues and then, on a signal being given, the Englishmen, being masters of the "gunner-room" with the cannon and powder, would blow up the ship or kill their taskmasters one by one if they should open their cabins.

It was a daring plan and worthy of a man like Rawlins. But in all attempts at mutiny it is one thing to conceive a plan and it is another matter to know whom to entrust with the secret. In this respect Rawlins was as cautious as he was enterprising, and he felt his way so slowly and carefully that nothing was done hastily or impetuously or with excess of confidence.

CHAPTER XI

A WONDERFUL ACHIEVEMENT

RAWLINS knew he could rely on his fellow-countrymen, but at first he hesitated to say anything to the four Hollanders. At last, however, he found them anxious to join in with the scheme, and his next effort was equally successful, for he "undermined" the English renegado-gunner and three more, his associates. Last of all, the Dutch renegadoes of the "gunner-room" were won over and persuaded by the four Hollanders.

The secret had been well kept, and Rawlins resolved that during the captain's morning watch he would make the attempt. Now where the English slaves lay in the gunroom there were always four or five crowbars of iron hanging up. When the time was approaching when the mutiny should take place, Rawlins was in the act of taking down his iron crowbar when he had the misfortune to make such a noise with it that it woke up the Turkish soldiers, and they, in alarm, roused the other Moslems. Everything was in pitch darkness and it was uncertain as to what would happen. Presently the Turkish boatswain came below with a candle and searched all the parts of the ship where the slaves were lying, but he found nothing suspicious other than the crowbar, which had apparently slipped down. He then went and informed the captain, who merely remarked

A WONDERFUL ACHIEVEMENT

that there was nothing to cause uneasiness, as the crowbar not infrequently slipped down.

But with this unlucky beginning Rawlins deemed it best to postpone the undertaking for the present. He had intended, with the aid of his friends, knife in hand, to press upon the gunner's breast and the other English renegadoes, and either force them to help, or else to cut their throats. "Die or consent"—this was to be the prevailing force, and the watchword was to be, "For God and King James, and St. George for England." In the meantime the *Exchange* continued on her northerly voyage, farther and farther away from the coast of Barbary. Still cautious but keen, Rawlins went about the ship's company, and now had persuaded the gunners and the other English renegades to fall in with his project. This was one of the riskiest moments of his enterprise, but it resulted that there were "reciprocal oaths taken, and hands given" to preserve loyalty to each other: yet once again was Rawlins to be disappointed.

For after the renegado gunner had solemnly sworn secrecy, he went up the hatchway on deck for a quarter of an hour, after which he returned to Rawlins in the "gunner-room." Then, to Rawlins' surprise, in came an infuriated Turk with his knife drawn. This he presented in a menacing manner to Rawlins' body. The latter, cleverly feigning innocence, inquired what was the matter, and whether it was the Turk's intention to kill him. To this the Turk answered, "No, master. Be not afraid: I think he doth but jest." But it was clear to Rawlins that the other man had broken his compact and rounded on him. So, drawing back, Rawlins drew out his own knife and also stepped towards the gunner's side, so that he was able to snatch the knife from the gunner's sheath. The Turk,

A WONDERFUL ACHIEVEMENT

seeing that now the Englishman had two knives to his one, threw down his weapon, protesting that all the time he had been joking. The gunner also whispered in Rawlins' ear that he had never betrayed the plan nor would he do such a thing. However, Rawlins thought otherwise and kept the two knives with him all the night.

Very ingenious was the way in which this Rawlins was weaving his net gradually but surely around the ship. He succeeded in persuading the captain to head for Cape Finisterre, pretending that thereabouts they would be likely to come upon a ship to be pillaged. This was perfectly true, though the Englishman's intention was to get the *Exchange* farther and farther from the Straits of Gibraltar, so that it became less and less likely that the corsairs would send out reinforcements. On the 6th of February, when about thirty-six miles off the Cape, a sail was descried. The *Exchange* gave chase and came up with her, " making her strike all her sails: whereby we knew her to be a bark belonging to Torbay, near Dartmouth." She was laden with a cargo of salt, and her crew consisted of nine men and a boy. But it came on bad weather, so the *Exchange* did not then launch her boat, but ordered the Torbay ship to let down her boat. Her master, with five men and the boy, now rowed off to the *Exchange*, leaving behind his mate and two men in the bark. The Turkish captain now sent ten Moslems to man her. Now among these ten were two Dutch and one English renegadoes " who were of our confederacy."

Just as the latter were about to hoist out their boat from the *Exchange*, Rawlins was able to have a hurried conversation with them. He quickly warned them it was his intention that night or the next to put his plan into action, and he advised these men to inform the mate and

A WONDERFUL ACHIEVEMENT

two men of the Torbay bark of this plot and then make for England, " bearing up the helm, whiles the Turks slept and suspected no such matter." Rawlins reminded them that in his first watch, about midnight, he would show them a light by which the men on the bark might know that the plan was already in action. So the boat was let down from the *Exchange* and rowed off to the Torbay bark. The confederates then told the mate of their intention, and he entirely approved of the plan, though at first amazed by its ingenuity.

The fact was that the idea was really much simpler than was at first apparent. Being sailors the English "had the helm of the ship," for the Turks, being only soldiers and ignorant of sea affairs, could not say whether their vessel were sailing in the direction of Algiers or in the opposite direction. They knew nothing of navigation and practically nothing of seamanship, so they were, in spite of all their brutality, more at the mercy of the Christians than they had realised. But, resolved the plotters, if by any chance these Moslems should guess that the ship was sailing away from Algiers then they would at once cut the Turks' throats, and then throw their bodies overboard. It will be remembered that the master and some of the Torbay bark's crew were now in the *Exchange*, and Rawlins made it his business to approach these men tactfully and ask them to share in the plan. This they resolved to do.

So far so good. Now the number of Turks had been gradually diminishing since the beginning of the cruise. For, first of all, nine Turks and one English slave had been sent back to Algiers with the polacca prize; and now some more had been sent off to the Torbay bark. Had the *Exchange's* captain fully realised how seriously he was diminishing the strength of his own force, he could scarcely

A WONDERFUL ACHIEVEMENT

have done such a foolish thing. But throughout the whole plot he was, without ever suspecting it, being fooled by a clever schemer. Rawlins had all the tact and foresight of a diplomatist combined with the ability to know when to strike and the power to strike hard. And all this time, while the captain himself was diminishing the number of Moslems and simultaneously adding to the number of Englishmen by the arrival of the Torbay ship, Rawlins, in the most impudent manner, was going about the ship winning every one except the Turkish soldiers over to his side. One knows not which to admire most: his wonderful courage or his consummate skill. For had he made one single error in reposing confidence in the wrong man, the death of the Englishman would have been both certain and cruel.

And the following step in Rawlins' diplomatic advance was even more interesting still. When morning came again—it was now the 7th of February—the Torbay prize was quite out of sight. This annoyed the captain of the *Exchange* intensely, and he began both to storm and to swear. He commanded Rawlins to search the seas up and down; but there was not a vestige of the bark. She was beyond the horizon. In course of time the captain abated his wrath and remarked that no doubt he would see her again in Algiers and that all would be well. This remark rather worried Rawlins, as he began to fear the captain would order the *Exchange* to return to the Straits of Gibraltar. But Rawlins did not allow himself to worry long, and proceeded below down into the hold. Here he found that there was a good deal of water in the bilges which could not be sucked up by the pump. He came on deck and informed the captain. The latter naturally asked how this had come about that the pump would not discharge this, and Rawlins explained that the ship was too

A WONDERFUL ACHIEVEMENT

much down by the head and needed to have more weight aft to raise her bows more out of the water.

He therefore ordered Rawlins to get the ship trimmed properly. The captain was swallowing the bait most beautifully; presently he would be hooked. Rawlins explained that "We must quit our cables and bring four pieces of ordnance" further aft, and that would cause the water to flow to the pump. The captain, being quite ignorant of the ways of a ship, ordered these suggestions to become orders, and so two of the guns which usually were forward were now brought with their mouths right before the binnacle. In the ship were three decks. Rawlins and his mates of the "gunner-room" were warned to be ready to break up the lower deck; and the English slaves, who always lay in the middle deck, were likewise told to watch the hatchways. Rawlins himself persuaded the gunner to let him have as much powder as would prime the guns, and quietly warned his confederates to begin the mutiny as soon as ever the gun was fired, when they were to give a wild shout and hand on the password.

The time appointed for the crisis was 2 p.m., and about that time Rawlins advised the master-gunner to speak to the captain that the soldiers might come on the poop deck and so bring the ship's bows more out of the water and cause the pump to work better. To this suggestion the captain readily agreed, so twenty Turkish soldiers came aft to the poop, while five or six of the confederates stole into the captain's cabin and brought away various weapons and shields. After that Rawlins and his assistants began to pump the water. Later on, having made every preparation and considered all details, in order to avoid suspicion the members of the "gunner-room" went below and the slaves in the middle deck went

A WONDERFUL ACHIEVEMENT

about their work in the usual way. Then the nine English slaves and John Rawlins, the five men and one boy from the Torbay bark, the four English renegades, the two Dutch and the four Hollanders "lifting up our hearts and thanks to God for the success of the business" set to work on the final act of the cleverly conceived plot.

About noon Roe and Davis were ordered by Rawlins to prepare their matches, while most of the Turks were on the poop weighing down the stern to bring the water to the pump. The two men came with the matches, and at the appointed time Roe fired one of the guns, which caused a terrific explosion. Immediately this was followed by wild cheering on the part of the confederates. The explosion broke down the binnacle and compasses, and the soldiers were amazed by the cheering of the Christian slaves. And then they realised what had happened—that there had been a mutiny, that the ship had been surprised. The Turks were mad with fury and indignation. Calling the mutineers "Dogs," they began to tear up planks of the ship and to attack the confederates with hammers, hatchets, knives, boat's oars, boat-hook and whatever came into their hands. Even the stones and bricks of the "cook-room," or galley, were picked up and hurled at Rawlins' party.

But the carefully arranged plot was working out perfectly. Below, the slaves had cleared the decks of all the Turks and Moors, and Rawlins now sent a guard to protect the powder, and the confederates charged their muskets against the remaining Turks, killing some of them on the spot. The Moslems, who had been such tyrannical taskmasters, now actually called for Rawlins, so he, guarded by some of his adherents, went to them. The latter fell on their knees and begged for mercy, who had shown no

A WONDERFUL ACHIEVEMENT

mercy to others. Rawlins knew what he was about, and after these tyrants had been taken one by one, he caused them to be killed, while other Turks leapt overboard, remarking that "it was the chance of war." Others were manacled and then hurled overboard. Some more had yet to be killed outright, and then at length the victory and annihilation were complete. By careful plotting and good organisation and a firmness at the proper time, the whole scheme had been an entire success.

It happened that when the explosion had taken place, the captain was in his cabin writing, and at once rushed out. But when he saw the confederates and how matters stood and that the ship was already in other hands, he at once surrendered and begged for his life. He reminded Rawlins "how he had redeemed him from Villa Rise," and that he had since treated him with great consideration. Rawlins had to admit that this was so, so he agreed to spare the captain his life. As before mentioned, the captain was an English renegade whose real name was Henry Chandler, he being the son of a chandler in Southwark. So this man was brought back to England, as well as John Goodale; Richard Clarke, gunner (*alias* Jafar in Turkish); George Cook, gunner's mate (*alias* Ramedam in Turkish); John Browne (*alias* Mamme in Turkish); and William Winter, ship's carpenter (*alias* Mustapha in Turkish); "besides all the slaves and Hollanders, with other renegadoes, who were willing to be reconciled to their true Saviour, as being formerly seduced with the hopes of riches, honour, preferment, and suchlike devilish baits to catch the souls of mortal men and entangle frailty in the tarriers of horrible abuses and imposturing deceit."

The Englishmen now set to work and cleared the ship

A WONDERFUL ACHIEVEMENT

of the dead Moslem bodies, and then Rawlins assembled his men and gave praise to God "using the accustomed Service on shipboard; and, for want of books, lifted up their voices to God, as He put into their hearts or renewed their memories." And after having sung a psalm, they embraced each other "for playing the men in such a deliverance." The same night they washed the ship of the carnage, put every thing in order, repaired the broken quarter which had been damaged by the explosion, set up the binnacle again and made for England. On the 13th February the *Exchange* arrived at Plymouth, where they "were welcomed like the recovery of the lost sheep, or as you read of a loving mother that runneth with embraces to entertain her son from a long voyage and escape of many dangers."

As for the Torbay bark, she too had got back to England, having arrived at Penzance two days before. Her story is brief but not less interesting. The mate had been informed of Rawlins' plan, and he and his friends had agreed. But the carrying out of this had been a far simpler and neater matter than that which had taken place on the *Exchange*. For once again mere landsmen had been fooled at the hands of seamen. It happened on this wise. They made the Turks believe that the wind had now come fair and that the prize was being sailed back to Algiers. This they believed until they sighted the English shore, when one of the Turks remarked that "that land is not like Cape St. Vincent." To this the man at the helm replied very neatly, "Yes; and if you will be contented and go down into the hold, and turn the salt over to windward, whereby the ship may bear full sail, you shall know and see more to-morrow."

Suspecting nothing the five Turks then went quietly

A WONDERFUL ACHIEVEMENT

down. But as soon as they had gone below into the hold, the renegadoes, with the help of two Englishmen, nailed down the hatches and kept the rascals there till they reached Penzance. But one of the other Turks was on deck, and at this incident he broke out into great rage. This was but short-lived, for an Englishman stepped up to him, dashed out his brains and threw his body overboard.

All the other prisoners were brought safely to England and lodged either in Plymouth gaol or Exeter, "either to be arraigned according to the punishment of delinquents in that kind, or disposed of as the king and council shall think meet." We need not stop to imagine the joy of welcoming back men who had been lost in slavery. We need not try to guess the delight of the west-countrymen that at last some of these renegadoes had been brought back to be punished in England. There is not the slightest doubt of this story of the *Exchange* being true, but it shows that even in that rather disappointing age which followed on immediately after the defeat of the Armada, there were, at a time when maritime matters were under a cloud, not wanting English seamen of the right stamp, men of courage and action, men who could fight and navigate a ship as in the spacious days of Queen Elizabeth. Happily the type of man which includes such sailor characters as Rawlins is not yet dead; the Anglo-Saxon race still rears many of his calibre, and it needs only the opportunity to display such nerve, daring enterprise and tactful action.

CHAPTER XII

THE GREAT SIR HENRY MORGAN

ABOUT the year 1636 a certain London mariner, named Dunton, had an experience somewhat similar to that which we related in the last chapter concerning Rawlins. Dunton had the bad luck to be taken by the Sallee pirates, who then sent him out as master and pilot of a Sallee pirate ship containing twenty-one Moors and five Flemish renegadoes. The instructions were that Dunton should sail to the English coast and there capture Christian prisoners. He had arrived from Barbary in the English Channel and was off Hurst Castle by the Needles, Isle of Wight, when he was promptly arrested as a pirate and sent to Winchester to be tried by law. He was given his release at a later date, but his ten-year-old boy was still a slave with the Algerines.

Now about the year when this was taking place, there was born into the world Henry Morgan, who has become celebrated in history and fiction as one of the greatest sea-rovers who ever stepped aboard a ship. His career is one of continual success, of cruelties and amassing of wealth. He was a buccaneer, and a remarkably clever fellow who rose to the position of Governor-General of one of our most important colonial possessions. Adventures are to the adventurous, and if ever there was a Britisher who longed for

THE GREAT SIR HENRY MORGAN

and obtained a life of excitement, here you have it in the story of Henry Morgan. It would be easy enough to fill the whole of this book and more with his activities afloat, but as our space is limited, and there are still many other pirates of different seas to be considered, it is necessary to confine ourselves to the main facts of his career.

The date of his birth is not quite certain, but it is generally supposed to belong to the year 1635. He first saw light in Glamorganshire, and his existence was tinged with adventure almost from the first. For whilst he was a mere boy, he was kidnapped and sold as a servant at Barbados. Thus it was that he was thrust on to the region of the West Indies, and in this corner of the world, so rich in romance, so historic for its association with Spanish treasure-ships of Elizabethan times, so reminiscent of Drake and others, he was to perform deeds of daring which as such are not unworthy to be ranked alongside the achievements of the great Elizabethan seamen. But he differed from Drake in one important respect. The Elizabethan was severe even to harshness, but he was a more humane being than Morgan. All the wonderful things which the Welshman performed are overshadowed by his cruel, brutish atrocities. In a cruel, inhuman age Morgan unhappily stands out as one of the wickedest sailors of his time. And yet, although we live in an epoch which is somewhat prone to white-washing the world's most notorious criminals, yet we must modify the popular judgment which prevails in regard to Morgan. To say that he was a pirate and nothing else is not accurate. At heart he certainly was this. But as Sir John Laughton, our greatest modern naval historian has already pointed out, he attacked only those who were the recognised enemies of England.

I admit that in practice, especially in the case of men

THE GREAT SIR HENRY MORGAN

of such piratical character as Henry Morgan, the difference between privateering and piracy is very slight. The mere possession of a permission to capture the ships belonging to other people is nothing compared to a real sea-robbing intention. Morgan was lucky in having been required for a series of certain peculiar emergencies. His help happened at the time to be indispensable, and so he was able to do legally what otherwise he would have done illegally. All those seizures were legalised by the commission which he was granted at various times. But this is not to say that without those commissions he would not have acted in a somewhat similar manner.

We are accustomed to speak of Morgan and his associates as buccaneers. Now let us understand at once the meaning of this term. Originally the word meant one who dried and smoked meat on a "boucan." A "boucan" was a hurdle made of sticks on which strips of beef newly salted were smoked by the West Indians. But the name of buccaneers was first given to the French hunters of S. Domingo, who prepared their meat according to this Indian custom. From the fact that these men who so prepared the flesh of oxen and wild boars were also known for another characteristic, namely, piracy, the name was applied in its widest sense to those English and French sea-rovers of the seventeenth and eighteenth centuries who employed their time in depredating Spanish ships and territory of the Caribbean Sea. Hence from signifying a man who treated his food in a certain fashion, the word buccaneer came to mean nothing more or less than a robber of the sea.

After young Morgan had finished his time in service at Barbados, he joined himself to these buccaneer-robbers after arriving at Jamaica. It should be added that Morgan's uncle, Colonel Edward Morgan, went out from England in

THE GREAT SIR HENRY MORGAN

1664 to become Governor-General of Jamaica, but his death occurred in the following year. There are gaps in Morgan's life, and there has been some confusion caused by others possessing the same surname. But it appears pretty certain now that in the year 1663 Henry Morgan was at sea in command of a privateer. Even by this time he had begun to be an expert in depredation and in sacking some of the Caribbean towns, and striking terror into the hearts of the wretched inhabitants. We may pass over these minor events and come to the time when, his uncle having died, Sir Thomas Modyford was sent out from England as Lieutenant-Governor. Bear in mind that intense hatred of the Spanish prevailing at this time, and which had not been by any means quenched by the defeat of the Armada. To put it mildly, the Caribbean Sea was an Anglo-Spanish cockpit where many and many a fight had taken, and was still to take, place. Modyford wanted the island of Curaçoa to be taken, and there was then no better man to do the job than a very celebrated buccaneer named Edward Mansfield. Sir Thomas therefore commissioned Mansfield to seize this island. He got together a strong naval expedition and accomplished the task early in the year 1666, Henry Morgan being in command of one of Mansfield's ships.

Off the Nicaraguan coast lies an island which has been called at different times Santa Catalina or Providence Island. This had been taken from the English by the Spaniards more than twenty years before, and Morgan was also present when Mansfield now recaptured it. A small garrison was left to occupy it, and Mansfield returned with his ships to Jamaica. But before long Santa Catalina fell again into the hands of the Spaniards, and Mansfield died. It is now that Morgan's career begins to come into the

THE GREAT SIR HENRY MORGAN

limelight. For after Mansfield's decease the buccaneers, bereft of their leader, thought the matter over and decided to make Morgan his successor, and the commissions which Mansfield had been accustomed to receive from Modyford now fell to the Welshman.

The first of these duties occurred when Modyford became aware of a rumour that the Spaniards were contemplating an invasion of Jamaica. It was nothing more than a rumour, but, as governor, he desired to find out the truth. He therefore despatched Morgan to ascertain the facts. He was directed to get ten ships together and to carry 500 men in this fleet. The ships gathered on the south side of Cuba and then, having accomplished their voyage, Morgan landed his men and found that the people had fled from the coast, driving all their cattle away. Morgan marched inland, plundered the town of Puerto Principe, and then was able to send information to Modyford that considerable forces were being collected and that an expedition against Jamaica was, in truth, being planned. He had fulfilled his commission as instructed.

His next big achievement occurred when he sailed to the mainland in order to attack Porto Bello, where levies were being made to attack Jamaica. Several Englishmen were known also to be confined here in grim dungeons. And if any further incentive were required, this would certainly rouse the ire and sharpen the keenness of Morgan and his men. Porto Bello relied for its defence on three forts, and it was likely to be no easy work to compel these to yield. But Morgan suceeeded in his object, and this is how he went to work: Arrived in the vicinity of Porto Bello, he left his ships and, under the cover of night, proceeded towards the shore with his men in about two dozen canoes. By three o'clock in the morning his force had crept

THE GREAT SIR HENRY MORGAN

into the shore and landed. The first fort was assaulted by the aid of ladders, and the garrison was slaughtered. So, too, the second fort was attacked. Hither the Spanish governor had betaken himself. For a time it offered a stout resistance, but Morgan had a number of ladders so made that they were wide enough to allow several men to climb up abreast of each other. By this means the castle walls were overcome, the castle itself taken, and the governor slain. The third fort surrendered, the town was sacked, and then, for over a fortnight, the buccaneers indulged themselves as was their wont in debauchery. I have no intention of suggesting the details either of these excesses nor of the abominable tortures to which the inhabitants were now subjected in order to compel them to reveal the places where their treasures were hidden. Not even the most unprincipled admirer of the buccaneers could honestly find it possible to defend Morgan and his associates against the most serious charges on the ground of common justice.

Morgan may not have been any worse than some of his contemporaries at heart, but whatever else he was, he was an unmerciful tyrant. As for his enemies, we cannot regard them with much admiration either. This Dago crowd were morally not much better than the Welshman, and though sometimes they put up a good fight, they were too often cowards. In this present instance they adopted that futile and weak plan of buying off the aggressor. You will remember that, unfortunately, our ancestors adopted this plan many hundreds of years ago when they sought to ward off the Viking depredators by buying peace. It was a foolish and an ineffectual method both then and in the seventeenth century in the case of Morgan. For what else does such an action mean than a confession of inferiority? Peace at this price is out of all proportion to the ultimate

THE GREAT SIR HENRY MORGAN

value obtained, and the condition is merely a temptation to the aggressor to come back for more. Stripped of any technicality, Morgan blackmailed these Panamanians to the extent of 100,000 pieces of eight, and 300 negroes. On these conditions, which were agreed upon, he consented to withdraw. So, very well rewarded for his trouble, Morgan returned joyfully to Jamaica, and for some time the buccaneers were able to indulge themselves in the pleasures which this booty was capable of affording them.

You will generally find that a buccaneer, a highwayman, a gambler, a smuggler or any kind of pirate by land or by sea is a spendthrift. There are certainly exceptions, but this is the rule. A man who knows that he can easily get more money when he runs short shows no reserve in spending, provided it affords him gratification. So with these buccaneers. At length they came to the end of their resources and were ready to go forth again. It is true that Modyford had been in two minds after Morgan's return from Porto Bello. He rejoiced at the success of his arms, but he was nervous of the consequences. The Welshman had certainly exceeded his commission, and there might be trouble, as a result, at headquarters.

And yet there was work to be done, and Morgan was the only man who could do it. So once more Modyford had to commission him to carry out hostilities against the Spaniards. To the eastward of Jamaica lies the island of S. Domingo, or as it was known in those days, Hispaniola. If you were to examine a chart of Hispaniola you would see in the south-west corner a bay and a small island. The latter is known as Vache Island. This was to be the meeting-place where Morgan was now to collect his ships. Apart from being a good anchorage, it was a convenient starting-place if one wished to attack either the mainland

THE GREAT SIR HENRY MORGAN

of Central America or Cuba. In the present instance the objective was in the latter. The ships got under way, Morgan arrived at the scene of operations, and positively ravaged the Cuban Coast, again striking terror wherever he went. But, important as this was, it is not to be reckoned alongside the achievement which he performed in the early part of 1669.

On the north coast of South America is a wide gulf which opens out into the Caribbean Sea. But as this gulf extends southward, the shores on either side narrow so closely that the shape resembles the neck of a bottle. The town here is named Maracaibo. But a little distance still farther south the shores on either side recede considerably like the lower portion of a bottle, and there extends a vast lagoon which takes its name from the town mentioned. It is obvious to any one that the strategical point is at the neck. And when I mention that here the navigation was both tricky and shallow, and that the channel was protected by a strong castle, the reader will instantly appreciate that any one who tried to bring his ships into the lake would have a very difficult task.

Now in the month of March, Morgan, with eight ships and 500 men, had arrived off this entrance. With great daring and dogged determination he was able to force his way in through this narrow entrance. He not only dismantled the fort, but he sacked the town of Maracaibo in his own ruthless manner; then he followed up his attack by scouring the neighbouring woods, and put the captured and terrified inhabitants to cruel tortures in order to compel them to reveal the hiding-places of their valuables. He captured many a prisoner and at length, very well satisfied with his success, after the lapse of three weeks decided to advance still farther. He had got his ships through the

THE GREAT SIR HENRY MORGAN

most difficult portion, and now he intended to navigate the lagoon itself.

At length he arrived at a town called by the inhabitants Gibraltar, after the European place of that name. Here Morgan again satiated himself with plunder, with cruelties and with debauchery until the time came for him to take his ships away with all the booty they could carry. But the serious news reached them that awaiting them off the entrance to the gulf were three Spanish men-of-war. Still more serious was the information that the castle at Maracaibo had now been efficiently manned and armed. That was more than awkward, for without the permission of the fort it was quite impossible for his ships to make their exit in safety. The situation would have puzzled many a fine strategist. Here was the buccaneer positively trapped with no means of escape.

But Morgan was quite equal to the occasion, and he set to work. His first object was to gain time, and so he began by opening negotiations with the Spanish Admiral Don Alonso del Campo y Espinosa. He knew these negotiations would prove fruitless, as indeed they did. But in the meantime Morgan had been busily employing his men in getting ready a fireship. In our modern days of steel hulls, fireships play no part in naval tactics, but in the time of oak and hemp this mode of aggression continued till very late. The fireship would first be filled with combustible material, and then released, the wind or current taking her down on to the enemy's ships. The grapnel irons projecting from her side would foul the enemy, and it would be no easy matter to thrust the fire-ship off until she had done considerable damage by conflagration. This method of warfare was one of the oldest tactics in the history of naval fighting. It was successful over and over

THE GREAT SIR HENRY MORGAN

again, and the reader can well imagine that the sight of a flaming ship rapidly approaching a fleet of anchored ships with the tide was really terrifying. And even if the attacked ships were under way and not brought up it made little difference: for the flames would immediately set on fire a ship's sails, and the tarred rigging would soon be ablaze, rendering the attacked ship disabled.

Of course it was possible at times for a fleet under way so to manœuvre as to get out of the direction towards which the fire-vessel was travelling. But Morgan was up to every eventuality. The fireship he disguised as a man-of-war, and she was not yet set alight. With this craft looking just like one of his own he took his fleet to look for the Spanish men-of-war. On the 1st of May he found them just within the entrance to the lagoon. He now made straight for them, and setting the fireship alight when quite near, sent her right alongside the Spanish flagship, a vessel of 40 guns. The latter was too late to shake her off, burst into flames and soon foundered. Another Spanish ship was so terror-stricken that her crew ran ashore, and she was burnt by her own men lest she should fall into the hands of the buccaneers. The third was captured after heavy slaughter. Some of the Spaniards succeeded in swimming ashore, among whom was the Admiral Don Alonso himself.

Morgan was able to capture a number of prisoners, and from these men he learned tidings which must have sent a thrill of great joy through his avaricious mind. The sunken ship had gone down with 40,000 pieces of eight! So the buccaneer took steps to recover as much of this treasure as he could, and salved no less than 15,000, in addition to a quantity of melted silver. His next work was to have the prize-ship refitted, and her he adopted as his

THE GREAT SIR HENRY MORGAN

own flagship. So far, so good. But he was still in the lagoon, and the door of the trap was yet closed as before, although the enemy's ships had been now disposed of. He again opened negotiations with Don Alonso, and it is surprisingly true that the latter actually paid Morgan the sum of 20,000 pieces of eight and 500 head of cattle as a ransom for Maracaibo. But, on the other hand, Don Alonso declined to demean himself by granting Morgan permission to take his ships out.

That, of course, set Morgan's brain working. He was determined to put to sea, and it was only a question of stratagem. He therefore allowed the Spaniards to gain the impression that he was landing his men so as to attack the fort from the landward side. This caused the Spaniards to move the guns of the fort to that direction, leaving the seaward side practically unarmed. That was Morgan's chance and he fully availed himself thereof. It was nighttime and there was the moon to help him. He waited till the tide was ebbing, and then allowing his ships to drop down with the current he held on until he was off the fort, when he spread sail and before long was well on his way to the northward. It was a clever device for getting out of a very tight corner.

So he sailed over the Spanish Main with rich booty from Gibraltar, with 15,000 pieces of eight from the wreck, with another 20,000 from Alonso, with a new ship and other possessions. Certainly the voyage had been most fortunate and remunerative. He reached Jamaica in safety, but again Modyford was compelled to reprove him for having exceeded his commission. But the same thing happened as before. The Spaniards were becoming more and more aggressive towards the English in the West Indies, and it was essential that they should be given a severe lesson before worse events

THE GREAT SIR HENRY MORGAN

occurred. Morgan was the only man for the task, and he was now appointed commander-in-chief of the warships of the Jamaican station, and sent forth with full authority to seize and destroy all the enemy's vessels that could be found. He was further to destroy all stores and magazines, and for his pay he was to have all the goods and merchandise which he could lay his hands on, his men being paid the customary share that was usual on buccaneering expeditions.

We find him, then, at the middle of August 1670, leaving Port Royal (now better known as Kingston), Jamaica, and as before his rendezvous was Vache Island. With this as his base he sent ships for several months to ravage Cuba and the mainland, and as usual "refreshed" himself, as an Elizabethan would have said, with the things he was in most need, such as provisions. But he was able also to obtain a great deal of valuable information, and at length sailed in a south-west direction till he came to that island of Santa Catalina which we mentioned earlier in this chapter as having been taken by the Spaniards. This he now recaptured, and thereafter he was to perform another wonderful feat. The object he had conceived was to capture Panama. It was another bold idea boldly carried out. First of all, then, he sent from Santa Catalina four of his ships, and a boat, and nearly 500 men, under the leadership of Captain Brodely. These, after a three days' voyage, arrived off Chagres Castle, which is at the mouth of the River Chagres, not far from where the modern Panama Canal comes out. In a remarkably short time Brodely was able to capture this castle: and presently Morgan arrived with the rest of his expedition.

Having made security doubly sure, he proceeded inland, taking his ships up the River Chagres. But after he had gone some distance it was found that, through lack of rain,

THE GREAT SIR HENRY MORGAN

the river had dried considerably. He therefore left 200 men behind to hold the place, and with the rest of his forces he set out to march on foot. He did not hamper his expedition with provisions, as he trusted to obtain supplies from the inhabitants whose dwellings he passed. On the tenth day he had arrived at his distination. Before him lay Panama and the Pacific. But the Spaniards were there on the plain to meet his forces with a considerable strength, consisting of 3000 infantry and cavalry as well as some guns.

But the Spaniards had also ready a unique tactic which seems almost ludicrous. We have already referred slightly to the cattle, which were a feature of this region of the globe. The Spaniards decided to employ such in battle. So, between themselves and the English, they interposed a vast herd of wild bulls, which were driven on in the hope of breaking the English ranks. The wild stampede of creatures of this sort is not likely to make for order, but, like the boomerang on land and the ram in naval warfare, such a device is capable of being less damaging to the attacked than to the attacker. For, as it happened, many of these bulls were shot dead by the English, and the rest of the animals turned their heads round and made for the Spanish, trampling many of them under foot. The English gained the day; the Spaniards were put to flight, and although the buccaneers lost heavily, yet the other side had lost 600 dead. The city of Panama was captured early in the afternoon, and yet again Morgan scooped in an amazing amount of booty. There was the same series of tortures, of threats, and there was a total absence of anything noble-minded in the way Morgan went about his way, satisfying his greed for gold. But he had just missed one very big haul, and this annoyed him exceedingly. For when the

THE BITER BIT

The Spaniards attempted to repel Morgan's men by a stampede of cattle, but the Englishmen completely turned the tables by shooting some of the animals, and turning the rest upon their foes. The Spaniards were put to flight with heavy loss.

THE GREAT SIR HENRY MORGAN

Spaniards saw their men were being defeated, they sent to sea a Spanish galleon which was full of money, church plate and other valuables, worth far more than ever Morgan had obtained from what was left in Panama.

The expedition started on its return journey overland, and after twelve days arrived at Chagres. Here the great quantity of booty was divided up among the crews; but the men were not satisfied with their share, protested that they had been cheated of their full amount, and much discontent ensued. There can be little doubt but that this was so, and that Morgan had enriched himself at the expense of his men. However, he managed to slip away to his ship, followed by only a handful of his former fleet, and once again found himself in Jamaica. Here he received the formal thanks of the governor, but there was trouble brewing. For while Morgan had been away, a treaty had been signed at Madrid concerning Spanish America. It is true that Modyford had, in those days of slow communication, known nothing of it; but he was recalled, and he returned to England a prisoner to answer for his having supported and encouraged buccaneering. The following year Morgan was also sent to England in a frigate, but Charles II. took a great liking to this dare-devil, and in 1674 sent him back again to Jamaica, this time with the rank of Colonel and with the title of knighthood, to be not a buccaneer but Lieutenant-Governor of Jamaica. If ever there was an instance of the ungodly flourishing, here it is. Fourteen years longer did Morgan continue to live in this island as a rich man possessing social prestige. It is true that he made a good governor, but although he had defeated Alonso, reduced Panama, made a clever escape from Maracaibo, taken Santa Catalina and been a veritable thorn in the side of the Spaniards, yet he had been a brute,

THE GREAT SIR HENRY MORGAN

and he died a brute. He was a blackmailer on a large scale, he was unmercifully a tyrant, and he was a profligate. It is only because he attacked the enemies of his own Government, and because he was lucky to obtain the commissions demanded by law, that he is prevented from being reckoned as a mere common pirate. But if there is honour among most thieves, what shall we say of Morgan's dishonesty and harshness in cheating the very men who had fought under him of their fair share of plunder when the battle was won? It is, perhaps, hardly fair to judge even a Morgan except by the prevailing standard of his time. But those who care to look up the details of Morgan's private life will find much to condemn even if there is something to admire in his exceptional cleverness and undoubted courage. The sea is a hard school and makes hard men harder, and in those days when might was right and every ocean more or less in a chaotic state of lawlessness, when poverty, or chance, or despair, or the irresistible longing for adventure drove men to become pirates, there was no living for a soft-hearted sailor. He had to fight or be fought: he had to swim with the tide, or else sink. The luckiest and cleverest became the worst terrors of the sea, while the least fortunate had either to submit to the strong or else end their days in captivity. Morgan having been kidnapped while young may have been driven to kidnap others by sea: or there may have been other causes at work. One thing, however, is certain: the world is not made the richer by the advent of such a man as this Welsh buccaneer.

CHAPTER XIII

"BLACK-BEARD" TEACH

THE sea-rovers whom we know by the name of buccaneers had an origin somewhat similar to that of the Moslem corsairs of Barbary. The reader will not have forgotten that the latter, after being driven out of Spain, settled on the north coast of Africa, and then, after being instructed in the nautical arts by the seamen of different nationalities, rose to the rank of grand corsairs.

So, likewise, the buccaneers were at first inoffensive settlers in Hispaniola, but, after having been driven from their habitations by the Spaniards, developed an implacable hatred of the latter and devoted themselves to infesting the shores of Spanish America and intercepting ships on their way over the sea. And just as the Moslem corsairs were a mixture of several nations—English, Dutch, Levantine, Italian and so on—in like manner the company of buccaneers before long was made up of various European seamen from many a different port.

But among the English buccaneers a special place must be reserved for a Bristol seaman named Edward Teach, better known as "Black-Beard" Teach, just as we remember the great Moslem corsair was known as Red-Beard Uruj, or Barbarossa. Teach left the west of England, and having arrived at Jamaica shipped as one of the crew of a privateer

"BLACK-BEARD" TEACH

during the French war, and was not long in showing that he was made of the right stuff of which those who rove the seas for booty are supposed to be. But it was not until a Captain Benjamin Hornigold gave him the command of a prize which he had taken that Teach began to have his full opportunity. In the spring of 1717 Hornigold and Teach sailed away from the West Indies for North America. Before they had reached their destination they had captured a vessel with 120 barrels of flour, which they distributed between their two vessels. A little later they seized two more vessels, from which they obtained a quantity of wine and treasure. The pirates next proceeded to the coast of Virginia, where they cleaned ship, and then, after these diversions, they captured a ship bound for Martinique.

Hornigold now returned with his prizes to the island of Providence, and presently surrendered himself to the King's clemency. But Teach went about his business as an independent pirate now. The vessel in which he sailed was fitted with forty guns, and he named her *The Queen Anne's Revenge*, and he began rapidly to accumulate wealth. One day, while cruising near the island of St. Vincent, he captured a large vessel called the *Great Allan,* pillaged her of what he fancied and then set her on fire. Only a few days later the *Scarborough* man-of-war hove in sight, and for several hours the two ships engaged. The former recognised that Teach was a pirate and was endeavouring to conquer him : but it is a fact that after a time the *Scarborough,* seeing she was not a match for *The Queen Anne's Revenge*, deemed it better to retire from the contest, thus allowing Teach to resume his piratical profession.

He next found himself encountering a sloop, which was commanded by a Major Bonnet, and Teach and Bonnet agreed to throw in their lot together. But as "Black

"BLACK-BEARD" TEACH

Beard" soon saw that Bonnet was inexperienced in naval matters the former gave the command of the sloop to one of the crew named Richards, whilst Bonnet transferred to the larger ship. And then the two craft went roaming over the seas with singular success. Indeed, were one to mention every ship that Teach captured, the reader would find the catalogue to be one of mere monotony. The pirate had but to give chase after a sail, hoist his black flag, and the fleeing ship would heave-to and surrender. But as I believe the reader would find it more interesting to become acquainted with the more interesting episodes rather than a complete list of every single engagement, I propose to confine myself to the former.

Teach cruised about the West Indies and off the southern portion of what are now the United States. He would anchor off Charleston (South Carolina), wait till an outward-bound ship emerged from the harbour, and then promptly seize her, or, just to vary matters, he would capture a couple of others as they were about to enter Charleston. The impudence of the man was amazing, and his audacity spread terror in the town and paralysed the trade of the port. No vessel dared to show her nose outside the harbour, and a whole fleet of ships was thus tied up inside unable to move. And then, like many of these pirates, Teach showed how remarkably clever and resourceful he was. By this time he had captured quite a large number of prisoners, and it became essential that medicine supplies should be procured by some means. To this end he had the remarkable impudence to demand a medicine-chest from the governor: and this request was made neither diplomatically nor even politely. He asked for it with consummate insolence. He sent some of his own crew ashore, together with several of the prisoners, demanding these medicinal stores, and it was

"BLACK-BEARD" TEACH

made quite clear to the governor that if these were not forthcoming and a safe return made to the ships, every prisoner should instantly be put to death, and the captured ships burnt to ashes. Whilst these negotiations were being carried on by the little deputation of prisoners, the pirate's crew were swaggering up and down the streets of Charleston, and not a hand dared to touch them.

The governor was in a dilemma and listened carefully to the insolent demand: but as he was anxious to prevent human carnage, he got together medicinal supplies to the value of over £300 and sent them aboard. But to show you what sort of a man Teach was, let it be said that as soon as the pirate obtained these goods and the safe return of his own men, he pillaged the captured vessels of all their gold and provisions, then put the prisoners back on their respective ships and set sail for North Carolina. On the way thither Teach began to consider how he could best secure the spoil for himself and a few of his especial friends among the crew, so he pretended that he was about to give his ship's bottom a scrub and headed for the shore, where she grounded. He then called to the sloop to come to his assistance. This they attempted, but the sloop also took the ground badly and both ships became total wrecks. Teach then took the tender, put forty hands therein, had about half of them landed on a lonely sandy island three miles from the shore, "where there was neither bird nor beast nor herb for their subsistence." Had it not been for Major Bonnet, who afterwards sent a long-boat for them, they would have died.

Meanwhile Teach, now very rich, with the rest of his crew, went and surrendered himself to the Governor of North Carolina. Why? Not for any other reason than in order to plan out bigger piracies. For he knew that the governor

"BLACK-BEARD" TEACH

would succumb to bribery, and by this official's influence a court of vice-admiralty was held and *The Queen Anne's Revenge* condemned as a lawful prize and the legal property of Teach, although it was a well-known fact that she belonged to English merchants.

It was not long before Teach was at sea again, and setting a course for Bermudas he pillaged four or five English and French merchantmen, and brought one of the ships back to North Carolina, where he shared the prizes with the governor who had already obliged him. Teach also made an affidavit that he had found this French ship at sea with not a soul on board, so the court allowed him to keep her, and the governor received sixty hogsheads of sugar for his kindly assistance. Teach was very nervous lest some one might arrive in the harbour and prove that the pirate was lying, so on the excuse that this ship was leaky and likely to stop up the entrance to the harbour if she sank, permission was obtained from the governor to burn her, and when that had been done, her bottom was sunk so that she might never exist as a witness against him.

But the time came when the piracies of this Teach could no longer be endured. Skippers of trading craft had already lost so heavily that it was resolved to take concerted action. The skippers knew that the Governor of Virginia was an honourable man, and they laid the matter before him, begging that an armed force might be sent from the men-of-war to settle these infesting pirates. The governor consulted the men-of-war captains as to what had best be done, and it was decided to hire two small vessels which could pursue Black Beard into all those inlets and creeks which exist on the American coast. These were to be manned by men from the warships, and placed under the command of Lieutenant May. A proclamation was also

"BLACK-BEARD" TEACH

issued offering a handsome reward to any who within a year should capture or destroy a pirate.

But before we go on to watch the exciting events with which this punitive expedition was concerned I want the reader to realise something more of the kind of pirate they were to chase. A few actual incidents will reveal his character better than many words. The story is told that on a certain night when Black Beard was drinking in his cabin with Israel Hands (who was master of *The Queen Anne's Revenge*), the ship's pilot and a fourth man, Teach suddenly took up a pair of pistols and cocked them underneath the table. When the fourth man perceived this, he went up on deck, leaving Teach, Hands and the pilot together. As soon as the pistols were ready, Teach blew out the light, crossed his arms and fired at the two men. The first pistol did not harm, but the other wounded Hands in the knee. When Teach was asked why he did this, he replied with an oath, "If I didn't now and then kill one of you, you would forget who I was."

And there is another anecdote which shows his vanity in a curious manner. Like most blackguards, he was anxious to pose as a person who set no limits to his endurance. Those were the days of braggadocio, of pomposity and hard drinking and hard swearing. It happened that on this particular occasion the ship was doing a passage, and Teach was somewhat high-spirited through the effect of the wine, and he became obsessed with the idea of making his crew believe that he was a devil incarnate. "Come," he roared to some of his men, "let us make a hell of our own, and try how long we can bear it." It was obviously the prank of a drunken braggart, but with several others he went down into the hold of the ship and closed up all the hatches. He then filled several pots full of brimstone

"BLACK-BEARD" TEACH

and other combustible matter and set it on fire. Quickly the hold became so bad that the men were almost suffocated, and some of them clamoured for air. The hatches were at last opened and Teach was as proud of having been able to hold out longest as if he had just captured a well-freighted prize. And, finally, you can also appreciate the man's vanity in a totally different manner. His name was derived from his long black beard, which caused him to look exceedingly repellent ; but he would sometimes even stick lighted matches under his hat, which, burning on either side of his face, lit up his wild fierce eyes and made his general appearance so repulsive that he exactly reflected his own character.

But to resume our story at the point where we digressed. About the middle of November 1717, Lieutenant Maynard set out in quest of Black Beard, and four days later came in sight of the pirate. The expedition had been fitted out with every secrecy, and care was taken to prevent information reaching Teach. But the tidings had reached Teach's friend, the Governor of Bermudas, and his secretary. The latter therefore sent a letter to warn Teach to be on his guard. But Teach had before now been the recipient of false news, and he declined to believe that he was being hunted down. In fact, it was not until he actually saw the sloops which had been sent to catch him that he could realise the true state of affairs.

Maynard had arrived with his sloops in the evening of a November day, and deemed it wiser to wait till morning before attack. Teach was so little concerned, however, that he spent the night in drinking with the skipper of a trader. Black Beard's men fully realised that there would be an engagement the next day, and one of them ventured to ask him a certain question. If, inquired the man, any-

"BLACK-BEARD" TEACH

thing should happen to Teach during the engagement would his wife know where he had buried his money? Black Beard's reply was short and concise. "Nobody but the devil and myself," he answered, "knows where it is. And the longest liver shall take all."

When the morning came, Maynard weighed anchor and sent his boat to sound the depth of water around where the pirate was lying. Teach then promptly fired at the boat, but Maynard then hoisted his royal colours and made towards Black Beard as fast as oars and sails could carry him. Before long both the pirate and two sloops were aground, but Maynard lightened his vessel of her ballast and water, and then advanced towards Black Beard, whereupon the pirate began to roar and rant. "Who are you?" he hailed, "and whence come you?" The naval officer quietly answered him. "You see from our colours we are no pirates." Black Beard then bade him send his boat aboard that he might see who he was, but Maynard simply answered this impudent request by replying, "I cannot spare my boat, but I will come aboard you as soon as I can with my sloop."

The swaggering pirate then raised his glass of grog and insolently drank to the officer, saying, "I'll give no quarter, nor take any from you." Maynard replied that he expected no quarter from him, nor, for his part, did he intend to give any. But whilst this exchange of courtesies went on, the tide had risen and the pirate's ship floated off. As fast as they could the sloops were being rowed towards Teach's ship, but as the ships drew near, Teach fired a broadside and so killed or wounded twenty of the naval men. A little later Black Beard's ship drifted in to the shore and one of the sloops fell astern. But Maynard, finding that his own sloop was carrying way on and that he

A FIERCE DUEL BETWEEN BLACK-BEARD AND MAYNARD

After exchanging shots, when Teach (Black-beard) was wounded, they drew their swords and fiercely attacked each other. Maynard's sword broke in his hand, and had it not been for one of his own men, who wounded Black-beard in the throat, the duel would have ended then.

"BLACK-BEARD" TEACH

would fetch alongside Teach's ship, ordered all his own men below, while he and the helmsman were the only two who remained on deck. The latter he managed to conceal so that only the officer was visible. But he ordered his crew to take their pistols, cutlasses and swords and to be ready for any duty immediately, and in order to make it possible for the men to regain the deck in the minimum time, he caused two ladders to be placed in the hatchway.

The sloop now came alongside the pirate, whereupon the latter had case-boxes, such as were discharged from cannon, thrown on board, having first been filled with powder, small shot, slugs and pieces of lead and iron. A quick match was placed in the mouth of these and then they were dropped on to the sloop's deck. These would, of course, be exceedingly destructive, but inasmuch as the naval crew were below at the time, they did but little harm. And when Black Beard saw that by now there were only a few hands on deck he believed that these three or four were the sole survivors. He exulted greatly and cried, "Let us jump on board and cut to pieces those that are alive." Now one of these case-boxes was causing a great cloud of smoke, so that Black Beard was able, together with fourteen of his men, to leap on the sloop's deck without being immediately perceived. But as soon as the smoke began to clear, Maynard ordered his men up from below, who were on deck in a flash.

Then there began a fierce fight, and between Maynard and Black Beard there was a magnificent hand-to-hand encounter. At first they exchanged shots, and the pirate was wounded. Then they drew their swords, and each man lunged at the other. Matters were proceeding in an exciting manner until, by ill-luck, the lieutenant had the misfortune to break his sword. In a moment Black Beard

"BLACK-BEARD" TEACH

would have dealt him a fatal blow, had not one of Maynard's men instantly given the pirate a terrible wound in the neck and throat. After this the onslaught became fiercer and fiercer. Both sides were releasing their pent-up rage, and it was by no means certain who would win the fight. There were twelve service men against fourteen of the pirates, not counting Maynard or Teach. It is to be stated that neither side lacked bravery, and the greatest valour was displayed on both sides. The deck presented a sickening sight, and blood was seen spilt everywhere. Teach, though he had been wounded by the shot from Maynard and the blow from one of the latter's men, as well as sundry other ugly cuts, still fought splendidly. But he was employing the very utmost of his physical resources, and finally, while in the act of cocking his pistol, fell down with a heavy thud to the deck dead.

In the meanwhile eight of his men had also perished, and most of the rest being wounded they clamoured for quarter, a request which was granted, seeing that Teach himself had been slain. Maynard severed the pirate's head from his body, and after affixing it to the end of his bowsprit, sailed away to Bathtown in order to obtain medical aid for his wounded men. On ransacking the pirate ship there were found a number of incriminating documents which showed the close connection between Teach and the Governor of Bermudas. After Maynard's men had their wounds attended to, the sloop left Bathtown, and with Black Beard's head still swinging at the bowsprit end, proceeded to Virginia, where there was great rejoicing that the pirate pest had at last been killed. The prisoners were brought off from the sloop, tried, condemned and executed, with the exception of two. Of these one had been taken by Teach from a trading ship only the day

"BLACK-BEARD" TEACH

before the fight, and he was suffering severely from no less than seventy wounds, but of these he presently recovered. The other man not executed was Israel Hands, who was master of *The Queen Anne's Revenge*, who had remained on shore at Bathtown, where he was recovering from that wound we mentioned just now which Black-Beard one night in a playful humour had dealt him from his pistol in the dark.

So the American colonists were able to breathe again, and the trading ships were allowed to go about once more without fear of this scoundrel. The blow had been dealt decisively and neatly. It only remains to add one other fact which well indicates the desperate nature of this pirate. When, during the engagement, it seemed likely that he would be overcome, he had placed a negro at the gunpowder door with instructions to blow the ship up the moment Maynard's men should come aboard. But inasmuch as Maynard's clever stratagem lured the pirate and his men on board the sloop, a terrible disaster was avoided which would have involved both ships and doubtless all the men of each contesting party.

CHAPTER XIV

THE STORY OF CAPTAIN KIDD

WE come now to another historical pirate, who, both in America and England, will long be remembered for his very interesting exploits. Following the modern tendency of endeavouring to whitewash notorious criminals of a bygone age, a recent writer has sought to dismiss the idea that Kidd was to be numbered among the pirates. I admit that at one time this man was an honest seaman, and that force of circumstances caused his career to become completely altered. But a pirate he certainly became, and no amount of juggling with facts can alter this.

The story of his life is as follows: He was a Scotsman who was born in Greenock, which has given to the world so many fine seamen in different generations, and so many handsome new ships both of wood and of steel. Sailing ships and steam-propelled liners have been built here during the past two hundred years by the score. After a while we find Kidd in North America. He became a resident of New York, and in 1691 married a widow. He became a prosperous shipmaster sailing out of New York, and they say that in his house in Liberty Street was the first Turkey carpet ever seen in New York. He was a man well-known to the local merchants, and for a time had command of a

THE STORY OF CAPTAIN KIDD

privateer cruising against the French in West Indian waters. This was the period during which William III. was at war with our French neighbours.

In the year 1695 Kidd had crossed to England and was in London, having command of the brigantine *Antigoa*, of New York. Now about this time the King had appointed the Earl of Bellomont to be governor of New England and New York. And the latter was especially instructed to suppress the prevailing piracy which was causing so much distress along the coast. Lord Bellomont, who had been governor of Barbadoes, suggested that Kidd should be entrusted with a man-of-war, as he was a most suitable person to send against these sea-rovers, knowing as he did every inch of the coast and the favourite hiding-places of the pirates. But the Admiralty did not esteem it suitable for Kidd to have a government ship under him, and there the matter ended. But Bellomont was one of those far-sighted men who ever had an eye for the main chance. He and his friends were well aware of the enormous amount of money which these pirates accumulated, and since the Admiralty would not give him a frigate, he resolved to form a small syndicate among his friends and fit out a private ship. He decided to appoint Kidd as captain. The latter was not anxious to accept this appointment, but Bellomont pointed out that if he did not, Kidd's own vessel would be detained in the Thames; so at last he consented.

In order to give the project a certain amount of status and in order to be able to enforce greater discipline over the crew, a King's commission was obtained for Kidd, authorising him "to apprehend, seize, and take into your custody" all "pirates, freebooters, and sea-rovers, being our subjects, or of other nations associated with them."

THE STORY OF CAPTAIN KIDD

But he was also given a "commission of reprisals." As it was then time of war, this second commission gave him justification for capturing any French ships he might encounter. The ship which had been purchased for him was called the *Adventure*, of 287 tons, 34 guns and 70 or 80 men.

In the month of May 1796, we find her sailing out of Plymouth Sound bound for New York. It should be mentioned that Kidd and a man named Robert Livingstone had undertaken to pay one-fifth of the expenses, whilst Bellomont, with the First Lord of the Admiralty, the Lord Chancellor and certain other gentlemen had put up the other four-fifths of the capital. On the voyage out, Kidd fell in with a French fishing craft off the Newfoundland banks and annexed her. Owing to the second of his commissions just mentioned, this was no act of piracy but perfectly legal as a privateer. Arrived in New York, Kidd made it known that he needed a number of additional hands as crew, and, as an incentive, he offered each man a share, reserving for himself and owners forty shares. He got an additional number of men, comprising now 155, and then sailed away. He had shipped a miscellaneous lot of rascals—naval deserters, pirates out of employment, fugitives from justice, brawlers, thieves, rogues and vagabonds. They had signed on, attracted by the chance of obtaining plenty of booty. He set a course across the Atlantic, and his first call was at Madeira, where he took on board wine and other necessaries. From there he proceeded to the Cape Verde Islands, where he obtained salt and provisions, and having all this done, steered in a southerly direction, rounded the Cape of Good Hope, and hauled up into the Indian Ocean till he found himself off Madagascar, which was a notorious hunting ground for pirates. It was now February of 1697, the

THE STORY OF CAPTAIN KIDD

Adventure having left Plymouth for New York the previous May.

But, as it happened, there were no pirate ships to be found off Madagascar, for they were somewhere out at sea looking for spoil. Therefore, after watering and taking on board more provisions, he steered to the north-east across the Indian Ocean till he came to the Malabar coast in the month of June. His ship was sadly in need of repairs, and he was in serious need of further stores. He had come a long way from New York to India, and his ship had not earned a penny since she left America. But he managed to borrow a sum of money from some Frenchmen who had lost their ship but had saved their effects, and with this he was able to buy materials for putting his ship in a seaworthy condition.

And now there came a change, and from being a privateer he became a pirate. Once more he crossed the Indian Ocean and arrived at Bab's Key, which is on an island at the entrance to the Red Sea. He began to open his mind to his crew and to let them understand that he was making a change. So far he had acted according to the law and his commission, though not a single pirate had he seen. He knew that the Mocha fleet would presently come sailing that way, and he addressed his men in these words: "We have been unsuccessful hitherto; but courage, my boys, we'll make our fortunes out of this fleet." There can be little doubt but that Kidd had been working at this idea as he came across the Indian Ocean. Before a man becomes a robber either by land or by sea, there is a previous mental process. A man cannot say that he acted on the spur of the moment without confessing that he had been entertaining the suggestion of robbery some time before. It would seem that Kidd originally had every intention of keeping to

THE STORY OF CAPTAIN KIDD

the terms and spirit of his two commissions. But as he had been sailing across the world without luck, he became despondent. He thought not merely of himself, or of his crew, but of Bellomont and the rest of the syndicate. Time and expenses had been running on, and there was nothing on the credit side beyond that one French ship of a year ago. He was utterly despondent, and as a man down on his luck thieves on land so he would now act on sea. The intention was thoroughly wrong, but it was comprehensible.

He waited for the Mocha fleet, but it came not; so he had a boat hoisted out, and sent her well-manned along the coast to bring back a prisoner, or at any rate obtain intelligence somehow. In a few days the boat returned, announcing there were fourteen ships ready to sail—English, Dutch and Moorish. He therefore kept a man continually on the look out at the mast-head lest the fleet should sail past without being seen; for Kidd was well-nigh desperate. And one evening, about four days later, the ships appeared in sight, being convoyed by two men-of-war—one English and one Dutch. Kidd soon fell in with them, got among them, and fired at the Moorish ship which happened to be nearest to him. Thereupon the two convoys bore down on him, engaged him hotly, and compelled him to sheer off. So, as he had begun to play the pirate, he resolved to go on. He crossed the Indian Ocean to the eastward yet again, and cruised along the Malabar coast, and at last he got a prize. She was a Moorish vessel, owned by Moorish merchants, but her master was an Englishman named Parker, and there was also a Portuguese named Don Antonio on board.

These two men Kidd forced to join him, the former as pilot and the latter as interpreter. Thus the commissioned privateer was now a full-fledged pirate; he had sunk deep down into the mire. And he acted with all the customary

THE STORY OF CAPTAIN KIDD

cruelty of a pirate. He hoisted his prisoners up by the arms, drubbed them with a naked cutlass in order that they might reveal where the money was hidden. But all that he obtained was a bale of pepper and a bale of coffee. But then he sailed along and touched at Carawar, where he discovered that already the news of the assault on the Moorish ship had arrived and was being discussed with great excitement by the merchants. Kidd was suspected, and two Englishmen came aboard and inquired for Parker and Don Antonio. Kidd denied that he knew such persons, and as he had taken the precaution to hide them away in a secret place down the hold, the visitors, still suspicious, went ashore without any definite tidings.

For over a week these two wretched men were kept in their hiding-place, and once more Kidd put to sea. A Portuguese man-of-war having been sent to cruise after him, he engaged her for six hours, but as he could not take her, and as he was the swifter sailer, he cleared off. Soon afterwards he became possessor of a Moorish ship by a very subtle quibble, which indicated the man's astuteness. The vessel was under the command of a Dutch skipper, and as soon as Kidd gave her chase, the pirate hoisted French colours. When the merchantship saw this, she also showed the French ensign. The *Adventure* soon overtook her and hailed her in French. The merchantship, having a Frenchman on board, answered in that language. Kidd ordered her to send her boat aboard, and then asked the Frenchman —a passenger—if he had a pass for himself. The latter replied in the affirmative. Kidd then told the Frenchman he must pass as captain, "and," he added, "you *are* captain." His intention was simply this. Remembering the terms of his commission, he was untruthfully insisting that the merchantman was French and therefore legally his

THE STORY OF CAPTAIN KIDD

prize. It was a bare-faced quibble, and one wonders why so unprincipled a man should deem it necessary to go out of his way to make such a pretence.

So he relieved the ship of her cargo and sold it later on. Presently, as he began to suffer from qualms of conscience and declined to attack a Dutch ship with which they came up, his crew mutinied, and one day, whilst a man named Moore, his gunner, was on deck discussing the Dutch ship, Moore so far lost control of his tongue as to accuse Kidd of having ruined them all. The pirate answered this complaint by calling him a dog, taking up a bucket and breaking the man's skull therewith, so that he died the next day. Kidd now cruised about the Malabar coast, plundering craft, taking in water and supplies from the shore, and pillaging when he liked.

And now he came up with a fine 400-ton Moorish merchantman named the *Queda*, whose master was an Englishman named Wright, for it was by no means rare for these Eastern owners to employ English or Dutch skippers, as the latter were such good seamen and navigators. Kidd as before chased her under French colours, and having got abreast of her compelled her to hoist out her boat and send it aboard. He then informed Wright he was to consider himself a prisoner, and he learnt that there were only three Europeans on board—two Dutch and one Frenchman—the rest being either Indians or Armenians. The last mentioned were also part-owners of the cargo. Kidd set the crew of this vessel ashore at different places along the coast, and soon sold about £10,000 worth of the captured cargo, so that each man had about £200, whilst Kidd got £8000.

Putting part of his own crew into the *Queda*, Kidd took the *Adventure* and the prize southwards to Madagascar, and when he had come to anchor a ludicrous incident occurred.

THE STORY OF CAPTAIN KIDD

For there came off to him a canoe containing several Englishmen who had previously known Kidd well. They now saluted him and said they understood that he had come to take them and hang them, "which would be a little unkind in such an old acquaintance." But Kidd at once put them at their ease, swearing he had no such intention, and that he was now in every respect their brother, and just as bad as they; and calling for alcohol he drank their captain's health. The men then returned on board their ship *Resolution*. But by now, after all her travels backwards and forwards over the ocean, the *Adventure* had become very leaky and her two pumps had to be kept going continuously. So Kidd transferred all the tackle and guns from her to the *Queda*, and in future made her his home. He then divided up the spoil on the sharing principle as before. About a hundred of his men now deserted him, and, with his forty men and about £20,000 in his ship, he put to sea, bound at last for America again, for he was under orders to report to Bellomont at the end of the cruise.

He arrived at the West Indies, called at one of the Leeward islands and learnt that the news of his piracies had spread over the civilised world, and he was wanted as a pirate. The date was now April 1699. He handed over the *Queda* to a man named Bolton who was a merchant at Antigua, and bought from him a sloop named the *San Antonio*, into which he put all his treasure. He must now press on and swear to Bellomont that he was innocent of piracy. Being anxious to communicate with his wife, Kidd steered for Long Island Sound, proceeded as far as Oyster Bay, landed, and sent her a message, and after going on his northward voyaging, transferred some of his treasure into three sloops. Towards the end of June he headed for Boston, arriving there on the 1st July, where he had

THE STORY OF CAPTAIN KIDD

various interviews with Bellomont. The sloop and her contents, as well as the other three sloops' goods were arrested, and Kidd was afterwards taken across to England. He and six others were tried at a sessions of Admirality at the Old Bailey in May 1701 for piracy and robbery on the high seas, and found guilty. Kidd was further charged with the murder of the man Moore in the bucket incident, and also found guilty.

Kidd's defence was that the man mutinied against him, that his accusers had committed perjury and that he was "the most innocent person of them all." But the Court thought otherwise, and a week or so later he and the other six men were executed at the Execution Dock, and afterwards their bodies were hung up in chains, at intervals along the river, where they remained for a long time.

Of the treasure which was brought by Kidd to America, and has frequently been sought for by treasure-hunters unavailingly, the exact total of gold dust, gold coins, gold bars; silver rings, silver buttons, broken silver, silver bars; precious stones—diamonds, rubies, green stones, and so on—reached the following enormous amount—

Gold	1111 oz.
Silver	2353 ,,
Jewels	17 ,,

A certain amount of plate and money was successfully retained by Kidd's wife, and of what was left of the booty after payment of the legal fees involved in his trial, the sum of £6472 was, by special Act of Parliament, handed over to Greenwich Hospital.[1]

[1] I wish to acknowledge my indebtedness for some of the facts here mentioned to an interesting article by Mr. Winfield M. Thompson in the *Rudder* for the year 1909.

THE STORY OF CAPTAIN KIDD

Surely, with such facts as these before one, it is a hopeless case for any modern enthusiast to pretend for a moment that the famous Captain Kidd was not a pirate. If his luck had turned out better, probably he would have contentedly remained a privateer. But opportunity is illustrative of the man, and if ever a sailor succeeded in showing himself to be a pirate with all the avariciousness and cruelty which the word suggests, here you have it in the life of Captain Kidd.

CHAPTER XV

THE EXPLOITS OF CAPTAIN AVERY

IF the sixteenth century was the "grand" period of the Moslem corsairs of the Mediterranean, the eighteenth will ever remain memorable for the manifold activities of those English seamen who took to piracy as a far more remunerative profession than carrying freights. If we look for any explanation of this, I think it is not far to seek.

You have to take into consideration several points. Firstly, it seems to me, in all phases whether political or otherwise, whether concerned with the sea or with land affairs, you must get at personal and national character—the very fount and origin of all human energies. Whatever else the seventeenth century was, it was not a very distinguished era. There were, of course, exceptions, but speaking broadly, it was a most disappointing period. Morally it was corrupt, politically it was degenerate, and artistically it was insincere and pompous. You have only to read the history of that period in its various aspects to realise this. This was the time when the reaction after the Puritan period had led to a dereliction of high principles, when intrigue and bribery had made such an onslaught on political life that votes were bought for money, that even admirals allowed petty politics to interfere with their loyalty when fighting at sea the nation's enemies. Smug respectability

THE EXPLOITS OF CAPTAIN AVERY

was the dominating high ideal, and there was no greater sin than that of being found out. High-handed actions by those in power and lawlessness by those who were covetous of obtaining wealth were significant of this period. And if you want to realise the humbug and insincerity of the eighteenth century, you have only to go into the nearest art gallery and examine the pictures of that period (excepting perhaps some portraiture), or to read the letters which the men and women wrote, or to read the books which the educated people of that time esteemed so highly. Religion and politics, domestic life, art and literature were in an unhealthy condition.

Now a man, whether a sailor or a politician, or whatever else, is very largely the child of his age. That is to say, given a lawless, unprincipled, corrupt period, it is more than likely that any particular individual will be found to exhibit in his activities the marks of that age. And therefore, bearing such facts as these in mind, it becomes perfectly comprehensible that the eighteenth century should have been the flourishing period of English sea-robbery. Add just one item more—the continual period of unrest caused by years of international wars and the rumours of war, and you are not surprised that the call of the sea was accepted by so many more hundreds of men than ever before in the history of the nation. But naval wars did not mean merely that more men were wanted to work the ship which fought our battles; there was such an encouragement and incentive to skippers and capitalists to undertake privateering that not even in the Elizabethan age had so many ships and men taken part in that kind of undertaking. So, instead of privateering being merely an exceptional activity during an occasional period of hostilities, it became, owing to long drawn-out wars, a regular, definite profession. There was

THE EXPLOITS OF CAPTAIN AVERY

in it every opportunity to indulge both personal and national hatred of the foreigner; to enjoy a series of fine adventures, and then to return home with an accumulation of glory and prizes. Side by side with this—and well illustrating the tone of the age—smuggling had become an almost irrepressible national evil.

In the history of smuggling you not infrequently found that the preliminary steps to this dishonest livelihood were as follows: First, the man was employed as an honest fisherman; then, finding this did not pay him, he became a privateer, or else in the King's service serving on board a Revenue cutter. Then, being more anxious for wealth, he threw in his lot with the very men he had been chasing, and became either an out-and-out smuggler or else a pirate. For, as has been insisted on more than once in previous chapters, the line of demarcation between privateering and piracy, though perfectly visible to lawyers, was not always sufficiently strong to keep the roving seaman within the limitations of legal livelihood. In a word, as it is always difficult suddenly to break a habit, and as this immense body of seamen had so long been accustomed to earning their money by attacking other ships, so in an age that had but little respect for what was lawful, it was really not surprising that dozens of ships put to sea as downright pirates or else as acknowledged smugglers. In this present volume we are concerned only with the first of these two classes.

Typical of the period was a notorious Captain Avery, whose doings became known throughout Europe. There was nothing petty in these eighteenth-century corsairs. They had in them the attributes which go to making a great admiral, they were born rulers of men, they were good strategists, hard fighters, brave and valorous, daring and

THE EXPLOITS OF CAPTAIN AVERY

determined. But as against this they were tyrannical, cruel and brutal; and, as is so frequently the case with all men, the acquisition of wealth ruined them, made them still more overbearing and swollen-headed, so that with no high principles, no lofty aims, they descended by degrees into debauchery and callousness. It was a thousand pities in many ways, for these were magnificent seamen who took their ill-designed, bluff, old tubs practically all round the world, keeping the sea for months at a time, and surviving terrible weather and many changes of climate. If these great disciplinarians had not become tyrants, and if their unquestioned abilities could have been legitimately employed, they had in them the ability which has produced great Empire makers, brilliant admirals and magnificent administrators. But their misfortune consisted in having belonged to the eighteenth century.

Avery, like many of the world's greatest seamen, was born in Devonshire, went to sea when quite young, and rose to the rank of mate in a merchant ship. It happened that there was a good deal of smuggling going on by the French of Martinique with the Spaniards of the American colonies. And in order to put a stop to this, the Spanish Government hired foreigners to act against the delinquents. A number of Bristol merchants accordingly fitted out a couple of 30-gun ships, and, well-manned, well-found in everything, sent them to Corunna to await orders. One of these ships was commanded by a Captain Gibson, and in the year 1715 Avery happened to be his mate. The Devonshire man possessed all the traditional seafaring instincts and that love of adventure for which his county was famous, and he was evidently not unpopular with the rest of the crew. For after he had won their confidence, he began to point out to them what immense riches could be obtained on the Spanish

THE EXPLOITS OF CAPTAIN AVERY

coast, and suggested that they should throw in their lot with him and run off with the ship. This suggestion was heartily agreed upon, and it was resolved to make the attempt the following evening at ten o'clock.

It should be mentioned that Gibson, like many another eighteenth-century skipper, was rather too fond of his grog, and on the eventful night he had imbibed somewhat freely and turned into his bunk, instead of going ashore for his usual refreshment. Those of the crew who were not in the present plot had also turned in, but the others remained on deck. At ten o'clock the long-boat from the other ship rowed off to them. Avery gave her a hail, and the boat answered by the agreed watchword thus: "Is your drunken boatswain on board?" Avery replied in the affirmative, and then sixteen able men came on board. The first thing was to secure the hatches, and then very quietly they hauled up the anchor and put to sea without making much noise.

After they had been under way some time, the captain awoke from his drunken sleep and rang his bell. Avery and one other confederate then went into the cabin. "What's the matter with the ship?" queried the "old man." "Does she drive; what weather is it?" For as he realised she was on the move he naturally was forced to the conclusion that the ship was sheering about at her anchor and that a strong wind had sprung up. Avery quickly reassured him, and incidentally gave his waking mind something of a shock. "No," answered the former mate, "no, we're at sea, with a fair wind and good weather." "At sea?" gasped the captain. "How can that be?" "Come, don't be in a fright, but put on your clothes, and I'll let you into a secret. You must know," he went on, "that I am captain of this ship now, and this is my cabin,

THE EXPLOITS OF CAPTAIN AVERY

therefore you must walk out. I am bound for Madagascar with the design of making my own fortune and that of all the brave fellows joined with me."

The captain began to recover his senses and to understand what was being said, but he was still very frightened. Avery begged him not to be afraid, and that if he liked to join their confederacy they were willing to receive him. "If you turn sober, and attend to business, perhaps in time I may make you one of my lieutenants. If not here's a boat, and you shall be set on shore." Gibson preferred to choose this last alternative, and the whole crew being called up to know who was willing to go ashore with the captain, there were only about half a dozen who decided to accompany him to the land.

So Avery took his ship to Madagascar without making any captures. On arriving at the north-east portion of the island, he found a couple of sloops at anchor, but when these espied him they slipped their cables and ran their ships ashore, while the men rushed inland and hid themselves in the woods. For these men had guilty consciences. They had stolen the sloops from the East Indies, and on seeing Avery's ship arrive they imagined that he had been sent to punish them. But Avery sent some of his own men ashore to say that the sloops' men were his friends, and suggested that they should form an amalgamation for their common benefit and safety. The men were well armed and had taken up positions in the wood, and outposts had been stationed to watch whether they were pursued ashore.

But when the latter perceived that two or three men were approaching unarmed, there was no opposition offered, and on learning that they were friends, the messengers were led to the main body, where they delivered Avery's

THE EXPLOITS OF CAPTAIN AVERY

message. At first the fugitives had feared this was just a stratagem to entrap them, but when they heard that Avery, too, had run away with his ship, they conferred and decided to throw in their lot. The next thing was to get the two sloops refloated, and then the trio sailed towards the Arabian coast. When they arrived at length off the mouths of the Indus, a man at the masthead espied a sail, so orders were given to chase. As they came on nearer, the strange vessel was observed to be a fine tall craft and probably an East Indiaman. But when they came closer she was found to be far more valuable and more worth fighting.

On firing at her the latter hoisted the colours of the Great Mogul and seemed prepared to fight the matter out. But Avery declined getting at close quarters and preferred to bombard from a safe distance, whereupon some of his men began to suspect that he was not the dashing hero they had taken him for. But the sloops attacked the strange ship vigorously, one at the bow and the other on her quarter. After a while they succeeded in boarding her, when she was now compelled to strike colours. It was found that she was one of the Great Mogul's ships, carrying a number of important members of his court on a pilgrimage to Mecca and most valuable articles to be offered at the shrine of Mahomet. There were large quantities of magnificent gold and silver vessels, immense sums of money, and altogether the plunder was very considerable. Everything of value having been taken out of her, and the entire treasure having been transferred on board the three ships, the vessel was permitted to depart.

When at last the ship returned to her home, and the Mogul learned the news, he was exceedingly wrathful and threatened to send a mighty army to drive out the English

THE EXPLOITS OF CAPTAIN AVERY

from their settlements along the Indian coast. This greatly alarmed the East India Company, but the latter managed to calm him down by promising to send ships after the robbers and deliver him into their hands. The incident caused great excitement in Europe, and all sorts of extravagant rumours spread about, so that at one time it was intended to fit out a powerful squadron and have him captured, while another suggestion was that he should be invited home with his riches and receive the offer of His Majesty's pardon, for he was reputed now to be about to found a new monarchy. But eventually these foolish notions were discovered to be baseless. Meanwhile the three treasure-laden ships were returning to Madagascar, where it was hoped to build a small fort, keep a few men there permanently and there deposit their ill-gotten treasure.

But Avery had another plan in his mind, and this well exhibits his true character. On the voyage he sent out a boat to each of the sloops, inviting each skipper to repair on board him. They came and he laid before them the following proposition. If either of the sloops were to be attacked alone, they could not be able to offer any great resistance, and so their treasure would vanish. As regards his own ship, he went on, she was such a swift ship that he could not conceive of any other craft overtaking her. Therefore he suggested that all the treasure should be sealed up in three separate chests, that each of the three captains should have keys, that they should not be opened until all were present, that these chests should then be kept on his own ship, and afterwards deposited in a safe place ashore.

It seems very curious that such wide-awake pirates should not have been able to see through such an obvious

THE EXPLOITS OF CAPTAIN AVERY

trick. But without hesitation they agreed with the idea, and all the treasure was placed aboard Avery's ship as had been suggested. The little fleet sailed on, and now Avery began to approach his crew in his usual underhand manner. Here was sufficient wealth on board to make them all happy for the rest of their lives. "What," he asked, "shall hinder us from going to some country where we are not known and living on shore to the end of our days in affluence?" The crew thoroughly appreciated the hint, so during the night Avery's ship got clear away, altered her course, sailed round the Cape of Good Hope and made for America. They were strangers in that land, they would divide up the booty and they would separate, so that each man would be able to live on comfortably without working. They arrived at the island of Providence, when it was decided that it would be wiser to get rid of such a large vessel. So, pretending she had been fitted out for privateering, and that, having had an unsuccessful voyage, Avery had received orders from his owners to sell her as best he could, he soon found a merchant who bought her, and Avery then purchased a small sloop.

In this craft he and his crew embarked with their treasure, and after landing at different places on the American coast where no one suspected them, they dispersed and settled down in the country. Avery had now immense wealth, but as most thereof consisted of diamonds and he was afraid of being unable to get rid of them in America without being suspected as a pirate, he then crossed to the north of Ireland, where some of his men settled and obtained the King's pardon. And now began a series of incidents which might well be taken to show the folly of ill-gotten gain. The reader has already seen that in spite of the vast affluence which these eighteenth-century

THE EXPLOITS OF CAPTAIN AVERY

pirates obtained, yet in the end such wealth brought them nothing but anxiety and final wretchedness.

Avery could no more dispose of his precious stones in Ireland than in America, so thinking that perhaps there might be some one in that big west-country town of Bristol who would purchase them, he proceeded to his native county of Devonshire and sent to one of his friends to meet him at Bideford. The "friend" introduced other "friends" and Avery informed them of his business. It was agreed that the best plan would be to place the diamonds in the hands of some wealthy merchants who would ask no awkward questions as to their origin. One of the "friends" asserted that he knew some merchants who would be able to transact the business, and provided they allowed a handsome commission the diamonds would be turned into money. As Avery could think of no other solution to the difficulty, he agreed with this, so presently the merchants came down to Bideford, and after strongly protesting their integrity they were handed both diamonds and vessels of gold, for which they gave him a small sum in advance. Avery then changed his name and lived quietly at Bideford, but in a short time he had spent all his money, and in spite of repeated letters to the wily merchants he could get no answer. But at last they sent him a small sum, though quite inadequate for paying his debts, and as he could barely subsist he resolved to go to Bristol and interview the merchants.

He arrived, but instead of money he was met with a firm refusal and a threat that they would give information that he was a pirate. This frightened him so much that he returned to Ireland, and from there kept writing for his money, which, however, never came. He was reduced to such a condition of abject poverty that he resolved, in

THE EXPLOITS OF CAPTAIN AVERY

his misery, to go back to Bristol and throw himself on the merchants' mercy. He therefore shipped on board a trading ship, worked his passage to Plymouth and then walked to Bideford. He had arrived there not many days when he fell ill and died without so much as the money to buy him a burial. So it was true that "there be land rats and water rats, land thieves and water thieves, I mean pirates." Avery had met a company of men who treated him in the way he had robbed others. Thus, the whole of his long voyaging from sea to sea, the entire series of events from the time when he had seized Gibson's ship, had been not only profitless but brought upon him the utmost misery, terror, starvation and ultimate death. He had fought, he had schemed, he had done underhand tricks, he had told lies and he had endured bitter anxiety: but all to no purpose whatever.

CHAPTER XVI

A "GENTLEMAN" OF FORTUNE

"IN an honest service there are commonly low wages and hard labour: in piracy, satiety, pleasure and ease, liberty and power; and who would not balance creditor on this side, when all the hazard that is run for it at worst is only a sour look or two at choking? No, a merry life and a short one shall be my motto."

Such was the remark which a certain Captain Bartholomew Roberts, a notorious seventeenth-century pirate, was said to have made, and no doubt there was a certain amount of truth in this statement. The low wages and hard labour in other spheres of life contrasted unfavourably with the possibilities of ease, plenty, liberty and power. This fellow, like the notorious Henry Morgan, was a Welshman and born in Pembrokeshire. He grew up to be a tall, dark, ingenious and daring seaman. For a time he led the hard but honest life of a sailor trading to the Guinea coast, but in the year 1719 he had the bad luck to be captured by Davis, another pirate captain. The latter constrained Roberts to lead this lawless form of life, and it is only fair to state that Roberts at first was distinctly averse from piracy and would certainly have deserted if an opportunity had been forthcoming. How-

A "GENTLEMAN" OF FORTUNE

ever, "preferment claimed his conscience and reconciled him to that which he formerly hated."

And when Davis ended his days by death in action, the pirate crew decided to choose Roberts as their skipper. "It is my advice," said one of these at the time of the election, "it is my advice, while we are sober, to pitch upon a man of courage, and one skilled in navigation—one who, by his prudence and bravery, seems best able to ward us from the dangers and tempests of an unstable element, and the fatal consequences of anarchy, and such a one I take Roberts to be: a fellow in all respects worthy of your esteem and favour." So the Welshman was prevailed upon to accept this new honour, adding that since he had dipped his hands in muddy water, and must be a pirate, it was better being a commander than a private man.

So the pirate ship sailed south along the Guinea coast with her new commander, captured a Dutch Guinea ship, emptied her of everything they fancied, sent her on her way again, and two days later took an English ship. From her, too, they extracted all that they desired, and since her crew were persuaded to join Roberts' ship the prize was burnt and the pirate, with a now much bigger company, set sail for the island of St. Thomas, which is in the South Atlantic some distance off the Congo coast. But as they had no further luck in these parts, they eventually resolved by vote to make for Brazil. After a twenty-eight-day voyage across the Atlantic they arrived off the South American shore and for nine weeks or so cruised about unsuccessfully, taking care to keep out of sight of land. But on the way to the West Indies, whither they were now bound, a little disappointed, they unexpectedly fell in with a fleet of forty-two Portuguese ships of Bahia. These

A "GENTLEMAN" OF FORTUNE

vessels were bound for Lisbon, and were now waiting for two 70-gun men-of-war to convoy them home.

Such a rich sight was too much for the pirate. He was sure that his one single ship would have but little chance against such a powerful fleet, especially as some of them were really powerful vessels. But a faint heart never made a prize, and he was minded to have a try. Among the many vicissitudes of these pirate wayfarers the reader must have been struck by the extremely able cunning which these lawless desperate fellows displayed in many of their captures. Somehow one does not associate skill with brutality. But it was very rare that these pirate skippers were at a loss for a stratagem. Force was employed and used without mercy at the proper time, but that was not allowed to take the place of ingenuity. So long as these corsairs remained sober and did not set foot on land, they very rarely met with defeat. They were terrified not by superior forces but by the possibility of being found out when ashore. The sea and its ways they understood: in that sphere they were at home. It was only when they became so foolish as to abandon their natural element that they fell on evil days.

So Roberts set about devising some means of getting what he wanted from this mighty fleet. He got his ship in their midst and kept his own rugged desperate crew concealed. He then took his ship close to one of the biggest Portuguese and hailed her to send her master aboard *quietly*. If the Portuguese should show the slightest resistance, or make any signal of distress, he would show them no mercy. This cool impudence was successful: for the master now coming on deck, and seeing the sudden flash of pirate cutlasses of the men who had for a time been concealed, there was nothing to do but submit quietly,

A "GENTLEMAN" OF FORTUNE

and the captain repaired on board the pirate as requested. Roberts saluted him in a friendly manner and told him he and his crew were gentlemen of fortune. All they desired from him was to be informed as to which was the richest ship of the fleet. If the captain informed them correctly, then he should be permitted to go back to his ship in safety: but if not, he must expect instant death.

So the Portuguese pointed out a 40-gun vessel which had a crew of 150 men. Certainly she appeared far too big a job for Roberts to tackle, but he made towards her, still keeping the Portuguese captain aboard. As they came alongside, the pirate ordered the Portuguese prisoner to hail her and inquire after the commander's health and invite him on board, as a matter of importance was waiting to be imparted to him. The reply came that the commander would come presently. But Roberts was not to be put off, for, observing signs of unusual activity on board her, he poured a heavy broadside into her, then ran his ship right alongside in the most approved Elizabethan manner, grappled and boarded her. In a short space of time she had been captured, and there were taken out of her into the pirate's hold large and valuable quantities of sugar, skins, tobacco, etc., and 4000 gold moidores.

After this, just as a dog which has stolen a piece of meat hurries off to find a secluded spot where he can eat his spoil in peace, so the pirates began to long for some safe retreat where they could spend their time in debauchery with the prizes to pay for the cost. They resolved to go to Devil's Island, on the river Surinam, in Dutch Guiana, and having safely arrived there were well received by the governor and inhabitants. But the pirates were sadly in need of provisions until they fell in with a sloop which was in the river. This craft, which was now seized, said that she had been

A "GENTLEMAN" OF FORTUNE

sailing in company with a brigantine loaded with provisions. The news gladdened the corsairs, and Roberts, believing the matter to be so important that he ought to attend to it himself, went in command of the sloop, taking forty men and leaving the pirate ship behind. He was sure the latter would be all safe, and he would not be away long. The brigantine would soon be espied and then he would return with the latter's welcome cargo.

But on this occasion Roberts was unlucky. He did not sight the brigantine, although he sailed for miles and miles during eight days, so at last he came to anchor off the coast somewhere, and sent a boat ashore to inform their shipmates left behind in the Surinam River. The boat was also to bring back provisions to the sloop: but when she returned, after an almost unbearable delay, she brought no provisions and the unwelcome knowledge that the lieutenant of the pirate ship had run off with her. Roberts had certainly been a fool not to have foreseen this probability, and in order to prevent such mutiny recurring he proceeded to draw up regulations for preserving order in his present craft. After that, he had to act. Provisions and water they must have at all costs, and so they must make for the West Indies.

They had not gone far, however, before they fell in with a couple of sloops, which they captured. These afforded them the necessary supplies. A few days later they also captured a brigantine and then proceeded to Barbadoes. Off Barbadoes they met a 10-gun ship heavily laden with cargo from Bristol. Her they plundered, but after three days allowed her to proceed. But as soon as the latter touched land and informed the governor of her misfortune, there was dispatched a 20-gun ship with eighty men, under the command of Captain Rogers, to seek out the pirates.

A "GENTLEMAN" OF FORTUNE

In two days they came up with her. Roberts was, of course, quite unaware that any vessel had been sent against him, and the two craft drew near. Roberts as usual fired a blank shot for the stranger to heave to, and was very surprised to observe that instead of striking his colours forthwith she returned his gun with a broadside. A sharp engagement ensued, but as Roberts was getting distinctly the worst of it, he threw some of his cargo overboard and hurried off as fast as his ship could travel, being very lucky to escape in this manner.

He next made for Dominica, in the Caribbean Sea, and bartered some of his cargo with the inhabitants for provisions. He watered his ship, and as he happened to meet fifteen Englishmen who had been left upon the island by some Frenchmen who had captured the Englishmen's vessel, Roberts persuaded these destitutes to join him, and this additional strength was by no means inappreciable. But his ship was very foul and badly needed her bottom scrubbed, so Roberts took her for this purpose southwards to the Grenada Islands. It was fortunate that he did not waste any time about his cleaning and that he put to sea immediately after, for the Governor of Martinique got to hear that the pirate was so near, and two sloops were sent to catch him. But Roberts and his ship had departed only the very night before the sloops arrived.

Setting a northerly course, the pirate now proceeded towards Newfoundland. His ship was well cleaned, so she could sail at her best pace. He arrived off the Banks in June of 1720, and entered the harbour of Trepassi with the black pirate's flag at her masthead, with drums beating and trumpets sounding. Twenty-two ships were lying in that harbour as Roberts came in, but as soon as they realised what sort of a visitor was amongst them, the crews forsook

A "GENTLEMAN" OF FORTUNE

the ships, and Roberts, with his men, destroyed them by burning or sinking, and then pillaged the houses ashore, behaving like madmen and fiends let loose.

He retained just one ship of the lot, which hailed from Bristol, and after leaving the harbour, encountered ten French ships off the Newfoundland Banks. All of these he also destroyed excepting one, which he took for his own use and named the *Fortune*. The Bristol ship he handed over to these Frenchmen, and then for some time, being in the very track of the shipping, made some important prizes, after which he sailed again for the West Indies, took in ample supplies of provisions and then determined to hasten towards the coast of Guinea, where previously they had been so successful. On the way they came up with a French ship, and as she was more suitable for piracy than his own, Roberts made her skipper exchange ships. They were some time getting towards Surinam, as they made a mistake in their navigation and got out of the trade winds. And then trouble overtook them. Water had been running short for some time, so that they became reduced to one mouthful a day. Famine, too, overtook them, so that with thirst also tormenting them many of the crew died, whilst the rest were extremely weak and feeble. Things went from bad to worse, and now there was not one drop of fluid for drinking purposes.

But, fortunately for them, they found they were in seven fathoms of water, so the anchor was lowered over, but as they were such a long way off the shore they despaired of relieving their thirst. But the ship's boat was sent away, and after a while, to their immense relief, the little craft returned with plenty of drinking water to end their sufferings. One would have thought that as an act of gratitude these men would then have given up their lawless

A "GENTLEMAN" OF FORTUNE

life and ceased their depredations. But they were a hardened lot of ruffians who feared neither God nor man, so as soon as they were able they were off to sea at their old game. They fell in with a ship which gave them all the provisions they required, and soon afterwards came up with a brigantine which not only afforded them still further supplies, but also a mate who joined their company. Then, as they learnt that the governor had dispatched two ships to capture them, they did a very impudent and a very cruel series of acts by way of revenge. It should be mentioned that it was the custom of the Dutch ships to trade with Martinique illegally. To prevent any trouble they would keep some distance off the island and then hoist their jacks. The inhabitants were on the look out for the signal and would row off to do their trading, there being always a sharp contest as to who should reach the ship first and so secure the pick of the goods.

The artful Roberts, always ready with some new device, was well aware of this custom, so when he arrived off the island he hoisted the Dutch jack and waited. The inhabitants of Martinique saw it and came off in their craft as fast as they could. As each man came on board he had him killed until there were only left those who had remained in the small ships which had come for the cargo. All these ships, to the number of twenty, he burned, excepting one: and into this one ship he put the survivors and sent them back to Martinique with the doleful news. It was a cruel, heartless trick and the basest of all methods of revenge. Roberts' ships then put to sea once more.

And so the life of pillage went on. When they found themselves, after a successful period, well supplied with everything, they would indulge their bestial bodies in hard drinking : in fact, it was deemed a crime among them not to be in

A "GENTLEMAN" OF FORTUNE

this condition of inebriety. And then finding their wealth diminishing they set a course across the South Atlantic once more to the Guinea coast in order to forage for gold. They fell in with two French ships, of which one was a 10-gunner and the other a 75. The former carried sixty-five men and the latter seventy-five. But so soon as these cowards recognised the black flag they surrendered. So, taking the two prizes with them, the pirates went on to Sierra Leone. One of the new ships Roberts named the *Ranger*: the other he used as a store-ship.

After six more weeks spent at Sierra Leone in excesses, they put to sea, and after more captures and more enjoyment of their wealth found that their resources were still in need of replenishment. Festivity and mirth had made a big hole in their capital, so that if they were to keep alive they must needs get busy forthwith. Therefore they cruised about, held up unprotected merchant ships, relieved them of their cargoes and then burnt or sunk those strong hulls which had been the pride of many a shipbuilder and many an owner. But the time of reckoning was at hand, for H.M.S. *Swallow* and another man-of-war had now been sent to capture both Roberts and his craft. Definite news had been gained as to where the pirates were likely to be found, and the matter was to be dealt with firmly. Just a little to the south of the Equator, where the "line" touches the west coast of Africa, is a bold promontory known as Cape Lopez. Off this point lay Roberts.

Now the *Swallow* was fortunate enough to know that the man he wanted was here and came up as fast as she could to that locality. Those who were serving under the pirate saw this strange sail in the offing, and so Roberts sent one of his ships to chase her and bring her back. The pirate had heard that two men-of-war were sent out to seek him, but

A "GENTLEMAN" OF FORTUNE

he had so successfully escaped their vigilance so far that he became over-confident and careless. And in the present instance he judged her to be merely one more unhappy merchantman that was to add to his list of victims. But when the pilot of the *Swallow* saw the detached pirate craft approaching, he effected a smart stratagem. He altered his course and ran away from her, but he gave her a good long run for her trouble, and managed to allow her gradually to overtake the man-of-war. But this was not until the pirate had got well away from her mother ship.

As the pirate came up, full of confidence that the prize would shortly be hers, she hoisted out her black flag as usual and then fired. But when it was now too late they discovered that this was a man-of-war and much more than a match for the pirate. The latter was too far from Roberts' ship to be assisted, and so, seeing that resistance would be futile, she cried for quarter. This was granted and her crew promptly made prisoners, but not till she had lost already ten men killed and twenty wounded, whereas the *Swallow* had not received one single casualty.

The pirate admiral was still lying near the Cape, and one morning her crew looked up and saw a sight which gave them no pleasure. Over the land they could see the masts of the *Swallow* as the ship bore away to round the Cape. At the time Roberts was below having breakfast, and some of the crew came down to inform him of the sight. But Roberts was far more interested in his meal than in the ship and declined to get excited. She might be a Portuguese craft, or a French slaver, or it might be their own *Ranger* coming back. But as the ship came on nearer and nearer the crew began to get exceptionally interested. That was the man-of-war *Swallow*. It was useless to dispute the point, for there was among the pirate crew a man named

A "GENTLEMAN" OF FORTUNE

Armstrong, who had previously served aboard the naval ship and deserted. He knew her too well to take any heed of others who disputed her identity. But Roberts was still not nervous, and stigmatised those as cowards who were disheartening his men. Even if she were the *Swallow*, what did it matter? Were they afraid to fight her?

But if there was a man aboard the pirate who still possessed any doubt, that uncertainty was instantly set at rest when the *Swallow* was seen to be hoisting up her ports and getting her guns ready for action. Out went the British colours, and even Roberts thought it was time to be doing something. He had driven matters pretty fine, so he had to slip his cable, got under way, and ordered his men to arms. All the time he showed no timidity, but dropping an occasional oath he meant to be ready for all that the *Swallow* would be willing to attempt. The pirate's sails were unloosed and the ship had gathered way. Roberts never lost his head, although he was not in a good humour at having had to interrupt his morning meal. He called Armstrong to him and questioned him as to the trim of the *Swallow*. Armstrong informed him that she sailed best upon a wind, so that, if Roberts wanted to get away, he would be best advised to run before the wind, as thus the *Swallow* would not easily overtake him.

But the two ships were getting very near to each other and there was no longer time for thinking out tactics. Quick but not hasty decision must be made, so this is what Roberts resolved to attempt: He would pass quite close to the *Swallow* under full sail, and receive her broadside before returning a shot. If the pirate should then have the misfortune to be disabled, or if his masts and sails were shot away, then the ship would be run ashore at the point, and every man could shift for himself among the natives.

A "GENTLEMAN" OF FORTUNE

But if this means of escape should turn out impracticable, Roberts intended to get his ship alongside the *Swallow* and blow the two craft up together. The reason why he intended such desperate measures was that old folly which has been the cause of so much disaster both to nations, fleets and individual ships. In a word, he was unprepared, so were his crew. He himself had not been expecting the *Swallow*, and his own men were either drunk or only passively courageous; in any case not the keen, alert crew who are likely to win an engagement.

But there was a curious old-time vanity about the man, which shows how seriously these pirate-skippers took themselves. Dressed in a rich crimson damask waistcoat and breeches, a red feather in his hat, a gold chain round his neck with a diamond cross depending, he stood on his deck, sword in hand, and two pairs of pistols hanging at the end of a silk sling flung over his shoulders, as was the custom of the pirates and such as one sees in the old prints of these men. He played the part of commander grandly, giving his order with boldness and spirit. When his ship closed with the *Swallow*, he received her fire and hoisted his black flag, returning the man-of-war's fire. He set all the sail he could, and, as the ship tore through the water, blazed away at the *Swallow*. It was a pity for his own sake that he did not follow Armstrong's advice and run his ship off before the wind. Had he done so he might have escaped. But either through the wind shifting or else through bad steerage in the excitement of the contest, his sails, with the tacks down, were taken aback, and for a second time the *Swallow* came quite close to him. From now onwards there would have been a very desperate fight, but a grape shot struck him in the throat, and presently he died. He laid himself on the tackles of one of the ship's guns. The man at the

A "GENTLEMAN" OF FORTUNE

helm observing him there, and seeing that he was wounded, ran towards him and swore at him, bidding him stand up and fight like a man. But when the sailor found to his horror that his chief was already dead, he burst into tears, and hoped that the next shot might settle himself. Presently the lifeless body of the daring, plucky, ingenious Roberts was thrown over the side into the water with his arms and ornaments still on, just as he had repeatedly expressed the wish to be buried during his lifetime.

The rest is quickly told. The pirate ship was now soon captured, and the crew arrested. The latter were strictly guarded while on board the man-of-war, and were taken to Cape Coast Castle, where they underwent a long trial. Like many of the old smugglers, these pirates remained defiant and impenitent for a long time, but after some experience of the dull confinement in the castle and the imminence of death, they changed their disposition, "and became serious, penitent, and fervent in their devotions." Their acts of robbery on sea had been so flagrant that there was no difficulty in bringing in a verdict of guilty.

CHAPTER XVII

PAUL JONES, PIRATE AND PRIVATEER

WE come now to consider the exploits of another historical character whose life and adventures will ever be of unfailing interest on both sides of the Atlantic. And yet, perhaps, this amazing Scotsman is to-day better known in America than in Great Britain. Like many another before him he rose from the rank of ordinary seaman to become a man that was to be had in great fear if not respect. His fame has been celebrated in fiction, and very probably many a story of which he has been made the hero had no foundation in fact.

There is some dispute concerning his birth, but it seems pretty certain that he was the son of John Paul, head gardener on Lord Selkirk's estate near Kirkcudbright. Paul Jones first saw light in the year 1728. Brought up on the shores of the Solway Firth, it was only likely that he gave up being assistant to his father and preferred the sea to gardening. In his character there developed many of those traits which have been such marked characteristics of the pirate breed. To realise Paul Jones, you must think of a wild, reckless nature, burning with enthusiasm for adventure, yet excessively vain and desirous of recognition. He was a rebel, a privateer, a pirate and a smuggler; he was a villain, he was quarrelsome, he was petty and mean. Finally, he

PAUL JONES

was a traitor to his country. When he died he had lived a most varied life, and had seen service on merchantman, slaver and man-of-war.

After making several voyages to the West Indies in a merchantman as ordinary and able-bodied seaman, he was promoted to rank of mate, and then rose to the rank of master. Soon after the rupture between England and America he happened to be in New England, and then it was that he succumbed to the temptation to desert his own national standard and to throw his aid on to the side of the revolutionists—for which reason he changed his real name of John Paul to that of Paul Jones. Notwithstanding that Jones has been justly condemned by biographers for having been a traitor, yet my own opinion is that this change arose far less from a desire to become an enemy of the British nation than from that overwhelming *wanderlust*, and that irrepressible desire for adventure to which we have already called attention. There are some men who have never had enough fighting. So soon as one campaign ends they are unhappy till another begins, so that they may find a full outlet for their spirits. To such men as these the daily round of a peaceful life is a perpetual monotony, and unless they can go forth to rove and wander, to fight or to explore, their very souls would almost cry out for freedom.

So, I am convinced, it was with Paul Jones. To such a man nationalities mean nothing more than certain artificial considerations. The only real differences are those between the land and the sea. He knew that in the forthcoming war he would find just the adventure which delighted him; he would have every chance of obtaining booty, and his own natural endowment, physical and mental, were splendidly suitable for such activities. He had a special knowledge of British pilotage, so he was a seaman distinctly worth having

PAUL JONES

for any marauding expeditions that might be set going. So in the year 1777 we find him very busy as commander, fitting out the privateer *Ranger*. This vessel mounted 18 guns as well as several swivel-guns, and had a desperate crew of 150 able men.

He put to sea and made two captures on the European side of the Atlantic, sending each of these prizes into a French port. The following spring he went a step further in his character as a rebel, for he appeared off the Cumberland coast and began to attack a part of England that must have been singularly well-known to him. He had made his landfall by daylight, but stood away until darkness set in. At midnight he ran closer in, and in grim silence he sent away his boats with thirty men, all well armed and ready to perform a desperate job. Their objective was Whitehaven, the entrance to the harbour being commanded by a small battery, so their first effort must obviously be to settle that. Having landed with great care, they rushed upon the small garrison and made the whole lot prisoners. The guns of the battery were next spiked, and now they set about their next piece of daring.

In the harbour the ships were lying side by side, the tide being out. The good people of the town were asleep in their beds, and all the conditions were ideal for burning the shipping where it stood. Very stealthily the men went about their business, and had laid their combustibles on the decks all ready for firing as soon as the signal should be given. But just then something was happening. At the doors of the main street of the little town there was a series of loud knockings, and people began to wake and bustle about; and soon the sound of voices and the sight of crowds running down to the pier. The marauders had now to hurry on the rest of their work, for the alarm had been

PIRATE AND PRIVATEER

given and there was not a moment to lose. So hastily the privateer's men threw their matches on the decks, then made for their boats and rowed off quickly to their ship.

But, luckily, the inhabitants of Whitehaven had come down just in time. For they were able to extinguish the flames before serious damage had been done. What was their joy was keen annoyance to the privateer's men. But who was the good friend who had taken the trouble to rouse the town? Who had at once been so kind as to knock at the doors and to despoil the marauders of their night's work? When the shore party of the privateer mustered on deck it was found that one man was missing, and this was the fellow who, for some conscientious or worldly motive, had gone over to the other side, and so saved both property and lives.

So Jones went a few miles farther north, crossed his familiar Solway Firth and entered the river Dee, on the left bank of which stands Kirkcudbright. He entered the estuary at dawn and let go anchor off Lord Selkirk's castle. When the natives saw this warlike ship in their river, with her guns and her formidable appearance generally, they began to fear she was a man-of-war come to impress men for the Navy. It happened that the noble lord was away from home in London, and when the men-servants at the castle espied what they presumed to be a King's ship, they begged Lady Selkirk for leave to go and hide themselves lest they might be impressed into the service. A boat was sent from the ship, and a strong body of men landed and marched to the castle, which, to the surprise of all, they surrounded. Lady Selkirk had just finished breakfast when she was summoned to appear before the leader of the men, whose rough clothes soon showed the kind of fellows they were. Armed with pistols, swords, muskets, and even an

PAUL JONES

American tomahawk, they inquired for Lord Selkirk, only to be assured his lordship was away.

The next request was that all the family plate should be handed over. So all that was in the castle was yielded, even to the silver teapot which was on the breakfast table and had not yet been washed out. The silver was packed up, and with many apologies for having had to transact this " dirty business," as one of the officers called it, the pirates went back to their ship rather richer than they had set out. But the inhabitants of the castle were as much surprised as they were thankful to find their own lives had not been demanded as well as the plate. The ship got under way some time after, and put to sea without any further incident. Now the rest of this story of the plate runs as follows, and shows another side to the character of the head-gardener's son: for, a few days after this visit, Lady Selkirk received a letter from Jones, apologising for what had been done, and stating that this raid had been neither suggested nor sanctioned by him. On the contrary he had used his best influence to prevent its occurrence. But his officers and crew had insisted on the deed, with a view to capturing Lord Selkirk, for whose ransom they hoped to obtain a large sum of money.

As an earnest of his own innocence in the matter, Paul Jones added that he would try to purchase from his associates the booty which they had brought away, and even if he could not return the entire quantity he would send back all that he could. We need not stop to wonder whether Lady Selkirk really believed such a statement; but the truth is that about five years later the whole of the plate came back, carriage paid, in exactly the same condition as it had left the castle. Apparently it had never been unpacked, for the tea leaves were still in the tea-

PIRATE AND PRIVATEER

pot, just as they had been taken away on that exciting morning.

But to come back to the ship. After leaving the Solway Firth astern, Jones stood over to the Irish coast and entered Belfast Lough, amusing himself on the way by burning or capturing several fishing craft. But it happened that he was espied by Captain Burdon of H.M.S. *Drake*, a sloop. Seeing Jones' ship coming along, he took her to be a merchantman, and so from her he could impress some seamen. So the officer lowered a boat and sent her off. But when the boat's crew came aboard Jones' vessel they had the surprise of their lives, for instead of arresting they were themselves arrested. After this it seemed to Jones more prudent to leave Belfast alone and get away with his capture. Meanwhile, Captain Burdon was getting anxious about his men, as the boat had not returned. Moreover, he noticed that the supposed merchantman was now crowding on all possible sail, so he at once prepared his sloop for giving chase and prepared for action, and, on coming up with the privateer, began a sharp fire.

Night, however, intervened, and the firing had to stop, but when daylight returned the engagement recommenced and continued for an hour. A fierce encounter was fought on both sides, and at length Captain Burdon and his first lieutenant were killed, as well as twenty of the crew disabled. The *Drake's* topmast was shot away and the ship was considerably damaged, so that there was no other alternative but to surrender to the privateer.

But as both sides of the Irish Channel were now infuriated against Jones, he determined to leave these parts, and taking his prize with him proceeded to Brest, where he arrived in safety. In the following year, instead of the *Ranger* he had command of a frigate called the *Bon Homme*

PAUL JONES

Richard, a 40-gun ship with 370 crew. In addition to this vessel he had also the frigate *Alliance*, of 36 guns and 300 crew; the brig *Vengeance*, 14 guns and 70 men; a cutter of eighteen tons; and a French frigate named the *Pallas*. All except the last mentioned were in the service of the American Congress. A little further down the coast of the Bay of Biscay than Brest is L'Orient, and from this port Jones sailed with the above fleet in the summer of 1779, arriving off the Kerry coast, where he sent a boat's crew ashore to bring back sheep. But the natives captured the boat's crew and lodged them in Tralee gaol.

After this Jones sailed to the east of Scotland and captured a number of prizes, all of which he sent on to France. Finally he determined to attempt no less a plan than burn the shipping in Leith harbour and collect tribute from the undefended towns of the Fifeshire coast. He came into the Firth of Forth, but as both wind and tide were foul, he let go under the island of Inchkeith. Next day he weighed anchor and again tried to make Leith, but the breeze had now increased to a gale, and he sprung one of his topmasts which caused him to bear up and leave the Firth. He now rejoined his squadron and cruised along the east coast of England. Towards the end of September he fell in with a British convoy bound from the Baltic, being escorted by two men-of-war, namely, H.M.S. *Serapis* (44 guns), and H.M.S. *Countess of Scarborough* (20 guns). And then followed a most memorable engagement. In order that the reader may be afforded some opportunity of realising how doughty an opponent was this Paul Jones, and how this corsair was able to make a ship of the Royal Navy strike colours, I append the following despatch which was written by Captain Pearson, R.N., who commanded the *Serapis*. The *Countess of Scarborough* was under command

PIRATE AND PRIVATEER

of Captain Thomas Piercy, and this officer also confirmed the account of the disaster. The narrative is so succinct and clear that it needs no further explanation. The letter was written from the Texel, whither Pearson was afterwards taken:—

"*PALLAS* FRIGATE IN CONGRESS SERVICE,
TEXEL, *October* 6, 1779.

" On the 23rd ult. being close in with Scarborough about twelve o'clock, a boat came on board with a letter from the bailiffs of that corporation, giving information of a flying squadron of the enemy's ship being on the coast, of a part of the said squadron having been seen from thence the day before standing to the southward. As soon as I received this intelligence I made the signal for the convoy to bear down under my lee, and repeated it with two guns; notwithstanding which the van of the convoy kept their wind with all sail stretching out to the southward from under Flamborough-head, till between twelve and one, when the headmost of them got sight of the enemy's ships, which were then in chase of them. They then tacked, and made the best of their way under the shore for Scarborough, letting fly their topgallant sheets, and firing guns; upon which I made all the sail I could to windward, to get between the enemy's ship and the convoy, which I soon effected. At one o'clock we got sight of the enemy's ship from the masthead, and about four we made them plain from the deck to be three large ships and a brig! Upon which I made the *Countess of Scarborough's* signal to join me, she being in-shore with the convoy; at the same time I made the signal for the convoy to make the best of their way, and repeated the signal with two guns. I then brought-to to let the *Countess of Scarborough* come up, and cleared ship for action.

" At half-past five the *Countess of Scarborough* joined me, the enemy's ships bearing down upon us with a light breeze at S.S.W.; at six tacked and laid our head in-shore, in order to keep our ground the better between the enemy's

PAUL JONES

ships and the convoy; soon after which we perceived the ships bearing down upon us to be a two-decked ship and two frigates, but from their keeping end upon us in bearing down, we could not discern what colours they were under. At twenty minutes past seven, the largest ship of the two brought-to on our lee-bow, within musket shot. I hailed him, and asked what ship it was? They answered in English, the *Princess Royal.* I then asked where they belonged to? They answered evasively; on which I told them, if they did not answer directly I would fire into them. They then answered with a shot, which was instantly returned with a broadside; and after exchanging two or three broadsides, he backed his topsails, and dropped upon our quarter, within pistol-shot; then filled again, put his helm a-weather, and ran us on board upon our weather quarter, and attempted to board us, but being repulsed he sheered off: upon which I backed our topsails in order to get square with him again; which, as soon as he observed, he then filled, put his helm a-weather, and laid us athwart hawse; his mizen shrouds took our jib-boom, which hung for some time, till it at last gave way, and we dropt alongside each other head and stern, when the fluke of our spare anchor hooking his quarter, we became so close fore-and-aft, that the muzzles of our guns touched each other's sides.

" In this position we engaged from half-past eight till half-past ten; during which time, from the great quantity and variety of combustible matters which they threw upon our decks, chains, and, in short, into every part of the ship, we were on fire not less than ten or twelve times in different parts of the ship, and it was with the greatest difficulty and exertion imaginable at times, that we were able to get it extinguished. At the same time the largest of the two frigates kept sailing round us during the whole action, and raking us fore and aft, by which means she killed or wounded almost every man on the quarter and main decks. At half-past nine, either from a hand grenade being thrown in at one of our lower-deck ports, or from some other accident, a cartridge of powder was set on fire, the flames of which running from cartridge to cartridge all the way aft, blew up

PIRATE AND PRIVATEER

the whole of the people and officers that were quartered abaft the main mast; from which unfortunate circumstance all those guns were rendered useless for the remainder of the action, and I fear the greatest part of the people will lose their lives.

"At ten o'clock they called for quarters from the ship alongside, and said they had struck. Hearing this, I called upon the captain to say if they had struck, or if he asked for quarter; but receiving no answer, after repeating my words two or three times, I called for the boarders, and ordered them to board, which they did; but the moment they were on board her, they discovered a superior number lying under cover, with pikes in their hands, ready to receive them; on which our people retreated instantly into our own ship, and returned to their guns again until half-past ten, when the frigate coming across our stern, and pouring her broadside into us again, without our being able to bring a gun to bear on her, I found it in vain, and in short impracticable, from the situation we were in, to stand out any longer with any prospect of success; I therefore struck. Our main-mast at the same time went by the board.

"The first lieutenant and myself were immediately escorted into the ship alongside, when we found her to be an American ship of war, called the *Bon Homme Richard*, of forty guns, and 375 men, commanded by Captain Paul Jones; the other frigate which engaged us, to be the *Alliance*, of forty guns, and 300 men; and the third frigate, which engaged and took the *Countess of Scarborough*, after two hours' action, to be the *Pallas*, a French frigate, of thirty guns, and 275 men; the *Vengeance*, an armed brig, of twelve guns, and 70 men; all in Congress service, under the command of Paul Jones. They fitted out and sailed from Port l'Orient the latter end of July, and came north about. They have on board 300 English prisoners, which they have taken in different vessels in their way round since they left France, and have ransomed some others. On my going on board the *Bon Homme Richard* I found her in the greatest distress, her quarters and counter on the lower deck being entirely drove in, and the whole of her lower-deck guns dismounted; she was also on fire in two places, and six or seven feet of water in her hold, which kept increasing upon them all night and next day, till they were obliged to quit her. She had 300 men killed and wounded in the action. Our loss in the *Serapis* was also very great.

"My officers, and people in general, behaved well; and I should be very remiss in my attentions to their merit were I to omit recommending them to their Lordships' favour.

"I must at the same time beg leave to inform their Lordships that Captain Piercy, in the *Countess of Scarborough*, was not the least remiss in his duty, he having given me every assistance in his power; and as much as could be expected from such a ship in engaging the attention of the *Pallas*, a frigate of thirty-two guns, during the whole action.

"I am extremely sorry for the accident that has happened, that of losing His Majesty's ship which I had the honour to command; but at the same time I flatter myself with the hope that their Lordships will be convinced that she has not been given away; but, on the contrary, that every exertion has been used to defend her, and that two essential pieces of service to our country have arisen from it: the one, in wholly oversetting the cruise and intentions of this flying squadron; the other is rescuing the whole of a valuable convoy from falling into the hands of the enemy, which must have been the case had I acted any otherwise than I did. We have been driving about the North Sea ever since the action, and endeavouring to make to any port we possibly could; but have not been able to get into any place till to-day we arrived in the Texel. Herewith I enclose you the most correct list of the killed and wounded I have as yet been able to procure, from my people being dispersed among the different ships, and having been refused permission to make much of them.

"R. Pearson.

"*P.S.* I am refused permission to wait on Sir Joseph Yorke,[1] and even to go on shore.

[1] The British Ambassador.

PIRATE AND PRIVATEER

"The killed were—1 boatswain, 1 master's mate, 2 midshipmen, 1 quarter-master, 29 sailors, 15 marines—49.

"Wounded—second lieutenant Michael Stanhope, Lieutenant Whiteman, marines, 2 surgeon's mates, 6 petty officers, 46 sailors, 12 marines—total, 68."

It is obvious that the British Officers had fought their ships most gallantly, and the King showed his appreciation by conferring the honour of knighthood on Captain Pearson, and soon after Piercy was promoted to the rank of Post-Captain, and promotion was also granted to the other officers. But recognition was shown not merely by the State but by the City, for the Directors of the Royal Exchange Assurance Company presented Pearson with a piece of plate valued at a hundred guineas, and Piercy with a similar gift valued at fifty guineas. They further voted their thanks to the officers for having protected the rich fleets under their care.

The British Ambassador, Sir Joseph York, had considerable difficulty in procuring the release of the prisoners which Paul Jones had made from His Majesty's ships, and although he strenuously urged the States General to detain Jones and his ships as a rebel subject with unlawful ships, yet the squadron, after being carefully blockaded, succeeded in escaping one dark night to Dunkirk. Jones had lost his ship the *Bon Homme Richard* as a result of the fight, and now made the *Alliance* his flagship.

The story of Paul Jones from now is not capable of completion. For a period of several years his movements were somewhat mysterious, although it is known that on one occasion he sailed across the Atlantic in the remarkable time of three weeks with despatches from the American Congress. Then the fame of this remarkable fellow begins to wane. After peace was concluded the active brain and

PAUL JONES

fervent spirit of this Paul Jones were not required, and he chafed against the fetters of unemployment. It is true that he offered his services to the Empress of Russia in 1788, but he seems very soon to have gone to Paris, where he spent the rest of his life. There was no employmeut for him in the French Navy, and finally he was reduced to abject poverty and ended his days in the year 1792. The reader will doubtless have in mind that less than ten years ago the United States had the body of Paul Jones brought across the Atlantic and re-buried in North America.

It is not quite easy, altogether, to estimate the character of a man so contradictory as Paul Jones. Had he been born in another age and placed in different circumstances, there is no telling how illustrious he might not have become. He was certainly a magnificent seaman and fighting man, but over and above all he was an adventurer. Idolised as a hero both in America and France, he struck terror in Britain. His latest biographer has stated that the skull and crossbones never fluttered from his masthead and that he never sailed with a letter of marque. But that being so it can only be a mere quibble which can save him from being reckoned among the most notorious pirates of history. A pirate is a person who performs acts of piracy. It seems to me that it makes little difference whether he hoists the conventional black pirate flag or not. It is not the flag which makes a pirate, but the deeds and intentions of which he is responsible. And if his biographer is correct in saying that Jones was never commissioned as a privateer, that is still one more proof that in raiding Whitehaven, the coasts of Scotland, Ireland, England; capturing and burning merchant or fishing craft on the seas; taking their crews into bondage,—he was acting without any shred of legality, and therefore a pirate pure and simple.

PIRATE AND PRIVATEER

A pirate—and a very daring pirate—he certainly was, though he was primarily a sailor of fortune. As one can see from his life his devotion of adventure was far superior to his devotion to nationality—Scotch, English, French, American or Russian. He was willing and anxious to go wherever there was fighting, wherever glory could be obtained. He was a man who despised those who did not keep their word, and in the incident of his fulfilment of the promise made to Lady Selkirk in respect of the family plate, we have, at any rate in the life of Paul Jones, a proof that sometimes there is honour among thieves. But his death in abject poverty is but another illustration of the tragic ending which was customary in the lives of many notorious pirates.

CHAPTER XVIII

A NOTORIOUS AMERICAN PIRATE

THE notorious sea-robber of whom we are to speak in the following chapter has an especial interest for English and American readers, from the fact that he was a member of the *Chesapeake* during her historic duel with the *Shannon*. This Charles Gibbs was born in the State of Rhode Island in the year 1794. From the sulky, refractory character which he exhibited as a child any reader of human nature could have guessed that his career promised none too well, and when his full powers had been developed he developed finally into a singularly cruel robber of the sea. From one cruelty to another he sunk lower and lower until the inevitable gallows were ready to put an end to his atrocities.

Possessed of that roving spirit which was ever an early characteristic of those who were destined to become pirates, he threw up his work as farm-hand at the age of fifteen, ran away from home and signed on as one of the crew in the United States sloop-of-war *Hornet*. Off the coast of Pernambuco this ship was in action and captured H.M.S. sloop *Peacock*. The commander of the former was Captain Lawrence, and on his return he was promoted to command the *Chesapeake*, and to that ship Gibbs accompanied him. When the *Shannon* emerged from the fray victorious, the

A NOTORIOUS AMERICAN PIRATE

survivors were taken as prisoners and imprisoned in Dartmoor, among them being Charles Gibbs. When prisoners were exchanged, he returned to Boston, Captain Lawrence having fallen in the engagement.

For a time Gibbs now abandoned the sea and set up in business, but he was unable to lead a respectable life ashore, so back he went to sea, this time on board a privateer belonging to Buenos Ayres; but a quarrel arising between the officers of the one part and the crew regarding the division of prize-money, there ensued a mutiny. The mutineers won the victory and took possession of the ship. They proceeded to the coast of Florida, landed some of the ship's company, and thence sailed to the West Indies to perform their piratical exploits, and in a short time had captured more than twenty ships and murdered about four hundred human beings, Havannah being used as the port where they could conveniently dispose of their plunder. It is difficult to speak of a man like Charles Gibbs in cold blood. He was not a mere pirate, but a blackguard and murderer of the vilest type. Of him it may be said in very truth that with his death the world lost nothing, but was the gainer. A pirate who in the heat of the moment, when he is being violently opposed by another, kills his aggressor, is a criminal whom we can understand though not acquit. But a human fiend who, for no particular reason, unnecessarily sheds blood and bereaves women of husbands and children of fathers, is a devil incarnate. Such was Gibbs.

In the year 1819 he departed from Havannah and returned to the United States, his accumulated wealth, as a result of so many piracies, amounting to about £6000. After passing some time in New York and Boston he sailed for England on the *Emerald*, but in 1826 was back again in the United States. Hearing of the war between Brazil

A NOTORIOUS AMERICAN PIRATE

and the Buenos Ayres republic, he sailed from Boston to fight, if possible, on behalf of the republic. He made himself known to Admiral Brown, and presently received a lieutenant's commission, being assigned to a 34-gun ship. For four months he served in this ship, and then, as a result of his satisfactory conduct, he was given command of a privateer schooner which carried two 24-pounders and forty-six men. Sailing from Buenos Ayres he made a couple of successful privateering cruises, and then was able to purchase a half-share in a Baltimore schooner. But after putting to sea he was captured seven days out and taken into Rio de Janeiro, where he remained until the declaration of peace and eventually returned to New York.

There followed another year's interval in roaming about from place to place, and then the French campaign against Algiers attracted him, not to fight on behalf of the French but for the pirates. He accordingly embarked on a ship that landed him at Barcelona, whence he crossed to Port Mahon and tried to make his way to Algiers; but the vigilance of the French fleet prevented him from getting any nearer than Tunis, and at last returned from Marseilles to Boston. A few days later he went to New Orleans, and there he signed on as one of the crew on board the *Vineyard* brig. Up till now he had led a restless, wandering, wicked life of self-indulgence. He had robbed and murdered. But now we come to the climax and decline of his career. The details which follow are essential to the story, and they indicate better than any number of words the type of character to which Gibbs belonged.

The skipper of this brig was William Thornby. She sailed away from New Orleans, bound for Philadelphia, with a valuable cargo of cotton, sugar, molasses, as well as over £10,000 in dollars. When the ship was about five days

A NOTORIOUS AMERICAN PIRATE

out from her port the crew began to talk about the money on board, and some of them, including Charles Gibbs, made up their minds to seize the ship. Before attaining this object they realised they would have to kill the captain and mate. On the night of the 23rd of November, soon after midnight, the opportunity for putting this dastardly deed into action arrived. One of the crew named Dawes was at the helm. As the brig was ploughing her way over the lonely sea, rolling her masts across the star-specked sky, the steersman suddenly saw the steward emerge from below with a light in one hand and a knife in the other. He set down the light, and then, taking the top of the pump, struck the captain on the head. The latter cried "Murder!" but he was then seized firmly by Gibbs and the cook at the head and the heels, and without further delay hove overboard.

Roused by the unwonted noise on deck, the mate now came up the hatchway, but, as he approached, two others of the crew named Atwell and Church were waiting for him, and struck him over the head just as he was asking for the reason of the noise. The mate then rushed back into his cabin, followed by Gibbs, who, by reason of the darkness, could not find him. So the murderer ran on deck, fetched the binnacle light, with the aid of which the helmsman was steering, and returned below. This time he found his victim, and two others of the crew knocked him down and then dragged him on deck. Dawes, since he could not now see his compass to steer by, left the helm to see what was going on. And as the other men were hauling the mate along, they called to Dawes to assist them. In a few moments the mate was thrown over the side alive and was even heard to cry out from the water twice. He was never picked up, so must have been drowned.

A NOTORIOUS AMERICAN PIRATE

Dawes was terrified beyond expression at these two incidents, so that he scarcely knew what to do. The confederates then ordered him to call a man named James Talbot who had declined to take part in the plot. Talbot was in the forecastle saying his prayers. He came up, and the confederates did not instantly put him to death, as he had quite expected, but, on the contrary, gave him some grog. The captain and mate being now out of the way, the confederates then got up a keg containing dollars. They then divided the captain's clothes, the sum of eight pounds, which he possessed, and a gold watch. Dawes was ordered to go back to the helm and to steer for Long Island, while Talbot was likewise compelled to do as he was told. The next day several more kegs of specie, amounting to £1000 each, were divided and the specie placed into bags and sewn up. After this the money was divided up without counting it.

Gibbs had been acting as captain ever since the two murders, and when they arrived about fifteen miles south-southeast of Southampton Light the ship's boats were ordered out, half the money was placed in each, and the survivors got in. Before doing so, however, the ship was scuttled and set fire to in the cabin, so that before long she would founder and so not exist as possible evidence against the assassins. But after the boats had rowed away towards the shore, soon after daylight, they stuck on the bar. One of them was saved by throwing overboard about £1000 in dollars, but the other was seen to fill and founder as the men in her vainly sought to cling to the masts of the craft. Those in the other craft, however, were more fortunate and landed on Barron Island, buried the money in the sand and soon afterwards fell in with a man who took them to the only house on the island.

A NOTORIOUS AMERICAN PIRATE

But justice, if delayed, advanced with sure and certain steps. In the month of February 1831, Charles Gibbs and a man named Wansley, who had been one of the confederates, were brought up for trial in New York on a charge of murdering Captain Thornby. Wansley was a negro and was found guilty and condemned to death. Gibbs, in his defence, said that when the ship started out from New Orleans he was a stranger to all on board excepting Dawes and one other. He pretended that it was not he himself who first suggested taking the money, but that after the subject had been discussed for some days he agreed to join in the plot. He even protested, he alleged, that it would be better to give up the plan, as it was a serious thing to take human life and commit piracy. This, be it remembered, was Gibbs' version of the affair, but having regard to his past record there is every reason to suppose that he was now adding lies to his other guilt. Three days later, he averred, the murder took place, and all that he did was to help throw the captain's body overboard after he had been struck, when he presumed he had been killed. He protested further that he was innocent of the mate's murder.

But the judge pointed out that even if Gibbs had not actually done the deed, he was there strongly instigating the murderers on without stretching out a hand to save them. "It is murder as much to stand by and encourage the deed as to stab with a knife, strike with a hatchet or shoot with a pistol. It is not only murder in law, but in your own feelings and in your own conscience." So spoke the judge, and he who had spent a life of licence and piracy, marked by murders with only occasional legitimate fighting, was condemned to the scaffold. To the end Gibbs, while admitting his guilt of piracy, yet insisted that he was innocent of the

A NOTORIOUS AMERICAN PIRATE

charge of murdering the captain, although "it is true I stood by and saw the fatal deed done, and stretched not forth my arm to save him." Wansley, however, frankly admitted the justice of the sentence and died penitent. We need say no more, but if there are any to-day who have still a secret affection for the pirates of yesterday, we can only suggest that although few of these pirates were cowards yet there is not one who showed himself little more than a vulture in human form. Very rare indeed does one find instances of these rude fellows giving mercy. There is now and again such an occasion, but it is like the stray blade of herbage in a wilderness. Personal vanity—the determination to get rich at all costs—has brought many a crime in its wake, and if men are still dishonest in other ways, we can at least be thankful that the wholesale murders of the days of the pirates have long since ended.

CHAPTER XIX

THE LAST OF THE ALGERINE CORSAIRS

AND now let us take a final look at that pestilential spot, Algiers. We have seen how that during the sixteenth and seventeenth centuries it had been constantly attacked and conquered, but before long the Algerines had again broken out into piracy. So soon as their invaders withdrew their forces the corsairs rebuilt their walls, fitted out their new craft and went roving the seas and harassing innocent ships. They had pillaged the coastline of the French Riviera, burning and killing and destroying in their ruthless manner. And then the French had been compelled to send Admiral Du Quesne against them, who had bombarded the place for a time until bad weather had caused him to withdraw his ships from Algiers.

The pirate trouble had therefore begun afresh, and the Dey had sent to Louis the impudent message that if the French monarch would give him half the money the last French expedition had cost, the Dey would be pleased to burn down his city! So once more Du Quesne had been sent out, who had bombarded Algiers and caused wholesale destruction. Then he had consented to cease firing and discuss terms, but in the meantime the Dey had been assassinated by his own followers, who now elected a new one and ordered the Algerine flag to be re-hoisted on their

THE LAST OF

walls. With greater fervour hostilities were now resumed, and in a few days the place was reduced to ashes and large numbers of the Algerines had perished. This so infuriated the new Dey that he ordered all the French captives to be cruelly murdered, and with great brutality caused Father Vacher to be bound hand and foot, tied to a mortar and fired off like a bomb against the French fleet outside.

Du Quesne had then brought his ships as near in as possible, destroyed all their shipping, fortifications and buildings, and, having done all that he could, sailed away, leaving the Algerines plenty of subjects for meditation. And yet it was not long before these pirates had regained their good spirits and were again engaged in piracy. Was it not their profession and calling? Was it not by such methods that they kept themselves alive? They knew perfectly well they were rogues, but as other men were traders so they were pirates. Therefore, diplomatic measures being obviously impotent, the only way to treat with them was to keep on sending expedition after expedition. In 1700 Captain Beach attacked seven of their craft, drove them on shore and burnt them. Less than a hundred years later ten American ships had been seized by these corsairs and 150 men from their crews taken into captivity. In order to obtain these men back, the Americans had to pay a heavy ransom, and build the Dey a 36-gun frigate, but thereby they also received protection for the American ships and the right of free trade with Algiers.

At an earlier stage of this book I have had occasion, in discussing the Moslem corsairs, to refer to the port of Bona, a little to the east of Algiers. In the year 1816 there was an establishment here for carrying on the coral fishery under the protection of the British flag. Hither came a number of Corsican, Neapolitan and other Italian fishercraft.

THE ALGERINE CORSAIRS

Ascension Day in that year fell on the 23rd of May, and as the fishermen were about to attend Mass there was a gun fired from the castle, and simultaneously there rushed into sight 2000 infantry and cavalry, consisting of Moors, Turks and Levanters. Fire was opened on the poor fishermen, and practically the whole lot were massacred. The English flags were then torn to pieces and trampled on, the British Vice-Consul's house was pillaged, as well as the supplies of coral which had been obtained by the fishermen.

As soon as news of this incident reached England the country was roused to immediate action, and a punitive expedition was got together and sent out under Admiral Lord Exmouth. He had been delayed by head winds, but got under way in the last week of July. His flagship was the 120-gun *Queen Charlotte*, Rear-Admiral Sir David Milne being second in command in the 90-gun *Impregnable*. There were also three 74-gun ships in addition to a number of frigates, brigs, bombs, fireships and several smaller ships well supplied with shrapnel and the ordinary means of warfare of those times. By the 9th of August the fleet had arrived and anchored at Gibraltar, where it was joined by the Dutch fleet of five frigates and a corvette under Admiral Van Cappillen. Meanwhile H.M.S. *Prometheus* had been dispatched ahead to Algiers to bring away the British Consul and his family, but did not succeed in the entire task. By disguising them in midshipmen's uniform the Consul's wife and daughter were able to escape, but the Consul had been seized by the Dey and thrown into chains. For the Algerine had learnt from French papers of the forthcoming British expedition, and having heard of the escape of Mrs. and Miss Macdonell, he immediately ordered the detention of two of the boats from the *Prometheus*

THE LAST OF

which chanced to be ashore. The crews were thrown into slavery; but when this information reached the ears of Lord Exmouth, this, if anything were wanting, completed his eagerness to wipe out the plague-spot of European civilisation.

So the fleet left Gibraltar and arrived before Algiers on 27th August. An interpreter was sent ashore with Lieutenant Burgess (the Admiral's flag-lieutenant), under a flag of truce, with a letter to the Dey demanding reparation, and while this was being done the fleet, taking advantage of a light breeze springing up, came into the bay and hove to about a mile from Algiers. But after waiting beyond the stipulated time, since no answer was forthcoming, Mr. Burgess and the interpreter returned to the flagship, where every one was ready and anxious for the order to blaze away at the enemy. The Admiral now made a signal to know whether all the ships were prepared, and the affirmative answer being returned, the *Queen Charlotte* led the line towards the shore, and to the amazement of the enemy ran across all the batteries without firing or receiving a single shot. She then brought up within eighty yards of that mole which the reader will recollect had been built long years before by Christian captives. The spot selected by the Admiral was where an Algerine brig was seen lying. The rest of the fleet, including the Dutch vessels, then took up their assigned positions in regular order.

The position of the *Queen Charlotte* had been selected with great foresight, for here she was exposed to only three or four flanking guns, while her own broadside swept the whole of the enemy's batteries. But so far not a shot had been fired, and the shore batteries were lined with spectators who gazed in astonishment at the quiet order

THE BOMBARDMENT OF ALGIERS

When Lord Exmouth attacked this den of piracy and cruelty, even the British women served at the same guns as their husbands, and never shrank.

THE ALGERINE CORSAIRS

with which the ships had each come to her berth in such close proximity to the defensive works. For a time Lord Exmouth was in hopes that the Dey would yield to his lordship's demands, but this delay was not caused by any such intention on the part of the enemy but owing to the fact that the Algerines were completely unprepared for such a sudden approach, and their guns were not even shotted. It was only as the fleet came to anchor that the gunners ashore could be seen getting busy. To the last minute the British Admiral was minded to spare human life and even was seen on the quarter-deck repeatedly waving his hat as a warning to the crowd to retire from the mole.

So at 2.45 p.m. the enemy opened fire at the *Queen Charlotte*. Before the sound of the firing reached his ears, and while the first smoke was visible, Lord Exmouth gave the order to fire, and then three broadsides were fired in about six minutes, the rest of the fleet following the example. This caused terrible devastation ashore, as many as 500 people being killed or wounded. Then the attack began in deadly earnest. It was a repetition of the history of the sixteenth century. On the one hand, the Christian forces of Europe: on the other, the infidel corsairs and enemies of the human race. Both sides fought with the same fierceness which had marked their contests in many a previous generation. In the hot, overpowering sun, with the last vestige of breeze vanished away, the gunners blazed away in fine style. Algerine vessels in close proximity to the English fleet burst forth into flames and for a time endangered the wooden walls of England. On both sides frightful slaughter was taking place. The Dey had 500 guns mounted and doing their work to our great loss, but our own men and guns were hurling death into the nest of

THE LAST OF

pirates in a manner that surprised the Algerines. There was in the breasts of the invaders, not merely the hatred of the Algerines as infidels and pirates, but the fact that these men had been responsible for the capture of so many Christian ships and the cruelties to so many European seamen, sufficed to increase the determination and enthusiasm with which the destruction was being dealt out to these poisonous wasps.

But if the enemy was clearly suffering heavy losses, the attackers were not without heavy casualties. About sunset Rear-Admiral Milne made a signal to Lord Exmouth announcing the losses on the *Impregnable* alone as 150 killed and wounded, and requesting that if possible a frigate might be sent to take off some of the enemy's fire. The *Glasgow* was therefore ordered to go, and actually got up her anchor, but the wind was so scant that she was obliged again to let go, though in a rather more favourable position. But meanwhile on shore flames were bursting out and making an end to matters. One of the enemy's frigates had been gallantly boarded and set on fire, but now all the Algerine ships in the port were in flames, and thence the fire spread with all-devouring force to the arsenal and storehouse, causing a marvellous sight against the background of darkness. Our shells had been splendidly aimed, and although in some cases they had to be fired right across our own men-of-war, yet never an accident occurred to our ships as they went to find their billet in the home of the Algerine pirates. And then, as if to bring about the climax of this hot battle, the attacking fleet had brought near to the battery of the enemy the special ship which had been specially charged with explosives. And as she blew up there was another wealth of damage done to the cause of the defenders. And so by midnight the

THE ALGERINE CORSAIRS

enemy's batteries had been silenced, and in the morning the Dey was compelled to surrender.

The net result of Lord Exmouth's fine attack was as follows. Twelve hundred Christians were released from their terrible slavery, all the demands were complied with, the British Consul had been indemnified for his losses, and the Dey, in the presence of all his officers, made an apology for the insults offered. Even though, a few years later, the French had further trouble with these Algerines, yet Exmouth's expedition had the effect of giving the death-blow to a monster that had worried Europe for about three centuries. The scourge of the tideless Mediterranean had been obliterated: the murders and enslavery of so many thousands and thousands of European Christians of past centuries had been avenged, and a universal enemy which neither Charles v., nor Andrea Doria, nor many another had been able to exterminate was now laid low. The combined squadrons of those two historic maritime nations—Great Britain and Holland—had shown that even a race so long accustomed to the sea as the Algerine pirates could not resist for all time. In the history of the world few nations have ever done so much for the development of ships and sea-power as these two northern peoples, and the chance which enabled them to combine forces against a common evil of such antiquity was singularly happy.

CHAPTER XX

PIRATES OF THE PERSIAN GULF

WE have seen throughout this volume that there have always been certain geographical areas which have been favoured by pirates as their suitable sphere for roving. Madagascar, Malabar, the north coast of Africa, the West Indies—these and others have been the scene, not of one piratical incident, but of scores.

The Persian Gulf is to this day not quite the peaceful corner of the globe that undoubtedly some day it will become. It is still patrolled by the Royal Navy for various reasons, including the prevention of gun-running. Just how long the Persian Gulf has been navigated it would be impossible to say : but there is every reason to suppose that if the first kind of boat which ever floated was seen on the Tigris or Euphrates, the first sea-going craft was observed in the Persian Gulf. At any rate it is certain that the Arabians who occupy that peninsula which separates the Red Sea from the Persian Gulf were in the early stages of history the greatest navigators and seamen anywhere. Even right down to the Middle Ages, for scientific navigation, with the aid of those nautical instruments which were the forerunners of our modern sextant, there were no mariners who could find their way across the trackless seas so skilfully as these inhabitants of Arabia.

PIRATES OF THE PERSIAN GULF

From time immemorial there have dwelt on the west side of the Persian Gulf an Arabian tribe named the Joassamees, engaged in maritime pursuits either in trading, or pearl-fishing, or as pilots to strange ships entering the Gulf, or else acting as pirates. For it was obvious to them that this last mentioned occupation held out much that was tempting. So the Joassamees began in a small way, pillaging the coasting vessels of the Gulf, and as they found their efforts in this respect were so successful they aspired to bigger things. We are speaking now of that fascinating period of the sailing ship which belongs to the end of the eighteenth and the beginning of the nineteenth centuries.

The reader will instantly call to mind those fine ships of the East India Company, so smart and similar to the ships of the Royal Navy in appearance, and so similar in discipline and actual build. Shortly before the close of the eighteenth century the *Viper*, a 10-gun East Indiaman, was lying at anchor in the Bushire Roads. (Bushire is a port on the east or Persian side of the Gulf.) In the same harbour there were at anchor also a few dhows. Up till now these pirates had never molested an English ship : they had confined their attentions to native craft, so no efforts had been made to deal with them.

Now the skippers of these dhows had applied to the Persian agent of the East India Company for a supply of gunpowder and cannon shot to last them out their cruise, and, as the agent had no suspicions whatever, he gave them an order to the commanding officer on board for the desired quantity. It happened that the *Viper's* captain was ashore, so the order was produced to the officer in charge, the quantity mentioned was handed over, and the dhows began to make sail. The *Viper's* crew were breakfasting on deck, and the officers below, when, without any warning, a couple

PIRATES OF THE PERSIAN GULF

of these dhows began to cannonade the *Viper*, and the crews attempted to come aboard. No time was lost on the Indiaman, however, for the officers rushed up on deck, called the crew to quarters, cut the hempen cable, got sail on her so as to be ready for manœuvring, and a regular engagement began between the *Viper* and the four dhows which had plenty of men and big guns. It was a determined onslaught, and Lieutenant Carruthers, the commanding officer, was wounded in the lower part of the body, but bravely kept on, until he was killed by a ball in the forehead.

The command now fell on Mr. Salter, midshipman, who continued the fight not less courageously, and, after a keen encounter, drove the pirates off and chased them out to sea. This gave them a severe lesson, so that years passed by before another similar attempt was made on the British flag. But in the year 1804 there was a renewed attempt, and the following story, though a little involved, is of real interest. It begins with the East India Company's cruiser named *Fly*, and the scene is still the Persian Gulf. At the time we are speaking of this ship was off the island of Kenn when she had the bad fortune to be attacked by a French privateer. In order, however, to prevent the enemy boarding her, she was purposely run on to a shoal, and the Government dispatches which she was carrying, together with some treasure, were thrown overboard in $2\frac{1}{2}$ fathoms, cross-bearings having first been taken so that perhaps these might be recovered at some future date. The passengers and crew were taken to Bushire and set at liberty.

They then purchased a dhow by subscription, fitted her out and sailed down the Gulf bound for Bombay. On their way they stopped near Kenn Island to recover the dispatches and treasure. The former they managed to get

PIRATES OF THE PERSIAN GULF

up again, and as there was no time to waste they left the treasure and were hurrying on to their goal. But when they got to the south of the Gulf they had even worse fortune, for they were attacked by a fleet of Joassamee pirates and taken into the port of Ras-el-Khyma, which was to these Arabian rovers what Algiers had been to the corsairs of the Mediterranean. Here the English remained in the hope of being ransomed, but no such opportunity occurred. Months went by, and at last they determined to do what they could. They informed the pirate-chief of the treasure which lay sunk in the Gulf, and assured him that having taken good cross-bearings of the spot by the marks on shore the wealth could be recovered if some of these Arabians, so accustomed to pearl-diving, would assist them. The arrangement was that if the treasure was recovered the English should regain their liberty.

So English and Arabian sailed to the spot, and anchored where the cross-bearings indicated. The first divers who went down were so successful that all the crew dived down to the bottom of the fifteen feet in turns. And then came the great chance of escape. While practically all these men were below the water on the floor of the sea, it seemed that the real opportunity was at hand after all those months to get away. The picture is not without humour—the prisoners above in the craft, while the captors are left behind with no alternative but to swim ashore. But the best laid schemes of mice and men often work out differently from mere theory. The cable was cut, and either the splash of the rope in the water, or some suspicious instinct in these primitive people betrayed the plot, so the divers rushed up again to the surface and prevented the consummation of the prisoners' desires.

But for all that, the pirates kept their word. The

PIRATES OF THE PERSIAN GULF

treasure had been recovered, so the prisoners were given their liberty. The promise was kept *literally* and no more. For being placed on the island of Kenn there was no means of escaping from this limited freedom; and, further, there was practically nothing to eat. The pirates came ashore at the same time and put to death all the inhabitants, and the Englishmen, thinking it might be their own turn next, took to hiding in the rocks as best they might, going out under cover of night to steal a goat or whatever food might fall into their hands. But when at last the pirates had completed their bloody work they departed, leaving the Englishmen the sole inhabitants.

It was clear to the latter that if they wished to keep alive, they too must quit the island; but what were they to do for a boat? And here again we have one of those instances which, in fiction, would be far-fetched. When they were most in despair they had the good fortune to find a wrecked boat on the beach which might be capable of being repaired. Through the silent, deserted town the mariners searched until they were able to bring down to the beach an adequate supply of timber for patching up the boat and for making also a raft. In a few days both of these were ready, and the party in two sections began to endeavour to cross to the Persian shore. But one of the sections foundered and were never seen again, while the other reached the mainland and then, following the line of coast, obtaining food and water from the villages through which they passed, they arrived at length after terrible privations at Bushire, still having preserved their Government dispatches. Thence they proceeded to Bombay, but out of the whole company there were only two that survived, though the bag of dispatches was brought at last into safety.

PIRATES OF THE PERSIAN GULF

In the following year two English brigs were also captured by these pirates, while the former were sailing from Bombay to Bussorah, and the crew taken to an Arabian port, whence they succeeded in escaping, though the piracies now continued unabated. By the year 1808 these Joassamees were becoming exceedingly strong and impudent. Their many successes had made them more desperate than ever, and the time-honoured practice of heaving the resisting captain overboard was, of course, resorted to. One of the most daring attacks was that on the *Sylph*, an East India Company's cruiser of 60 tons, mounting 8 guns. She was bound from Bombay to Persia, and when she had arrived in the Gulf she was attacked by a fleet of these Arab dhows. The commander of the *Sylph* was a Lieutenant Graham. He, of course, observed these craft approaching him, but he had been previously warned by the Bombay Government not to fire upon any of these dhows until he had first been fired at.

Under the circumstances one would have thought that was a clear instance when orders might have been disobeyed: for before he had even time to hoist his colours to indicate his nationality, the dhows had thrown themselves against the *Sylph*, poured in a shower of stones, wounded many of the crew, and then leapt aboard and captured the vessel before a single shot had been fired. Those whom they had not killed were now slain with the sword, and the enemy being in sole possession made sail and took the ship along triumphantly, their dhows bearing them company. But before long the Commodore of the squadron hove in sight, cruising in the frigate *Nereid*. Seeing the *Sylph* with so many dhows alongside, he correctly surmised that the East Indiaman had fallen a victim to the pirates. So giving chase to this assorted

PIRATES OF THE PERSIAN GULF

fleet he soon came up to the East Indiaman, and the Arabs having leapt again into their dhows, the Commodore was able to regain the *Sylph*, though he was unable to capture either dhow or Arab.

And then the East India Government began to realise that something ought to be done to end these repeated attacks: so an expedition was sent from Bombay consisting of a frigate and a 38-gun ship as well as eight East India Company's cruisers, four large transports and a bomb-ketch. These at length arrived at Ras-el-Khyma, anchored before the town and landed the troops. The Arabs assembled in crowds to attack the invaders, but the trained troops were too great a match for them. The regular volleys and the charge at the point of the bayonet caused very heavy losses to the enemy. The place was burnt down, sixty of their dhows and boats as well as an English ship which they had previously captured were also consumed in flames, and the troops were allowed to plunder all that they found. With very small loss to the invaders the whole place had been wiped out, though it was thought that the treasures had been taken inland by the pirates.

The expedition afterwards sailed to Linga, another of these pirate ports, and burnt it to the ground. And after an exciting encounter yet another port, named Luft, was also overcome. It happened on this wise. Because the channel was very difficult and narrow, the ships had to be warped to their anchorages. The troops were then landed, and it was hoped to have been able to blow up the gate of the fortress with a howitzer specially brought for such a purpose. The fortress's walls were fourteen feet thick, so it would have been a tough business to have razed them to the ground. But the English were picked off by the enemy so disastrously from the loopholes of the fortress

PIRATES OF THE PERSIAN GULF

that a general flight took place of our men, and the howitzer was left behind. The troops lay hidden till darkness came on, and were thus enabled to make for the beach, where they embarked without further assault from the enemy. But as the dawn came, judge of the surprise of the invaders when they saw a man on the top of the fortress walls waving the Union Jack! The whole squadron marvelled and rubbed their eyes in amazement. Who was it, and how had he remained there alive, and what were the enemy doing? The answer was soon found. This gallant gentleman was Lieutenant Hall who was in command of the *Fury*, one of the ships nearest to the shore. During the darkness he had put off from his ship, landed alone with a Union Jack and advanced to the castle gate. Here he found the fortress had been for the most part abandoned, but there were a few of the enemy still remaining. When they saw the British officer these presumed that there were more of his followers coming on, so they fled precipitately. All that the officer now had to do was to take possession single-handed. It was a plucky, cool act, and well worthy of remembrance.

The fleet got under way again, bombarded for several days another pirate stronghold named Shenaz. A breach was made in the castle walls, and even now a stubborn resistance was made, the Arabs fighting finely till the last, but the town was overcome and left a mere ruin. And such was the effect of this protracted expedition, that for some years following the pirates were compelled to reverence the British flag whenever they were tempted to attack our ships at sea. But as it was with Algiers, so with these Arabian pirates. The respite did not continue long, and by the year 1815 the Arabian dhows were infesting the entrance of the Red Sea. Under their admiral, Ameer

PIRATES OF THE PERSIAN GULF

Ibrahim, a fleet of them, the following year, captured near the Straits of Babelmandeb four British vessels richly laden with cargo from Surat.

So again a British squadron had to be sent against them. This consisted of H.M.S. *Challenger* and the East India Company's cruisers *Mercury*, *Ariel* and *Vestal*, which were dispatched to the port of Ras-el-Khyma, where a demand was presented for the return of the four Surat ships or, if not forthcoming, then the payment of four lacks of rupees, coupled with the handing over of Ameer Ibrahim. This town stands on a narrow tongue of sandy land, pointing to the north-east, presenting its north-west edge to the open sea and its south-east edge to a creek which ran up to the south-west and affords a safe harbour for small craft. Round towers and isolated walls were seen, but no continuous wall. There were about 10,000 inhabitants in the town, and the port boasted of 60 dhows manned by crews of from 80 to 300 men. In the present instance they were assisted by another 40 dhows from other ports. In short, the concentrated force amounted to about 100 dhows and 8000 fighting men.

After some fruitless negotiations, the signal was made to the British squadron to get up anchors and stand in close to the shore. This was followed by another signal to engage with the enemy, and the squadron bore down nearly in line before the wind, under easy sail, till they got near where four dhows were lying at anchor, the depth of the water gradually shoaling till they found themselves in $2\frac{1}{2}$ fathoms. At this sounding the squadron anchored with springs on the cables, so that each vessel lay with her broadside to the shore. Fire was now opened against these four of the enemy's craft, the latter seething with men, brandishing their weapons in the air. At first some of our shells reached the shore and buried themselves in the sand, others

ATTACKING A PIRATE STRONGHOLD

A breach was made in the wall by the British, but a stubborn resistance was made, the Arabs fighting finely till the last, but the town was overcome and left a mere ruin.

PIRATES OF THE PERSIAN GULF

fell across the bows of the Arab craft. On all the forts were seen the Arabs' colours flying, and crowds of armed men were visible on the beach. But, unhappily, the whole of this bombardment availed nothing and a bloodless battle was brought to an end.

In the year 1818, as these pirates had assumed such strength and daring to the great menace of commercial shipping, another fleet had to be sent against them. For the Arab dhows had not merely plundered ships at sea but ravaged the sea-coast towns on islands as well as mainland. But the British ships now dispatched intercepted them and drove them back into the Gulf. In one day as many as seventeen dhows were being chased by one of ours, but the wind just suited the Arabian craft so that they managed to get away. And so we might continue. For years these pirates caused grievous trouble, and for years they had to be dealt with. Perhaps the time will come when the Persian Gulf will be as safe for navigation as the English Channel is to-day, with regard to the elimination of pirate craft. Matters have, thanks to the patrolling by the Royal Navy, improved considerably : but that there is still danger is well-known, and it would be foolish to ignore it. For we must remember that it is a hard task to exterminate such an ancient profession as piracy, and especially when the practice is carried on by such an historic race of seamen as the Arabs. When any community has been accustomed for centuries and centuries, either in the Persian Gulf or the Red Sea or the Arabian Sea or the Indian Ocean, to gain their living by sea robbery; when they have made such a careful study of the local navigation and the habits of their potential victims,—it is no easy matter for these men suddenly to relinquish their previous habits and to give up their hard-earned knowledge. It would be just as easy for a

PIRATES OF THE PERSIAN GULF

Brixham or Lowestoft fisherman to give up his vocation and take to farming or manufacture, as it has been for the Arab slaver and pirate to become a law-abiding seaman. But as so many of the notorious piratical seas in the past have been cleansed beyond all expectation, so, doubtless, the time will come when the last sea-robber has disappeared from both hemispheres and the pirate has become as extinct as the dodo. But whether the story of the sea will thereby be as interesting and exciting as in previous ages is quite another matter.

CHAPTER XXI

THE STORY OF AARON SMITH

IF the expression had not been used already so many thousand times, one might well say of the following story that truth is indeed stranger than fiction. Had you read the yarn which is here to be related you would, at its conclusion, have remarked that it was certainly most interesting and exciting, but it was too exaggerated, too full of coincidences, too full of narrow escapes ever to have occurred in real life. But I would assure the reader at the outset that Smith's experiences were actual and not fictional, and that his story was carefully examined at the time by the High Court of Admiralty. The prelude, the climax and the conclusion of this drama with its exciting incidents, its love interest and its happy ending; the romantic atmosphere, the picturesque characters, the colours and the symmetry of the narrative are so much in accord with certain models such as one used to read in mere story-books of one's boyhood, that it is well the reader should be fully assured that what is here set forth did in very truth happen. In some respects the narrative reads like pages from one of Robert Louis Stevenson's novels, and yet though I have, by the limits of the space at my disposal, been compelled to omit many of the incidents which centred around Smith and his pirate associates, yet the facts which are set forth

THE STORY OF AARON SMITH

have been taken from contemporary data and can be relied upon implicitly.

The story opens in the year 1821, and the hero is an English seaman named Aaron Smith. In the month of June, Smith departed from England and embarked on the merchant ship *Harrington*, which carried him safely over the Atlantic to the West Indies. Subsequent events induced him to resign his billet on that vessel, and as he found that the West Indian climate was impairing his health, he made arrangements to get back home to England. Being then at Kingston in the island of Jamaica, he interviewed the captain of the British merchant ship *Zephyr* and was appointed first mate. The *Zephyr*, like many of the ships of the eighteenth and early nineteenth centuries, was rigged as a brig, that is to say with square sails on each of her two masts, with triangular headsails and a quadrilateral sail abaft the second mast much like the mainsail of a cutter-rigged craft. Brigs nowadays are practically obsolete, but at the time we are speaking of they were immensely popular in the merchant service and for carrying coals from Newcastle-on-Tyne to London.

The *Zephyr*, after taking on board her West Indian cargo together with a few passengers, weighed anchor in the month of June 1822—just a year after Smith had left Europe—and set sail for England. From the very first Smith saw that things were not quite as they should be. The pilot who took the ship out into the open sea was a very incapable man, but his duties were soon ended and he left the ship. The name of the *Zephyr's* captain was Lumsden, and even he was far from being the capable mariner which one would have expected in a man whose duty it was to take a ship across the broad Atlantic. Presently, before they had left Kingston far astern, a strong breeze

THE STORY OF AARON SMITH

sprang up from the north-east, and a heavy easterly swell got up, which made the brig somewhat lively. Most people are aware that the navigation among the islands and in the tricky channels of the West Indies needs both great care and much knowledge, such as ought to have been possessed by a man in Lumsden's position. Judge of Smith's surprise, therefore, when the latter found his captain asking his advice as to which passage he ought to take.

Whatever else Smith had in his character, he was certainly extremely shrewd and cautious, and he replied in a non-committal answer to the effect that the "windward" passage might prolong the voyage but that the "leeward" one would expose the ship to the risk of being plundered by the pirates, which in those days were far from rare. Lumsden weighed the pros and cons in his mind, and at last resolved to choose the "leeward" passage. About two o'clock one afternoon Smith was pacing up and down deck when he suddenly espied a schooner of a very suspicious appearance standing out from the land. Not quite happy as to her character, he then went aloft with his telescope and examined her closely. In the case of a man of his sea experience it did not take long for him to realise that the schooner was a pirate-ship. Lumsden was below at the time, so Smith called him on deck and, pointing out the strange vessel, suggested to the captain that it would be best to alter the brig's course to avoid her. But Lumsden, like most ignorant men, was exceedingly obstinate, and stoutly declined the proffered advice. With characteristic British sentiment he opined that "because he bore the English flag no one would dare to molest him." The skipper of the schooner, as we shall presently see, did not think of the matter in that way.

Half an hour passed by, the brig held on her original

THE STORY OF AARON SMITH

course, and the two ships drawing closer together it was observed that the schooner's deck was full of men. Clearly, too, she was about to hoist out her boats. This gave cause for alarm even in the stubborn breast of Lumsden, and now he gave orders for the course to be altered a couple of points. But the decision had been arrived at too leisurely, for the stranger was already within gun-shot. Before much time had sped on, the sound of voices was heard from the schooner, and short, sharp orders came across the heaving sea, ordering the *Zephyr* to lower her stern boat and to send the captain aboard the schooner. Lumsden pretended not to understand, but a brisk volley of musketry from the stranger instantly quickened the skipper's comprehension, and he promptly gave orders to lay the mainyard aback and heave-to.

The boat which had been lowered from the schooner was quickly rowed alongside the brig, and nine or ten men, ferocious of appearance and well-armed with knives, cutlasses and muskets, now leapt aboard. It was obvious before they had left the schooner's deck that these were desperate pirates, such as had many a dark, cruel deed to their consciences. With no wasting of formality they at once took charge of the brig and ordered Lumsden, Smith, the ship's carpenter, and also a Captain Cowper who was travelling as a passenger, to proceed on board the schooner without delay. In order to hurry them on, the pirates gave them repeated blows over the back from the flat part of their cutlasses, accompanying these strokes with threats of shooting them. So the company got into the schooner's boat and were rowed off; Lumsden recollected having left on the cabin table of the *Zephyr* the ship's books containing an account of all the money aboard the brig.

THE STORY OF AARON SMITH

Arrived alongside the schooner, the prisoners were ordered on deck. It was the pirate captain who now issued the commands, a man of repulsive appearance with his savage expression, his short, stout stature. His age was not more than about thirty-two, his appearance denoted that in his veins ran Indian blood. Standing not more than five and a half feet high, he had an aquiline nose, high cheek bones, a large mouth, big full eyes, sallow complexion and black hair. The son of a Spanish father and a Yucatan squaw, there was nothing in him that suggested anything but the downright brigand of the sea.

But with all this savage temperament there was nothing in him of the fool, and his wits and eyes were ever on the alert. Already he had observed a cluster of vessels in the distance, and he questioned Lumsden as to what kind of craft they might be. On being informed that probably they were French merchantmen, the pirate captain gave orders for all hands to get the schooner ready to give chase. Meanwhile the *Zephyr*, with part of the pirate crew on board, made sail and stood in towards the land in the direction of Cape Roman, some eighteen miles away. And as the schooner pushed on, cleaving her way through the warm sea, the pirate applied himself to questioning the skipper of the brig. What was his cargo? Lumsden answered that it consisted of sugars, rum, coffee, arrowroot, and so on. But what money had he on board? Lumsden replied that there was no money. Such an answer only infuriated the pirate. "Don't imagine I'm a fool, sir," he roared at him. "I know that all vessels going to Europe have specie on board, and "—he added—" if you will give up what you have, you shall proceed on your voyage without further molestation." But Lumsden still continued in his protestations that money there was

THE STORY OF AARON SMITH

none: to which the pirate remarked that if the money were not forthcoming he would throw the *Zephyr's* cargo overboard.

Night was rapidly approaching, and the breeze was certainly dying down, so that although the schooner had done fairly well through the water, yet the pirate despaired of ever coming up with the Frenchmen. Disappointed at his lack of success, he was compelled to abandon the chase, and altered his course to stand in the direction of the *Zephyr*. When night had fallen the pirates began to prepare supper, and offered spirits to their captives, which the latter declined. The pirate captain now turned his attention to Smith, and observed that as he was in bad health, and none of the schooner's crew understood navigation, it was his intention to detain Smith to navigate her. We need not attempt to suggest the feelings of dismay with which Smith received this information. To resist forceably was obviously out of the question, though he did his best to be allowed to forego the doubtful honour of being appointed navigating officer to a pirate-ship. Lumsden, too, uneasy at the thought of being bereft of a man indispensable to the safety of his brig, expressed a nervous hope that Smith might not be detained. But the pirate's reply to the last request came prompt and plain. "If I do not keep him," he growled at Lumsden, "I shall keep you." That sufficiently alarmed the brig's master to subdue him to silence.

The captives sat down to supper with their pirate captain and the latter's six officers. The meal consisted of garlic and onions chopped up into fine pieces and mixed with bread in a bowl. From this every one helped himself as he pleased with his fingers, and the coarse manners of the schooner's company were in keeping with the brutality

THE STORY OF AARON SMITH

of their profession. A breeze had sprung up in the meanwhile and they began fast to approach the *Zephyr*. When at length the two vessels were within a short distance, the pirate ordered a musket to be fired and then proceeded to tack shorewards. This signal was answered immediately by the pirates on board the brig, and the *Zephyr* then proceeded to follow the schooner. One of the brig's crew who had been brought aboard the schooner at the time when Lumsden and Smith were taken, was now ordered to heave the lead and to give warning as soon as the schooner got into soundings. It is significant that whatever else these pirates may have been, they were brigands first and sailormen only a bad second, who had taken to roving less through nautical enthusiasm than from a greed for gain and a means of indulging their savage tastes. Thus, although on waylaying a merchant ship their first object was to pillage, yet they made it also their aim to carry off any useful members of the trader's crew who were expert in the arts of seamanship or navigation.

As soon as the leadsman, then, found bottom at fourteen fathoms, the pirate commanded a boat to be lowered and therein were placed Lumsden and some of the crew which had belonged to the *Zephyr*. Smith, however, and with him the brig's carpenter, were detained on the schooner. The pirate captain himself accompanied Lumsden, left the latter on board the brig and brought back the crew of the pirate, who in the first instance had been left to take charge of the *Zephyr*. They also brought away to the schooner a number of articles, including Cowper's watch, the brig's spy-glass, Smith's own telescope, some clothes belonging to the latter and a goat. To show what kind of cruel rascals Smith had now become shipmate with may be seen from the fact that as soon as the animal had been brought aboard,

THE STORY OF AARON SMITH

one of the pirate's crew instantly cut the goat's throat with his knife, flayed the poor creature alive, and promised the same kind of treatment to his friends if no money were found in the *Zephyr*. Even the most stalwart British sailor could not help his heart beating the more rapidly at such cowardly and bullying treatment.

By now the schooner had stood so near to the shore that she was in four fathoms and the anchor was let go. The *Zephyr* also let go and brought up about fifty yards away. Relieved from work, the pirates now began to exult and to congratulate each other on their fine capture. Night came on again and a watch was set. Smith and Cowper, still in the schooner, were ordered to sleep in the companion-way, but with the fearful anxiety imminent and the possibility of never being allowed to wake again, they never relapsed into unconsciousness. Conversation was kept up stealthily between them, and Cowper, knowing that the *Zephyr* carried a quantity of specie and that Lumsden had hoodwinked the pirate captain, dreaded lest this should be found out. With the certain assurance in his mind of being put to death, a horrible night of suspense and fear was passed by the two seamen.

When daylight came, some of the pirates were seen on the brig's deck beating the *Zephyr's* crew with their cutlasses. Great activity of a most business-like nature was being manifested on the English ship, boats were being hoisted out, a rope cable—those were still the days of hemp—was being coiled on deck, the hatches were being removed and all was being made ready for taking out the *Zephyr's* cargo. The pirate commanded Smith to go aboard the brig and fetch everything that might be essential for the purposes of navigation, for the former was most determined to retain the former mate of the English merchantman. To accentu-

THE STORY OF AARON SMITH

ate his determination the half-caste brute raised his arm into the air and, brandishing a cutlass over poor Smith's head, threatened him with instant death if he showed any reluctance. "Mind and you obey me," he taunted, "or I will take off your skin."

We need not stop to depict Smith's feelings, nor to suggest with what dismay he found himself compelled to obey the behests of a coarse, ignorant freebooter. It was humiliating to the last degree for a man who had been mate and served under the red ensign thus to have to submit to such abominable treatment. But there was no choice between submission and death, though from what eventually followed it was obvious that Smith was not a coward and was not so proud of his skin as to fear death. He proceeded aboard the brig, discovered that she had been well ransacked and with a heavy heart began to collect his belongings. He brought off his gold watch and sextant, packed his clothes and then returned to the schooner. But before doing so he acted as a man about to pass out of the world and anxious to dispose of his remaining effects. With almost humorous pathos, one might remark, he set about this last duty. "My books, parrot and various other articles I gave in charge to Mr. Lumsden, who engaged to deliver them safely into the hands of my friends, should he reach England:" and it needs no very gifted imagination to see the sentimental sailor of the great sailing-ship age painfully taking a last look at these cherished possessions.

The cargo having been transferred to the schooner, the pirates indulged themselves in liquor and became intoxicated. But meanwhile the crew of the brig were not allowed to stand idle. The pirate captain was going to get all that he could from his capture, and ordered the *Zephyr's*

THE STORY OF AARON SMITH

fore t'gallant mast and yard to be sent down, and these, together with whatever other spars might seem useful, were to be sent on board the schooner. The merchant ship was positively gutted of everything the pirates fancied. There was not left even so much as a bed or a blanket : even the ear-rings on the ears of the children passengers were snatched from the latter. In addition to this the whole of the live stock such as an ocean-going ship carried in those days prior to the invention of refrigerating rooms and tinned food was transferred to the schooner and a certain amount of drinking water.

But the pirates had not yet concluded their dastardly work. Lumsden and Cowper were warned that unless they produced the money, which the pirate was convinced still remained, the *Zephyr*, with all her people in her, should be burnt to the water's edge. It is to the credit of these two men that they strenuously declined to oblige the pirate. This only served as fuel to the latter's temper, and he sent them below and began a series of heartless tortures which were more in keeping with some of the worst features of the Middle Ages than the nineteenth century. Determined to attain his object, no matter what the cost, he caused the two men to be locked to the ship's pumps and proceeded to carry out the threat which he had just promised. Every preparation was made for starting a fire, combustibles were piled round about the unfortunate men, and the light was just about to be applied when Lumsden, unable to endure the torture any longer, confessed that there was money. He was accordingly released, and rummaging about produced a small box of doubloons.

This, however, far from satisfying the pirate's thirst, merely increased his desire for more. Lumsden protested that that was all. So again the skipper was lashed to the

THE STORY OF AARON SMITH

pumps, again fire was ordered to be put to the fuel, and again the victim was about to be immolated. Once more, at the last minute, Lumsden yielded and offered to surrender all that he had. Thereupon, for the second time he was released, and producing nine more doubloons declared that this money had been entrusted to his care on behalf of a poor woman. Such human sentiments, however, rarely fell on more unsympathetic ears. "Don't speak to me of poor people," howled the pirate. "I am poor, and your countrymen and the Americans have made me so. I know there is more money, and I will either have it or burn you and the vessel."

Following up his threat with deeds, he once more ordered Lumsden below, yet again had the combustibles laid around. But the Englishman stood his torture well: his being was becoming accustomed to the treatment and for a while he never flinched. Then the monsters of iniquity applied a light to the fire, and the red and yellow flames leapt forward and already began to lick the skipper's body. For a time he endured the grievous pain as the fire burnt into his flesh. With agonising cries and heart-rending shouts he begged to be relieved of his tortures—to be cut adrift in a boat and left solitary on the wide open ocean—anything rather than this. Money he had not: already he had given up all that he possessed. And after this slow murder had continued for some time the stubborn dulled intellect of the pirate captain began to work, and seeing that not even fire could call forth more money from a suffering man, he was inclined to believe that the last coin had now been yielded up. Then turning to some of his own crew, he ordered them to throw water on to the flames, and the long-suffering Lumsden, more dead than alive, racked by physical and mental tortures, was released

THE STORY OF AARON SMITH

and allowed to regain his freedom. As if to accentuate their own bestial natures the pirates then proceeded to carouse once more and to exult again in their ill-gotten treasures.

But even in the most villainous criminal there is always at least one small trait of human nature left, and it is often surprising how this manifests itself when circumstances had seemed to deny its very existence. It was so in the case of this pirate captain. Everything so far had indicated the most unmitigated bully and murderer without one single redeeming feature of any sort whatever. And yet, in spite of all the vain entreaties of Lumsden for mercy, the pirate showed that the last spark of human kindness was not yet quenched. The reader will remember that among the articles which Smith had brought away from the brig was his gold watch. The pirate took this in his hands, examined it, and instead of promptly annexing the same, threw out a strong hint that he would like to retain it. Such moderation from one who had not hesitated to burn a man at the stake was in itself curious. But his inconsistency did not stop at that. Smith remarked that the watch was a gift from his aged mother, whom he now never expected to see again, adding that he would like to be allowed to send it to her by Lumsden, but was afraid that the pirates would take it away from the English captain if it were entrusted to him. It was then that the pirate manifested the extraordinary contradiction which his character possessed. "Your people," he began, "have a very bad opinion of us, but I will convince you that we are not so bad as we are represented to be; come along with me, and your watch shall go safely home." And with this he took Smith on board the *Zephyr* once more, handed the watch into Lumsden's keeping and gave strict orders

THE STORY OF AARON SMITH

that on no account was any one to take it away from the English captain.

Smith now took a final farewell of his old messmates, but lest he should take advantage of the indulgence which had been just granted him, the pirate captain instantly ordered him back to the schooner, and even impelled him forward at the point of his murderous knife. All this time the two ships had been lying alongside lashed together by warps. Being at last content with the ample cargo which he had extracted from the *Zephyr*, and being convinced that there was nothing else aboard of much value, the pirate now ordered the warps to be cast loose and informed Lumsden that he might consider himself free to resume his voyage. But, he insisted, on no account was he to steer for Havannah. Should he do so, the schooner would pursue him, and on being overtaken Lumsden and his ship should be destroyed without further consideration.

So at last the brig *Zephyr*, robbed of most of her valuables, lacking some of her gear and minus her mate, and with a tortured skipper, hove up her anchor, let loose her canvas and cleared out into the open sea.

CHAPTER XXII

SMITH AND THE PIRATE SCHOONER

WITH saddened gaze, Smith watched his old ship fade away into the invisible. There was but little wind, the sea was wonderfully calm and a thick fog came up which swallowed the wake of the *Zephyr* from his vision. In the whole of the western hemisphere there was no more miserable man alive at that moment than Aaron Smith. His ship had gone, his expectation of reaching England was torn from him, and his very life was liable to be taken away from him by force at any minute. He had no thought now for anything else than suicide. The pirate captain knew this, but it was not convenient to him to forfeit so able a seaman. He had other work for him to do yet, and threatened that should Smith attempt self-destruction he should be lashed to one of the schooner's guns and there left to perish slowly of hunger.

At daylight the next morning the schooner got under way, and after proceeding in a south-west direction, anchored in two fathoms in a beautiful harbour called Rio Medias. It is from this point that the second part of Smith's interesting story really begins. Arrived in this delightful anchorage, the schooner could afford to remain some time, and the pirate informed Smith that he expected a good many visitors on board, including two or three

SMITH AND THE PIRATE SCHOONER

magistrates with their families. The Englishman ventured the remark that he wondered the pirate was not afraid of magistrates coming on board a ship of that notoriety. But the pirate merely laughed and suggested that Smith did not understand the Spanish character. "Presents of coffee," he explained, "and other little things will always ensure their friendship, and from them I receive intelligence of all that occurs at the Havannah, and know every hostile measure in time enough to guard against it."

Before long the visitors came aboard, and the pirate, with something of the grand manner of an old-time Spaniard, received the ladies and gentlemen on his ship with great ceremony. Smith was brought forward and presented as an interesting English prisoner and attracted more than a little attention. It is customary with the Spanish-American people to conclude such social visits as this with a dance. Smith had little heart for such frivolity, but in small as in great matters he had no alternative but to obey, and was selected to dance with one of the daughters of a magistrate. However, in spite of enforced pleasure, he must have made himself singularly affable, for before the festivities had concluded, the lady and the Englishman had become more than mere acquaintances to each other. Womanlike, she began by taking pity on the European sailor, displayed unwonted interest in his story and determined to do her best to get him released. Mere pity and interest gave place to affection, but the utmost precaution and stealth had to be exercised lest the pirate captain or any individual member of his crew should so much as have the faintest suspicion that a plot for escape was being planned. The surname of the lady Smith did not learn, but her Christian name was Seraphina. She was a pretty brunette, with sparkling eyes and a kind, benevolent nature. In the monotony of her

SMITH AND THE PIRATE SCHOONER

West Indian life the advent of Aaron Smith had been as that of a person from another planet. The stories which she had learned of London had now the chance of being confirmed or refuted. She inquired eagerly about the grandeur of England's metropolis and asked naïvely " what sort of a building the immense church was that everybody went to see." A fresh interest had thus entered into her life, a man from the eastern hemisphere, a robust English sailor, with all the romance clinging thereto which an emotional Latin temperament was capable of conjuring up. But to the matter-of-fact mind of Aaron Smith all this embarrassing concern on the part of Seraphina suggested nothing less than treachery. It was difficult to believe that this was not part of the pirate captain's plot to entrap him. But the suspicion haunted him only at the first, and before long he was destined to find in the lady his best friend and commiserator. It would have been patent to any careful observer that these two individuals had fallen into that condition which is known as love at first sight.

The guests departed in due course, and the more serious business of the sojourn in the port was got in hand. The coffee and the other portions of the cargo which had been taken from the *Zephyr* were now unloaded and sold to the natives. This took some time and was spread over some days, varied by carousals and dancing. There was no lack of refreshment, and instead of every one helping himself with his fingers, as had been the case when first the schooner had been encountered, everybody was supplied with knives and forks and spoons which had been pillaged from the English brig. The wine flowed immoderately, and as usual most of the crew were soon in a state of intoxication. The sale of the cargo was proceeding, but as the men were flushed with wine it was not long before two of the crew

A Brave Man

Smith refused the pirate captain's treacherous proposal, so, having been lashed to the mainmast, gunpowder was sprinkled around him and then fired.

SMITH AND THE PIRATE SCHOONER

fell to quarrelling. High words were followed by a fierce duel with knives, and the sight was sickening. One of the combatants collapsed to the ground with a dull thud, severely stabbed in his left breast.

For some unexplained reason the crew of the pirate ship had in their minds the fixed idea that Smith was something of a doctor, and during the whole of his captivity no protestations of his could uproot that conviction. Probably he knew as many useful first-aid remedies as any average sailor of the early nineteenth century, and he was endowed with all the resource which a seaman usually possesses. Otherwise he had no expert knowledge of medicine or of surgery. And yet, as we shall see before we come to the end of our story, it was this imaginary healing power which rendered him the very greatest service.

It fell to Smith's lot, then, from the first to attend on the sick among his other duties, and in spite of his medical ignorance he was ordered to see to the wounded man, to staunch the blood and dress the horrible wound. When the injured man had recovered sufficiently to be able to converse, he sent a message begging the captain to come and see him, and then he told his tale. The cause of the quarrel, said he, was because his antagonist formed one of a party that was bent on assassinating the captain and crew. That being accomplished, they would then possess the ship and enrich themselves with the plunder. The man with whom he had been fighting had now gone to Havannah in order that he might get together more men to further his purpose. The pirate captain listened to the story with every attention, and was beside himself with rage that one of his own men should so far have dared to plot against him. Vowing certain destruction of them all, he summoned the crew on deck and informed them of the news. So soon as

SMITH AND THE PIRATE SCHOONER

they had heard it, the entire ship's company rushed madly below to where the suspected man was lying, dragged the fellow from his bunk on to the deck, cut off his legs and arms with a blunt hatchet, gashed at his body with their knives and then threw his half-dead remains overboard into the sea.

The next morning Smith was sent aloft to bend a new fore topsail, and about noon a ship being descried in the distance he was told to report as to what sort of vessel she might be. Looking through his spy-glass Smith replied that she was a schooner standing to the westward. " Is she a merchant or a man-of-war?" yelled the captain from the deck. "Mind you don't deceive me," he threatened, "for if you do, I will cut off your head. I have already killed several of your countrymen, and take care you don't add yourself to the number." This made Smith doubly cautious, but at last being certain in his mind he reported her as a merchantman. Already the pirate had got under way, and the receipt of these welcome tidings caused him to give chase. Smith remained aloft and observed that the merchantman had now guessed the pirate's intention and was altering her course to the nor'ard. Smith passed the information at once below, but the only thanks he got was abuse from the skipper for not having informed him sooner.

The sails filled to the meagre breeze as the pirate ship slowly sped onward. But when they had cleared the reef outside the pirate ordered the sweeps out, and with this auxiliary the ship began to travel fast over the smooth surface. Before long the lazy breeze began to stir, and soon both vessels were standing on under a smart press of canvas. For several hours the chase continued, and before dark the corsair was gaining rapidly. But she was yet a long way off and the pirate much feared that she might escape, as she

SMITH AND THE PIRATE SCHOONER

would assuredly alter her course during the night. At 10 p.m. the merchantman was well out of sight, and Smith was ordered below. The pirate then issued his instructions and remarked that he would keep on that tack until 2 a.m., and if the vessel was not then visible, he would alter his course to the east.

Meanwhile Smith, tired out with being tossed about whilst aloft, slept soundly until he was called. On coming on deck he found that every one was utterly at a loss to know the ship's position. Of any efficient navigation there had been practically nothing. The whole crew had been drunk, there had been no light in the binnacle, no log had been thrown to ascertain the ship's speed, so it was impossible to guess the distance travelled during the past night. The pirate therefore called upon Smith to help. Smith answered very properly that it was impossible to say exactly their position, whereupon the unscientific captain threatened him with instant death if he could not give the required information. Smith could not make an impossibility possible, and answered, "If you will wait till noon," he explained, "I will endeavour to do so." And the same threat was repeated in case he should fail to achieve this.

But Smith was certainly lucky for once in his varied life, for, as he said at a later date, "at this time the sun was in distance with the moon, and the sky being remarkably clear, the sea smooth, and the schooner making very little way, I had an opportunity at about nine o'clock to take a good lunar observation." So, after taking the sights—no one else on board had any knowledge of navigation, in fact, knew nothing better than seamanship and pilotage—he worked out his calculations and was able to find the true latitude, when, to his great surprise, he discovered they were

SMITH AND THE PIRATE SCHOONER

60 miles west-north-west of Cape Buonavesta, or 200 miles west of the position Smith had imagined.

The captain was informed of the position, who ordered Smith to direct the helmsman to the proper course and to have the sails trimmed accordingly. He questioned Smith as to when they would pick up the land, and the Englishman answered that if the wind was favourable they ought to do so in the afternoon. The captain demurred somewhat, then declared with an oath that if they did not then sight land he would punish Smith. Fortunately the breeze now freshened and became freer. Smith was nervously wondering whether he had made an error in his calculations, but at 4 p.m., to his great relief, the look-out man cried "Land!" This happily ended Smith's suspense, and the schooner's coast pilot complimented him on his skill, but the captain had nothing to say except abuse. "You rascal," he cried, "you pretended not to know where the vessel was: but you see you cannot deceive me, and I would advise you not to attempt it."

They had held on an easterly course for some time until at length they had come to an anchorage where they let go, and the following day proceeded into the harbour. While they were lying to their anchor a boat full of men was observed to be approaching the ship. As they came on it was seen to contain some of the men who, according to the man who had been wounded in that duel already narrated, had been plotting against the captain. The pirate was roused to fury on seeing them, and declared he would kill the lot of them. Then, ordering thirty muskets to be brought on deck, he awaited developments. When the boat got to within about two hundred yards, the men therein ceased rowing, and held up a white handkerchief as a signal for peace. This was answered by a similar

SMITH AND THE PIRATE SCHOONER

signal from the schooner, and thus encouraged the men laid to their oars again and pulled towards the ship. But they had not rowed many more strokes before the pirate gave orders to fire on the boat, and so deadly was the effect at such close range that of the six men five fell dead to the bottom of the boat, while the sixth leaped into the water and began to swim.

But it was no part of the pirate's intention to allow this man to escape, and dispatching a boat after him the fellow was soon hauled from the sea and brought aboard the schooner. From that moment began a series of cruelties and inhuman tortures of which it is difficult to write calmly. The captain commenced by remarking that he was well aware of the share which this survivor had in the plot that had been detected. Admonishing him to confess, he warned him that if he should not reveal the whole truth he would give him a cruel and lingering death. In vain did the terrified man protest his innocence, whereupon the captain had him stripped and exposed, naked and bleeding from the wounds already received, to the scorching heat of a West Indian July sun. Agony was piled on agony and the captain showed no hint of mercy. Smith, with great courage and humane feeling, entreated that the man might not be tortured so dreadfully, but the captain threatened him too with severest vengeance for his interference.

Then addressing himself to the suffering wretch, the pirate announced that he was now about to put him to death and advised him to prepare his soul for departure. Once more the man protested his innocence and begged for his life, but unavailingly. The next stage of terror began. Being placed in a boat, he was pinioned and his body lashed to the stern. Five men were told off to go in the

SMITH AND THE PIRATE SCHOONER

boat in addition to Smith. "You shall now see how I punish rascals!" exclaimed the captain as he gave orders to the Englishman, with the further instruction that the men were to row backwards and forwards up and down the narrow creek for the space of three hours. This creek was formed by a small strip of water that separated Cuba from a desert island. "I will see," exulted the brute, "whether the mosquitoes and the sandflies will not make him confess."

It was a brutal, inhumane form of torture worthy only of such a captain. The broiling sun shone fiercely on the warm sea. In the shade the thermometer registered as high as 90°, and from the side of the creek a waste of swamps was swarming with insects of a venomous and numerous kind. These settled in scores on the body of the pinioned man and sent him almost delirious with pain. His suffering body began to swell and he became blistered from head to foot—a ghastly sight for his beholders. Now and again in his agony he besought the boat's crew to put him out of his misery, but all save the Englishman laughed him to scorn and even imitated his heart-rending cries. After a while, owing to the solar heat and the stings of the mosquitoes and sandflies, his face became so swollen that he was utterly unrecognisable. His voice began to fail and his life was ebbing fast.

Smith had from the first believed that the story of the alleged conspiracy was false, and that it had been invented out of revenge by the man who had received the thrust of the knife. Unable to endure this loathsome sight any longer, the Englishman, believing fully in the man's innocence, at length prevailed on the crew to let the victim die in peace. They consented to go round to the other side of the island, where they would be secure from the captain's observation, untie the man and put something

THE FATE OF PIRATE MUTINEERS

The boat with the mutineers approached the vessel and waved a white handkerchief as a signal for peace. Encouraged by an answering signal, they drew nearer and were greeted by a shower of bullets which killed five men out of the crew of six.

SMITH AND THE PIRATE SCHOONER

over him to shelter from the violent rays of the sun. So they rowed to the spot, and laying upon their oars set him loose. But as soon as he felt the sea breeze on his parched face, he fainted right away. They then decided to tie him up as before, lest they might incur the fury of the captain for their lenience, and pulling back to the schooner they returned their prisoner. Instead of inspiring any feelings of pity, the sight of the moribund man caused the schooner's crew to break out into derisive laughter. As for the captain, he was disappointed that the fellow had not yielded any confession, and, turning to Smith, asked if he could now cure him of his ills. The Englishman replied that the man was actually dying. "Then he shall have some more of it before he dies," was the pirate's sharp answer.

So the victim was left in the boat, and the latter was moored within a few yards of the ship. Six of the schooner's crew were ordered to take their muskets and to fire at the wretch. This was done, but when they went to examine his body they were surprised to find him still breathing, so a pig of iron was fastened round his neck and he was cast into the sea, lucky to be freed from any further variety of torture. Then music broke out on the schooner's deck, and, with the callousness of the most hardened criminals, the guitars tinkled and songs were indulged in just as if nothing had happened to disturb their equanimity.

It is no pleasure to have to chronicle such incidents as these, which detract from the more romantic side of piracy at sea. But it would be as unfair to paint only the glamour of these rovers as it would be to select merely the harsh cruelties which they imposed. Whilst I can see little that is edifying in parading repellent details of blood and slaughter, yet it is part of one's duty to give some indication

SMITH AND THE PIRATE SCHOONER

of the lengths to which these miscreants allowed themselves to go. There are those who would do away with the too practical and unromantic steamship; there are those who would scrap the navies of the world; yet if all this were done we should soon find the seas become once more the happy sphere for pirates, and a recrudescence of robberies and cruelties would result. The person who is for ever *laudator temporis acti,* and while seeing nothing worthy of his praise except what he is pleased to call " the good old days," is the very individual who would have objected strongly to live in the insanitary houses of our forefathers, who would have protested most strongly against the inconveniencies of a protracted voyage in a sailing ship at the mercy of head winds, pirates and scurvy. It is too often that distance, coupled with a highly romantic temperament, which makes a page of black history appear with unwarranted attractiveness. In the story of the pirates there would be little to entertain us were we not able to feel that in this prosaic twentieth century we are at least free from this scourge of the sea.

CHAPTER XXIII

PLOT AND COUNTER-PLOT

ON the day following the incident of the above murder, Smith was busy on deck making a new gaff topsail for the schooner, when the cry came from the look out man, "A sail! A sail!" Well knowing that the Englishman was the most reliable of all his crew, the captain at once sent Smith aloft to scan the sea as the schooner was got under way.

Smith reported that the vessel in sight was a merchant brig, whereupon orders were given to go in pursuit. Ordered to return to the deck, the Englishman's advice was sought as to the best mode of fighting the brig in case she should resist. And while the schooner's pilot was occupied in taking the ship out to the open sea through the intricate channel, Smith was set to devise some suitable strategy. The pirate ship was not long in gaining on the brig, and, having come up to within a short distance, fired a gun and hoisted Spanish colours. This the brig answered by heaving-to and displaying the British ensign.

It should be mentioned that the brig rig was not confined to ships of the merchant service, but that the Royal Navy had similar vessels on its list. Let it be remembered that in those days of hemp and canvas there was not the smart distinction between a ship of war and a ship of commerce

PLOT AND COUNTER-PLOT

that there is to-day. No one in this present year of grace could possibly mistake a liner for a battleship, but a brig of the early nineteenth century might be naval or mercantile. Some of the merchantships carried guns for self-defence, and there was very little to distinguish them from the government vessels. And in those days the red ensign had not yet been entirely abandoned by the Navy to the use of merchant craft. Therefore we can well understand that when the schooner came near to this brig, the latter's painted ports and her smart figure-head caused the pirate to hesitate and to wonder whether this was not a man-of-war. If she were, then the contest would not be likely to favour the schooner.

But he was by no means certain, and being still a safe distance off, he ordered the foretopsail of his schooner to be laid aback and hove-to. By that time he was rather inclined to think the brig was after all a merchantman, and so, calling Smith, he informed him of the intention to send a boat to board her under the Englishman's directions. This announcement greatly alarmed the latter, and he pointed out that should he be captured it would be an ignominious death for a British sailor. As usual when any of his orders were likely to be disobeyed, the pirate became furiously incensed. "And what are you, sir," he taunted, "that you should not suffer as well as myself? The schooner shall never be captured: for when I can no longer defend her, I shall blow her up. If you do not instantly go," he threatened, "I will shoot you."

Smith knew that the pirate was a man who used no idle threats, and yet for an English sailor to attack an English ship was an unthinkable proposition. "You may shoot me if you please," was his brave answer, "but I will not commit an act that might subject me and my family to

PLOT AND COUNTER-PLOT

disgrace." The pirate now realised that Smith was as determined as he, and resort must be made to the measures which had been already employed so profitably. He therefore commanded his crew to blindfold Smith, to have him taken forward, and told the man himself to prepare for death. After a time the pirate came to Smith and asked him if he were now ready for death. "Yes," answered the man courageously and firmly. No sooner had this word been uttered than a sharp volley of musketry rang out.

But Smith was not shot: the captain's intention had been merely to strike terror into his brave heart. It was a great trial to his nerves, but the man never flinched from his resolution. The pirate, knowing how invaluable Smith had become to the efficient working of the ship, was reluctant to lose him, but for all that he was determined to break his independent spirit. Coming up to him after the firing of the volley, he inquired of the Englishman as to whether he were not seriously wounded. In answering in the negative, Smith begged that if it was the captain's intention to destroy him he would not trifle with him. "Death I prefer to disgrace," said he, but the pirate was adamant. The next command was to lash Smith to the mainmast and to remove the bandage from his eyes. The captain himself could be seen cutting up a number of cartridges, and the powder he placed around Smith by his feet on deck. A train was laid, and then the ship's cook was ordered to light a match and send it aft. Once more the pirate gave Smith a chance, but again the firm answer was returned.

A terrific explosion ensued, flames leapt into the air and encircled the man who preferred death to dishonour. Up and up blazed the fire, and with his hands pinioned he could do nothing to relieve himself of his sufferings. His cries of pain were met with ridicule, and the captain tauntingly and,

PLOT AND COUNTER-PLOT

like the veritable bully that he was, inquired of him, "Will you *now* obey me?" But there is a limit to human suffering, though many a man both before and after that incident has endured the flame to the end. It is in nowise a disgrace if Smith in his excruciating agony at length yielded to the pirate, and at length, acquiescence being extorted by the vilest form of torture, Smith gave in and was ordered to be released.

There are few acts which a virile man, and especially a sailor, hates more than to faint. And yet so grievous had been his sufferings that the Englishman promptly lost consciousness. Some of the crew carried him down below, and when he came to he found himself stretched on a mattress in the cabin with a racking pain that gave him no respite. In his frenzy and delirium he meditated self-destruction, and begged the steward to lend him his knife for a moment. He, however, like the sneaking cur that was so characteristic of this Dago crew, straightway went to inform the captain, who came below in another of his furious tempers. "You want to kill yourself, young man, I understand," was his salutation. "But I do not mean that you should die yet. I shall blow you up again, for I see it is the only way to make you obey me." But happily the threat was not immediately put into execution. Frankly, it was the intention of the pirate that his most useful man should regain his health as quickly as possible.

Smith's wounds were dressed, and the cook, who was the one man who seemed to have any sympathy, made Smith's bed for him. The latter was in great pain but was able to converse. He learned that by now the schooner had returned to her anchorage, for the pirate had eventually been so convinced that the brig was a man-of-war, and that Smith had intended to decoy the corsair into

PLOT AND COUNTER-PLOT

the hands of the British, that an attack on the brig had been deemed inadvisable, so immediately after Smith had been taken below the schooner had headed for harbour. The cook, at least, had the courage of his convictions, and openly expressed his opinion of the pirate captain as a man of the worst character, adding that the latter had already killed over twenty people with his own hand.

Meanwhile, the master of a coasting schooner who had entered the harbour brought news that the *Zephyr* had arrived at Havannah, and announced the circumstances of her capture by the schooner. The pirate captain, on the receipt of this intelligence, and remembering that he had admonished Lumsden not to call at Havannah, was beside himself with rage. Rushing into the cabin where the sick man lay, he exclaimed to Smith, "See what dependence can be placed on your countrymen. That old rascal has gone to the Havannah and broken a solemn promise. But this will be a lesson to me not to trust the English again, for I now find them as treacherous as the Americans. He thinks," proceeded the pirate with increasing anger, "he is out of my reach: but mark me, if he remains a few days longer at the Havannah, he shall never live to see England. I have three or four already on the watch to assassinate him." And the pirate usually carried out his threats of vengeance.

That same evening, while the crew were at their evening meal, accompanied by the usual carousing and guitar-playing, the merriment was suddenly brought to a halt by the sound of approaching oars. Instantly the men were sent to quarters, and every man stood in readiness to open fire. The boat was hailed in Spanish, and a Spanish voice returned the hail. The oarsmen were allowed to come alongside, and informed the captain that some more of the

PLOT AND COUNTER-PLOT

original members of the crew, who were accomplices of the man that had been accused of plotting, had now arrived and were prepared to revenge the deaths of those men whom the captain had killed in the creek as already narrated.

Now it should be mentioned at once that, following out his threat to have Lumsden assassinated, the pirate captain had already sent at least one man, whose name was Stromeda, overland to Havannah. This man was to procure a horse and to hurry to the port so that he might arrive before the *Zephyr* had cleared. This intention had reached the ears of the late members of the pirate's crew, and they in turn vowed, as a means of partially revenging themselves, to kill the man now on his way to Havannah. The story is indeed varied by so much plotting and counter-plot that it is not easy to unravel the main narrative. However, the receipt of this news caused great consternation among the schooner's crew, and to show how little, for their own part, they sympathised with any mutineers, ten of the ship's company now volunteered to go ashore to protect the man hurrying towards Havannah. The captain thoroughly approved of the suggestion, and well-supplied with arms and ammunition the party set forth. The oars dug into the water and the boat advanced to the shore.

About midnight the boat returned to the schooner, and the captain was informed that on the beach they had met a servant despatched post haste from the magistrate whom we have already mentioned as the father of Seraphina. This gentleman sent information that Stromeda was already a prisoner and about to be put to death. The captain was further informed that on hearing this news the men from the schooner had taken a circuitous route

PLOT AND COUNTER-PLOT

through the wood, had eluded the scouts of the mutinous gang that were seeking to kill Stromeda, and had surprised four of this gang while busy under a tree playing cards and drinking. These four men they had captured, and had next proceeded to the magistrate's house, into which they had fired their muskets through the doors and windows, and discharged their blunderbusses. The precise object of this action was difficult to ascertain, unless they had expected that other mutineers were there hiding, and they had — quite unintentionally — wounded the magistrate. But they found Stromeda lying bound hand and foot and, having released him, the latter was able to resume his journey to Havannah. It was found that two of the mutineers' party had been killed, two more were taken prisoners, and two others acting as scouts had escaped after wounding one of the schooner's crew.

Smith was approaching convalescence, but he was yet far from recovered. All the time that he had been lying on his bed of sickness many a thought had passed through his mind, many a longing to escape from this life as an involuntary pirate. Many times, too, he had thought of Seraphina and of her promise that if she could assist his escape she would fly with him to England. The accident to the magistrate was now the means of Smith having opportunity to see Seraphina once again. Were the circumstance not true and actual, one would have called the incident a rather far-fetched coincidence. But I have already emphasised the fact that this is no fiction. It was policy for the pirate captain and the magistrate to render every assistance to each other. Their aims and ambitions were in many respects identical. Therefore, on learning of the latter's injury, Smith—still supposed to possess a unique medical ability—was sent to dress the magistrate's wounds.

PLOT AND COUNTER-PLOT

The Englishman himself had not yet recovered from his own injuries, so reclining on a mattress with one of the ship's hatches underneath, he was transferred to a boat and rowed ashore. No time had been wasted, for it was now only 2 a.m. For most of three miles Smith was carried on the back of a horse through a forest until they arrived at the house of the magistrate. Having been carried into the house, the first sight to greet him was Seraphina, who, rushing to his embrace, cried, "Take me, for they have just killed my father." With this announcement she burst into tears. Smith was taken to the room where the magistrate was lying, attended by the latter's wife. "Oh, my dear mother," exclaimed Seraphina, "this is the good Englishman who has come to cure my father."

For in spite of the lady's lack of logic, the magistrate was not wounded mortally. Lying stretched out on his bed covered with blood he presented a sorry spectacle none the less. Lying on another bed was another man who had also been wounded during the same incident. It was seen that the magistrate's arm had been fractured by a ball which had passed through his shoulder and lodged in his arm. With no little skill Smith succeeded in extracting this ball and then proceeded to bind up the wound. Exhausted with his labours, Smith was afterwards allowed to recline in another room, and Seraphina, full of gratitude, came to attend on him. It had been some time since their first meeting, and the unfortunate accident to the magistrate had thus brought them together once again. On many an occasion Smith, during the period intervening, had been planning some means of escape, and now away from the schooner he was able to relate the experiences through which he had recently passed. He reminded the lady of her promise and her affection, to which she replied in terms which left no

PLOT AND COUNTER-PLOT

possible doubt in Smith's mind. "I have resolved," she answered, "to accompany you, and will remove every obstacle in the best way I can: but caution is necessary. You must therefore be patient."

A little later and the time came for Smith to be carried down by the pirates to the beach. Night had vanished and it was now broad daylight. Arrived back on the schooner, Smith found that this was not to be the last of such visits, as the pirate captain regularly sent him ashore to heal the magistrate's wounds on other occasions. On each of these visits Smith was able to obtain interviews with Seraphina, and to advance further their plans for flight. She had made every preparation, she said, to escape to England in his company. "I have arranged all," she went on. "The guide is in readiness, and it only remains for us to fix the time and find the opportunity." Many schemes were proposed and as many rejected, until at length it was agreed that Smith should come over late in the second evening under the pretence of performing some essential surgical operation on the magistrate. It was resolved that in the meantime she should have the horses and guide waiting a short distance away.

The best laid schemes of lovers, however, sometimes work out badly. For the guide proved to be treacherous, informed Seraphina's father and mother, and had it not been for the consummate skill of Seraphina herself in turning this accusation against the accuser, serious complications would have ensued. As it was, nothing worse happened than the loss of the fifty dollars with which the guide had been paid in advance. But on board the schooner the pirate captain was beginning to chafe a little at the magistrate's continued illness, and declared that as soon as Smith's services could possibly be dispensed with the

PLOT AND COUNTER-PLOT

Englishman was to be put to death: for there was a possibility that if he escaped, his knowledge, which he had now obtained of the channels through the dangerous reefs, would enable any English man-of-war to find her way into the harbour of the pirate. The captain's suspicions of a plot for Smith's escape had begun to take definite shape, and henceforth he resolved that, even if it were necessary for the magistrate to be attended by Smith, the former should, in the future be brought off to the schooner instead of Smith going ashore.

Stromeda, who had been able to reach Havannah in safety and to return to the schooner, came back with tidings which depressed the pirate captain. He had done his best to carry out the work of assassination, but, unfortunately for him, the brig, with Lumsden on board, had already left Havannah before Stromeda had reached there. So life on the pirate ship returned to its normal state. Smith was regaining his strength, but he had not lost anything of his intention to escape if chance should present itself. One day, whilst at anchor, a sail was descried in the offing, and the captain made her out to be an English brig with full quarters and the familiar white streak which was so much favoured in those days. The schooner was got under way and the deck cleared for action. Meanwhile, the gunner informed Smith that there were not enough cartridges made up for a long action in case the stranger should keep up a resistance, so the Englishman set to work to make some more. Before this had been done a second English brig was seen.

As the schooner continued to chase the first of these craft, which took not the slightest notice of the corsair although the latter fired several guns and hoisted American colours, the captain was fuming with rage. The chase kept

PLOT AND COUNTER-PLOT

on until the schooner's long gun was shotted and fired. This at last produced the desired effect and the brig hove-to. The schooner then hauled down the American colours which the pirate had hoisted, and showed a red flag in their place. A boat was lowered from the schooner, six armed men, a pilot, and Smith being sent away in her, for the latter had no thoughts again of resisting. But Smith was strictly enjoined to hold no conversation with the brig's crew or captain, and the pilot was instructed to throw the brig's skipper overboard, then tack the craft towards the shore and send Smith back to the schooner. However, Smith persuaded the pilot to disobey that mandate. On reaching the brig, the latter's captain met the pirates at the gangway, and inquired who they were, to which question nothing but an evasive answer was given. The brig was tacked towards the land and then, the corsair firing a musket, Smith was ordered to tell the captain and crew to get in a boat and proceed on board the schooner.

CHAPTER XXIV

CHANCE AND CIRCUMSTANCE

THE brig's skipper had been eyeing Smith for some time and now claimed acquaintance; but although his face was familar to Smith he could not guess the former's name. It surprised the brig's captain to be told this was a pirate ship, and on reaching the corsair's deck and being asked in a rough tone for his name, Smith heard the name "Cooke," and then recollected that he was slightly acquainted with the mariner. With more than a little tact he now claimed Cooke as his cousin, and begged the pirate that he would not maltreat him. In this request Smith succeeded, on condition that Cooke gave information as to what amount of money and cargo the brig had on board. Thereupon the man handed Smith the bills of lading, from which it was seen that the ship carried nothing but rum.

Cooke was questioned as to the other brig still in sight, and replied that she was either a transport with troops on board, or else she was the brig *Vittoria* from Black River, Jamaica. He thought more probably she was the former, but, on taking another look at her, changed his opinion in favour of the *Vittoria*. Chase was therefore given. Now the name of Cooke's ship was the *Industry*, and her crew were at once employed on board the schooner, and ordered to the corsair's guns. Rapidly the *Vittoria*

CHANCE AND CIRCUMSTANCE

was overhauled, and now the long gun was fired across her bows, which the brig answered by hoisting her colours and backing her mainyard. Smith and a pilot were sent aboard her, the brig's officers and part of her crew were as before sent off to the schooner, and the newest capture was steered to follow the corsair as she ran into the land near Cape Blanco.

But a change in the weather came, and instead of the clear, bright atmosphere, there followed a dense haze with rain. There was for a time almost a panic on the prize as the breeze freshened and the ship sped on: for suddenly, immediately astern out of the mist, appeared another schooner coming up fast and in the wake of the corsair. The man at the wheel was a bad steersman and sheered the vessel about a good deal. As the wind was free, steering-sails were set by the pilot's instructions in order to get away from the pursuer. One of the pirate's crew was pacing the deck with rage and in a state of nervousness lest the stranger should be a-man-of-war. He cursed the steersman for his bad helmsmanship, and this only made the sailor more confused and to steer a more erratic course than before. The corsair therefore turned round upon Smith and swore that if the latter did not make the helmsman handle the ship better he would take his knife and kill the Englishman. Smith accordingly did what he could, and later on in the day, as the weather fined down, the stranger was seen, with great relief to the pirate, to be no ship of war. Indeed, it was chiefly the corsair's bad helmsmanship which made it seem that any chase was occurring.

Every hour Smith's hopes for escape were being accentuated by a treatment that was barely endurable. One of the projects that now arose in his mind was a daring scheme, embracing the intention of killing the pilot and the

CHANCE AND CIRCUMSTANCE

other members of the schooner's crew and then take the ship to New Orleans. To have cheated the schooner's captain of the *Vittoria* would have been a fine thing, for the rest of the brig's crew would certainly have assisted Smith. However, the corsair's skipper was far too wide awake for any game of that sort, and at dusk the corsair's gunner was sent aboard the *Vittoria* while Smith was ordered back to the schooner, the prisoners were sent below into the hold and sentries placed on the hatchways, making escape impossible. All three ships had come to anchor outside the reef, consisting of the corsair, the *Industry* and the *Vittoria*. But later on Captain Cooke was permitted to get the *Industry* under way, as her cargo of rum was not deemed worth the corsair's attention. The *Vittoria* and the schooner, however, proceeded towards Rio O'Media, for the *Vittoria's* cargo of coffee was distinctly worth having.

The schooner was certainly no dull sailer, and on the way she outran the *Vittoria* by a long distance and soon reached her port. Hour after hour went by, and as the *Vittoria* had not arrived the next morning, the pirate began to be anxious. A few hours later a boat was seen rowing towards the schooner, containing that portion of the pirate's crew that had been left aboard the *Vittoria*, so it was then presumed on board the schooner that the brig had been recaptured and then abandoned. But what had happened was that, on sighting again the ship seen the day before (which had been supposed to be a man-of-war), they had become panic-stricken, and, fearful of being captured prisoners, had preferred to run the *Vittoria* on to the reef and abandon her.[1] The reader will rightly imagine

---

[1] Captain Hearn, the *Vittoria's* master, and his crew had also left the ship at the time of her abandonment, and were subsequently picked up by the *Industry*, whose master presently put them on board a British man-of-war.

CHANCE AND CIRCUMSTANCE

that this information did not please the choleric corsair. But a little later on the *Vittoria* was lightened of her cargo, floated off the reef, and taken into Rio Medias, where also the pirate schooner arrived.

There is reason to believe that the British Admiralty was somewhat remiss in those days in their duty of policing the seas of the West Indies, having regard to the number of pirates which were known to harass British shipping. It even became a joke among the pirates, who would laughingly remark that naval officers preferred to spend their time amusing themselves at Havannah rather than seek out these wasps of the sea. However, as it happened, just when the *Vittoria* had been floated and taken into harbour, the Jamaica fleet was observed under sail, and once more the pirates were afflicted with "nerves." They therefore deemed it best to make the poor *Vittoria* resemble a wreck, and she was for a second time drawn up on to the outer edge of the reef. Smith, for his own part, was smarting under the British neglect which could tolerate this sort of thing. For at the head of the Jamaica fleet he could espy a British man-of-war, and although she was passing within a league of the *Vittoria* and the schooner, yet no notice was taken of either. The pirates waited till the fleet had passed on their way, and then once more the *Vittoria* was hauled off the reef and taken to a mudbank. A couple of coasting vessels arrived from Havannah and speedily unloaded into their holds the rest of the *Vittoria's* coffee, to the great profit of the schooner's captain.

A week later the schooner was joined in harbour by the arrival of another piratical schooner, whose skipper asserted that he had successfully plundered three British ships. No one who has any knowledge of the depredations that were

CHANCE AND CIRCUMSTANCE

carried on at this time can deny that the life of a sea-robber was, if exciting, at least remunerative to the interested parties. Like the old smugglers the work was carried on in a business-like manner, with capitalists at the back of the concern. The principle on which this systematic piracy was conducted may be described as follows. The corsair-captain would agree with the owner of the ship to put guns, muskets and everything else necessary on board the pirate ship. This would be done with secrecy at Havannah, and the owner was probably a supposedly respectable citizen. The ship would then put to sea in charge of a master on the pretence that she was bound for a neighbouring port. But when night came on she would let go anchor not many miles farther on and close to the shore. The corsair-captain would now row off to her, take over the command and send the master ashore. As soon as the latter reached Havannah the owner would complain to the governor that while his ship was at sea she was attacked by pirates and seized. The master would then be brought as a witness to prove this assertion, and the story would be generally believed. And as it was known beforehand that the naval authorities would not show much activity, the owner might content himself with the knowledge that his ship was away earning handsome dividends as a pirate without interference on the part of the Government ships.

But on rare occasions the latter did bestir themselves. And it happened that whilst Smith was captive on board the schooner in Rio Medias, news came that the Governor of Havannah was about to adopt hostile measures against the pirates. Lumsden's narrative had not improbably something to do with this, and it was reported that five gunboats were to come down inside the reef within the

CHANCE AND CIRCUMSTANCE

next five days, and the magistrate, Seraphina's father, was ordered to render every assistance in his power. It should be mentioned that although the magistrate had up till now been visiting the schooner to have his wounds dressed in the cabin by Smith, yet the latter was no longer allowed ashore. And now that the schooner's captain had been told by the magistrate this warning news of the approaching naval advent, the former deemed it best to put to sea and cruise in the vicinity of Cape St. Antonio for an indefinite period. The visits of the magistrate had become even more frequent, since, in acting out his double life, he must needs keep the corsair fully up to date regarding the movements of the gunboats. Seraphina also used to come on board with him, and was able to smuggle the intelligence to Smith that the plans for escape were being pressed forward and a new guide had been engaged.

The reader will like to know what became of the ill-starred *Vittoria* before we pass on. This fine ship, after being so badly used and ignominiously cast upon reef or mud-bank, was now taken in hand by the magistrate, who, fearing that her presence when the gunboats visited Rio Medias might provoke awkward questions, had her destroyed. But in the meantime a change was coming over the schooner, and something important was about to happen. First of all a certain amount of ill feeling began to arise, generated by the suspicion that the pirate captain had secreted large sums of money for himself in the sharing of the prizes. The ship was therefore cleft into two discordant parties, and the differences were only settled by the arrival from Havannah of the two owners of the ship or capitalists.

But still a more important incident occurred which has a potent influence on the rest of Smith's career. For at

CHANCE AND CIRCUMSTANCE

last the pirate captain himself fell ill and was attacked by fever. It is significant in everyday life that he who is a bully is also a coward, and this brutish man who had terrorised and tortured others was now positively frightened that he would die. The pirate therefore sent for Smith, and such was his fear of succumbing that he promised the Englishman his liberty if he should succeed in curing him. But Smith had lived too long aboard the schooner to have much trust in any promise from a man of that character, and he resolved to take whatever advantage he could of this illness to make his escape, so long hoped for and planned, a reality. With no little resource, then, the Englishman insisted on confining the pirate to his cabin. The next afternoon it chanced that a couple of fishermen came aboard and exchanged their cargo of fish for a consignment of spirits, and as the evening turned out wet and stormy they decided to remain on board. The time was spent very pleasantly with the pirate crew, and there was no lack of alcohol. As the evening went on every man became intoxicated, and so the watch was neglected. Smith realised that here at last was his grand opportunity.

The only watchful man aboard was the fever-stricken captain, so, in order to settle him, Smith, in preparing the sick man's mess of arrowroot, was careful this time to add a quantity of opiate. He also caused him to drink a liberal amount of wine. The result was that at midnight the captain was fast asleep. Quietly and carefully Smith crept up on deck. There was no one there—every one was deeply wrapt in slumber. There was not a sound anywhere except the roar of the sea, the howling of the wind in the rigging and the slatting of the rain against the ship. It was a dirty night, with not a star visible in the whole heaven but the angry storm-rent clouds scudding across the arc. Smith

CHANCE AND CIRCUMSTANCE

seized his bag, into which he had been careful to place his navigating instruments and some biscuit. Then once more he mounted the companion-ladder with the stealth of a cat and crept aft to the schooner's stern, where the fishermen's canoe was made fast. With his heart thumping inside him and in trepidation lest the slightest noise might betray him, he let himself down the painter into the canoe, cut the rope and, in order to avoid making a sound, allowed the craft to drift for some way with the current. When once so far away as to be beyond hearing, he got the little ship trimmed, set the sail and began to steer for where he imagined Havannah lay. Then, committing himself to God, he held on his course as the frail craft sped on through the darkness.

Next morning he found himself forty miles away from the schooner's anchorage, so already he had obtained a fair start. Throughout the whole day it blew from the south-west, which was a fair wind: and this was supremely fortunate, for in those regions a breeze from that point of the compass is rare. All day long and through the following night he was sailing, and never a ship, pirate or merchant or man-of-war came into sight. With many an anxious look over his shoulder he glanced astern to see if he were being followed, but no sail came into sight. There was a big sea running and it was an adventurous voyage for so small a packet, but Smith was no novice at seamanship. Night and day did he keep her at it, and then, on his second morning out, at six o'clock, he came running into the port of Havannah, very fatigued with the nervous and physical strain, but a free man again and safe.

As he was entering, his eyes fell on a schooner lying in the harbour. A man was walking the deck whose face Smith knew. Running alongside, he found it was a Captain

CHANCE AND CIRCUMSTANCE

Williams, with whom he had been acquainted in America some years before, so in a few minutes Smith was allowed to clamber on board, received a hearty welcome and was refreshed with food. Then he turned in for a sleep, and, feeling better thereafter, proceeded ashore. But he had not gone far when whom should he encounter but one of the crew belonging to the pirate. So soon as the latter saw Smith he rushed off and presently returned with a Spanish officer and a guard of soldiers, who promptly arrested Smith as a pirate! The reader will instantly realise that the schooner's captain had, on hearing of Smith's escape, taken measures to be avenged, and the distance could be covered from Rio Medias to Havannah as well by land as by sea: but after such an exciting passage in a small boat the meeting was sheer bad luck for the Englishman. The officer had Smith thrown into prison, and for two days he was kept in a dark dungeon and then brought before the judge. An interpreter named Paine was employed, who proved to be an unprincipled Irishman. He told Smith that Lumsden had already made every particular known, but at this juncture the harbour-master came forward and declared that Lumsden had stated that Smith was detained forcibly. The result was that, after a few weeks' detention, Smith was brought before the governor and subsequently surrendered to the British Admiral of the Jamaica station.

The rest of the story is quickly told. Had this been romance and not real life it should have ended by Smith meeting again with Seraphina, marrying her and living happily ever after. As a fact, he never saw that lady since the occasion when we last mentioned her. After being taken on board the flagship *Sybelle*, the ship eventually crossed the Atlantic and arrived off the Isle of Wight. He was

CHANCE AND CIRCUMSTANCE

now put into irons again and in the same ship continued his voyage to Deptford. Thence he was sent to London and examined before the magistrate of the Thames Police Court, who committed Smith to Newgate. On the 19th of December 1823, he was tried before the High Court of Admiralty on a charge of piracy, with "seizing the ship *Vittoria*, the property of Hymen Cohen and others, and stealing 636 barrels of coffee, value £5000, and 100 barrels of coffee, value £1000," and also with seizing the ship *Industry* on the high seas on 7th August 1822. Several seamen and other witnesses were called by the prosecution who deposed to the active part Smith had taken in their capture.

Smith, in his defence, detailed the compulsory nature of his piratical actions, and declared that he would never have partaken in the unlawful booty had it been within his choice. He recounted with much feeling the circumstances of his captivity and the tortures which he had been forced to endure. He also called about twenty witnesses, who testified to his bravery and humanity and excellent character generally. Among these were Captain Hayes, commander of the ship on which Smith had for some time been mate; also his brother, John Smith, an officer in the Royal Navy. But a Miss Sophia Knight, a prepossessing lady who stated that she had for some time past been engaged to marry Aaron Smith, went into the witness-box. This lady's charm of manner, together with her attacks of bitter weeping, which also affected the prisoner, so overcame the jury that they acquitted Smith, so that if he had been prevented from marrying Seraphina, he was now free to fall into the arms of Sophia.

Subsequently Smith went to sea again, but before doing so he wrote an account of his amazing adventures,

CHANCE AND CIRCUMSTANCE

to justify himself in the eyes of the world and to prove that he was no pirate. This narrative appeared in the year 1824, and it is from his own story that I have taken this account of a real romance among the pirates of the sea.

CHAPTER XXV

THE CRUISE OF THE *DEFENSOR DE PEDRO*

IN the year 1827 a vessel called the *Defensor de Pedro* was being fitted out at Buenos Ayres for a voyage to the coast of Africa, whence she intended to obtain slaves and then smuggle them across the Atlantic into America. This trade of fetching negroes from West Africa to America was no new departure. It had been in vogue ever since the sixteenth century, and our own Hawkyns, in the reign of Queen Elizabeth, had, to his discredit, been engaged in the same disgraceful traffic. Even though we are writing in this present instance of the early nineteenth century the practice had not been discarded. The South American Portuguese had at that time the privilege of dealing in slaves on a certain part of the African coast, but it was the intention of the captain of the *Defensor de Pedro* to run farther down so that he might purchase slaves at a much cheaper price.

Among the crew which he shipped from Buenos Ayres were the very scum of the Latin races. French, Spanish, Portuguese and others of the very worst character came aboard, and among them was one arch-fiend named Benito de Soto, who had been born in a small village near Corunna in Galicia. He had taken to the sea as his occupation, and so, in the year of which we are speaking, he had found him-

THE CRUISE OF

self in Buenos Ayres. The ship and her crew of desperadoes crossed the Atlantic and duly arrived off the African coast, where a large number of slaves were shipped. In order to complete his cargo the captain went ashore, leaving the mate in charge of the ship. This mate was a villain of the most pronounced type, a man of reckless and ungovernable temperament. Seeing that in de Soto there was a kindred spirit he proposed to the latter a plan for seizing the ship and making off with her. De Soto cordially agreed.

The suggestion was now put before the rest of the crew, and after going about the matter in a cautious manner they had so influenced twenty-two of them as to promise to join in the plan. But the other eighteen declined to be won over in spite of threats and persuasions. The mate began to despair, but de Soto, acting on his own initiative, collected all the arms of the ship together, summoned the conspirators and handed to each a brace of pistols and a cutlass, having armed himself in a similar manner. He then advanced to the head of the gang, drew his sword and declared the mate to be the head of the ship and the confederates part owners. And when the resisters still held out, he ordered the ship's boat to be hoisted out, and then dramatically pointed to the land and cried, "There is the African coast. This is our ship. One or other must be chosen by every man on board within five minutes."

Still declining to submit, the eighteen got into the boat one by one. Only one pair of oars had been allowed them, and as the ship was now at sea ten miles from the shore they would in any case have had a hard row. At the time when they left the ship the weather was calm and fine: but soon afterwards a heavy gale sprang up and there was the full force of the heavy Atlantic sea to be encountered, with night coming on, and there can be little doubt that the

THE *DEFENSOR DE PEDRO*

boat never reached land but foundered in the terrible seas. The *Defensor de Pedro*, with her sails well bellied to the wind, rolled and plunged through the dark night. Outside the gale howled through the rigging, and all the fiends of storm seemed to have been let loose that night. So it was below in the 'tween decks, where those other fiends, made drunk with too much alcohol, raised a violent uproar. Argument and quarrelling for the mastery followed, and de Soto was not long in obtaining the mastery. The mate could not resist and the jealousy of the former was impossible to be constrained.

So, determined to have what he desired, this avaricious de Soto in one act made his own position doubly secure. Hitherto he had aided the mate: now he was going to end all that, and as the mate lay in his drunken sleep, de Soto put a pistol to the man's head and shot away his life. His next step was to conciliate the crew. He pointed out to them that he had done this deed for their benefit, and declared that he was now their leader, and promised them every success provided they should obey him. And as a mob always is swayed by the strongest character, the crew hailed him as their captain with acclamation and unanimity. As to the slaves, these poor creatures were confined below under the hatches, and de Soto steered for the West Indies, where he sold them at a good price, reserving one of them, a boy, as his servant.

They then proceeded to act the lives of ordinary pirates, plundering many a fine vessel. But bad as other pirates were, there is little or nothing to choose between the atrocities of this present crew and those others of which the Moslem corsairs, already narrated, were guilty. De Soto and his associates were devils incarnate, and it is past the wit of man ever to imagine such a gang should have

THE CRUISE OF

been allowed to mix with human beings. I have no intention of detailing all their abominable doings, but in order to convey some idea of the lengths to which they could go, the following will be found sufficiently indicative. A certain American brig had the misfortune to fall into their hands. From her they took all the valuables they could lay their hands upon, and then they sent all the people below, fastened the hatches and set the brig on fire.

One man—a negro—they had allowed to be excepted. Him they kept on deck for the villainous pleasure of seeing the man tortured. Having hove-to, the pirate ship watched the flames tearing through the brig, bursting up the decks and penetrating everywhere. Now it climbed the rigging, and the monsters laughed with joy to see the poor nigger leaping from rope to rope till he climbed even to the masthead and presently fell therefrom exhausted into the roaring furnace which filled the hold. But that was not the one solitary monstrous act in their piratical exploits, and the following is really a story in itself.

Every one knows of the island called Ascension which stands lonely in the South Atlantic some eight or nine degrees below the Equator. In the year 1828 a British ship named the *Morning Star* was homeward bound from Ceylon. That was, of course, many days prior to the opening of the Suez Canal, and in the days of oak and hemp. The *Morning Star* carried a valuable cargo as well as some passengers, including a major and his wife, two civilians and twenty-five invalid soldiers on their way to England. Some of the latter had their wives also with them. On the 21st of February, when near the island of Ascension, the *Defensor de Pedro* sighted the *Morning Star*, the two vessels proceeding in opposite directions. As soon as de Soto espied her, at daybreak, he summoned all hands and

THE *DEFENSOR DE PEDRO*

prepared for attack, having altered his course to give chase. At first he supposed that she was a Frenchman, but one of his crew named Barbazan, of French nationality, assured him the ship was British. This delighted de Soto, for he guessed there would be the more booty.

When the yards had been squared and the pirate ship ran before the wind, the *Morning Star* was about six miles away. The *Defensor de Pedro* was a fast ship, but, as the other had now set a great deal more canvas, the pirate was a long time coming up to her. This made de Soto like a wild animal, pacing the deck, muttering growls and exhibiting the utmost restlessness. The delay was lashing him into a wild orgie of oaths and curses and ill temper. The crew, however, were in a savage delight at the prospect of being able to capture so rich a vessel as she appeared to be. Barbazan was busy clearing for action, and seeing that the men had breakfast and then were well armed. The captain's black servant came up to ask if he would have his morning cup of chocolate, when de Soto, in his grossly irritable impetuosity, struck the boy violently with his telescope. And if any of the crew interrupted him as he paced up and down there was trouble for that unhappy man.

But now the stun'sls were set and the *Defensor de Pedro* was adding to her speed so nicely that she was perceptibly gaining on the *Morning Star*. This relieved the great monster of a load of anxiety, so that he went below and feasted heartily on cold beef and chocolate, and then sat down to enjoy his cigar. More and more gained the pursuer on the chase, so a gun was fired, with the customary blank cartridge, and British colours hoisted. But the *Morning Star* still held on her way. This infuriated the pirate. " Shoot the long gun," he commanded, " and give

THE CRUISE OF

it her point-blank." This was done, but the shot fell short, and he leapt from the deck to curse his men for bungling. When nearly abreast of the British ship, de Soto aimed the gun himself and fired again, as the pirate ran up Colombian colours. The people on the *Morning Star* were in a state of terror by now, though her captain did his best to restore confidence. Although one of his men had been wounded, yet he kept a smart press of canvas on the ship and was resolved not to strike to a pirate. Unhappily the weeping women and the nervous passengers prevailed upon him to heave to, for the invalid soldiers could not have made much of a resistance. De Soto was shouting through his speaking-trumpet: "Lower your boat down this moment, and let your captain come on board with his papers."

One of the passengers volunteered to go on board the pirate, but when the villains learnt he was not the captain, they sent him back after ill-using him, threatening that if the captain did not instantly come aboard they would blow the *Morning Star* up. So the captain came off forthwith, bringing with him the second mate, three soldiers and a sailor boy. De Soto was awaiting them with a cutlass near the mainmast. The mate was sent to the forecastle, and both he and the captain were immediately slain. De Soto then dispatched half a dozen men, including Barbazan, to row off to the *Morning Star* and put every one to death : after that they were to sink her. The six men, each with a brace of pistols, a cutlass and a long knife, went aboard as told. Picture these blackguards with their Latin features degenerated and their brutal expressions positively thirsting for human blood, longing to deal death or misery right and left. Their garments consisted of a coarse cotton chequered jacket and trousers, while their heads were covered with red woollen caps, and broad canvas waistbelts held their knives

THE *DEFENSOR DE PEDRO*

and pistols. Strong and vicious, merciless and coarse, they came aboard the Indiaman as the shrieks from the terrified women rent the sea-air. As the pirates jumped on deck they slashed about on either side, swearing and slaying at the same time. Before long there was scarcely a man left in the ship alive, though a mere handful took refuge below, while the long gun on the pirate ship was ready aimed to blow the *Morning Star* to splinters if any opposition were shown.

When the ghastly work was finished on the deck, the rascals went about their work of pillaging. Money, plate, valuable jewels, nautical instruments, charts — everything that was of any value was taken on deck and sent across to the *Defensor*. Even the clothes from the passengers' backs were torn off. The culprits, then, after two hours' rummaging, sat down in the cabin and were served with viands and sparkling wine by a reluctant steward. Unhappily a small piece of broken glass chanced to be found in the wine, so one of the pirates in a fury grasped the trembling steward by the throat, holding a pointed knife to his face. For some time they went on drinking, until the loud voice of de Soto recalled them to the ship. They had no time now to kill every one (as had been their orders), but were content with boring holes in the hull and leaving the surviving people to drown like rats.

Darkness came down over the saddened *Morning Star*. She presented a sight of the most poignant misery. Her decks were slippery with human blood. Her masts had been sawn off by the miscreants who had but recently left her. Her rigging had been cut away and her holds and cabins had been pilfered and left in disorder. When at last the deathly stillness convinced the imprisoned victims that they were alone, the ladies succeeded in forcing their way out of the cabin, where they had been left im-

THE CRUISE OF

prisoned to drown. But down in the hold were the captive men, and the hatches had been secured by heavy baulks of timber. The women shouted to them that the pirates had left, and then, with their united efforts, the timber was moved away and the hatches opened. At last they were restored to life. But it was not to be for long, they surmised, as they found the ship had already six feet of water in her. By working hard at the pumps she was kept afloat, yet what was the good when there were no sails or spars and they must eventually succumb to the fatigue of pumping. With shattered nerves and wounded bodies they were now to encounter a lingering death. But, by an act of God, the very next day they fell in with a vessel which picked them up and brought them safely back to England, where the arrival of these survivors created great excitement. But we must now return to follow de Soto and his gang.

The *Defensor* had sailed far into the night before de Soto learned that the people in the *Morning Star* had not been done to death but were only drowning. He raged like an infuriated monster robbed of its prey, cursed Barbazan and threatened his men with death. And even now he decided to put back and look for the *Morning Star*. He wanted to make quite sure they were dead, and after cruising about some time, as he could see no trace of her he concluded that she had already sunk to the depths below.

Thus gratified he headed for Europe, and on the way plundered and sunk a brig, murdering the entire crew, with the exception of one man, whom he brought aboard so that he might pilot them to Corunna, of which the stranger had special expert knowledge. And as soon as they came within near sight of the port the pirate came up to him as

THE *DEFENSOR DE PEDRO*

the latter steered and addressed him thus: "My friend, is this the harbour of Corunna?" "Yes," said the other. De Soto regarded him for a moment. "Then," said he, "you have done your duty well, and I am obliged to you for your services." And with that he drew his pistol and shot him dead. Then, flinging his still warm body over the ship's side, he took the steering himself and brought his ship into Corunna after her long and wicked voyage.

But the story is not yet complete. Hitherto the ungodly have prospered: now it is their turn to suffer. After de Soto had obtained ship's papers in a false name, after he had made a brief sojourn to sell most of his booty, he set sail again for Cadiz, where he hoped to be able to market the remainder of his spoil. It was not to be a long voyage: just down the coast, round Cape St. Vincent and so to his destination. He carried a fair wind all the way, too, until he was quite within sight of the neighbouring coast-line. But as night was approaching and he wanted daylight to go to his anchorage, he hove-to till the dawn should return. But during the night the wind backed to the westward and before long it was blowing the full force of a gale, making Cadiz a lee shore and the whole drift of the Atlantic to send in a cruel sea. De Soto luffed his ship all he could, so as to clear a point that stretched out from the shore. But all the time he was close-hauled trying to get to windward, his ship was making a lot of leeway, and he found it impossible to claw off from the land.

The weather got from bad to worse and the night was as black as a nigger's head. To windward the howling gale, to leeward the sound of the breakers, and over everything the impending doom of ship at the mercy of the wind. It was only a question of time now: the end was certain. And the *Defensor* struck the ground in the shallows with a

THE CRUISE OF

dull, sickening thud. For a moment she drifted a little nearer to the shore on the top of a succeeding wave, and then down she bumped harder than ever as her crew momentarily expected her back to be broken in twain. Aloft there was a miserable flapping of canvas and loose gear: on deck below, the men who had bullied others were now themselves craven cowards. At last their own destiny in this dark wild night had come. So it seemed.

But by Providential indulgence they were allowed to remain together all night in the wrecked ship: and in the morning they were able to row ashore. No other thought had de Soto now than to sell the wreck to the highest bidder, and to purchase another craft to renew their piratical endeavours. As the night and winds had passed, so had their own fears and good resolutions, and every member of the crew was ready to go afloat again with de Soto in a new ship, if they could obtain what they wanted. They therefore proceeded to Cadiz, and presenting themselves to the authorities, Soto pretended that they were poor shipwrecked mariners, that the captain had perished and that he himself was mate. The yarn was accepted with sympathy. As to the wreck she was sold for the sum of £350, or, to be more accurate, the contract had been signed for that amount. But just then, fortunately, the last act of the drama began and the plot took a new and unexpected turn. There were some inconsistencies in the accounts of the pirates' stories, so the money was not paid and six of the men were arrested on suspicion. De Soto and one of the crew became alarmed and fled from Cadiz, arriving at the neutral ground. Six others got right away.

The reader, in spite of his natural resentment of de Soto's character, cannot but admire the amazing ingenuity of the fellow and the consummate ease with which he could

THE *DEFENSOR DE PEDRO*

always invent some new stratagem to suit his change of fortunes, and now once more the pirate had to set his wits to work. He carried with him a letter of credit from Cadiz, and he wished to get into Gibraltar in order to obtain money. His companion decided not to attempt such a risky proposition and so escaped the fate which was de Soto's. By means of a false pass, de Soto obtained admission into the garrison and then took up his abode in a certain low tavern, where he remained a few weeks, pretending to the innkeeper that he had come to Gibraltar on his way to Cadiz from Malaga, and was waiting for a friend. He dressed expensively and seemed quite happy.

But after a while he was arrested and brought to court. There was plenty of evidence against him, and the pocketbook which had belonged to the captain of the *Morning Star*, together with certain other articles taken from that ship, were proved to have been found in de Soto's room in the tavern. Furthermore, that black boy whom he had retained from another ship, as narrated, and had been cruelly treated by de Soto, now came forward as a witness, and thus the chain of evidence was gradually completed to convict the lawless tyrant. The governor passed the sentence of death, and right up till the day of the execution the culprit still protested his innocence. But at length he was at the last moved to repentance, and if there is much to say against the man there is to be added—that in his final hour he showed amazing courage and played the man, even assisting his executioners in adjusting the halter.

In the life of such a man as de Soto there is little that can rouse one to enthusiasm. The romance of the days of piracy becomes clouded over by the horrible cruelties and unmerciful slaughter which accompanied the robberies by

THE *DEFENSOR DE PEDRO*

sea. Stripped of all its excitement and the glamour of brave deeds, such a story as that of this Dago is just one long account of avarice and its attainment. Neither Divine nor human laws, neither loyalty to his superior officers nor respect for his fellow-men—nothing did de Soto allow to stand in his way to fulfil his ambition. He plotted and schemed, he murdered and he pillaged, he fabricated falsehoods, and he collected fabulous wealth. But when the net benefit to himself is reckoned up, the reader may naturally ask the question *cui bono?* Whom did it benefit? Certainly not himself and certainly not his crew. It provided a life of excitement and debauchery: it caused misery and suffering to some and death to others. That, in a word, was the grand total of a wasted life. The pity of it is that all this wild energy, this daring, this ingenuity, this brilliant seamanship and fighting capability might not have been used to some better and more lasting purpose.

CHAPTER XXVI

THE PIRATES OF BORNEO

WE have seen already during the preceding chapters that there have been certain geographical spheres where piracy has been especially prevalent and persistent. Although, of course, there are some exceptions, yet as a rule the most suitable area is either at some spot where both sides of the land converge to make straits, such as Gibraltar or the entrance to the Red Sea, or in certain parts of the West Indies; or the area is an archipelago, where the multiplicity of islands can be used with advantage for convenient lurking-places. Of this we have excellent examples in the Ægean and Caribbean Seas, each of which has been a notorious haunt for pirates.

And now we come to yet another territory which for both of these separate reasons has been even in our own generation a well-known sphere of murder and robbery at sea. If you look at a chart or map of the Malay Archipelago, you will see how land nearly meets land at the Straits of Malacca, so that ships passing between Eastern and Western ports on the great highway become focused into one comparatively small area as at the Straits of Gibraltar, thus enabling the pirates to concentrate their attention on one particular spot with every assurance of reaping their cruel harvest. But also, where the three great seas, the

THE PIRATES OF BORNEO

Indian Ocean, the China Sea and the mighty Pacific meet, just to the north of the Australian continent you have here a perfect maze of islands, which, in the absence of any firm authority backed by adequate sea-power, are ready-made nests for the propagation of piracy and all which that term suggests.

Whatever else a pirate was, he was a master of strategy, not by education but by instinct. And the situation of the Malay Peninsula, Sumatra, Java and Borneo almost spells piracy, even if we were to be told that never in history had such a crime been hereabout perpetrated. The Malays were naturally sea-rovers by habit and instinct, and their native craft—the swift-flying prahu—was particularly suited for darting out from a snug lurking-place to harass the more cumbrous and slower merchant ship as she was passing over the sea. It was impossible to confine their energies to fishing or trading. Naturally warlike and roving, the convenient geographical position where they lived afforded them every opportunity of fulfilling their hearts' desire. Matters have altered a good deal during the last fifty or sixty years, but about the middle of the last century, before the modern steamship liner had conquered the world's trade-routes, no merchantman could voyage with safety through the region of which we are speaking. Simultaneously with the Malays there were the Dyaks of the north-west corner of the island of Borneo, who numbered thousands of warriors. These men, using spears and swords, were induced and trained by the Malays during the eighteenth century to become wily pirates too. These Dyaks became expert seamen with the facilities at their disposal, and built a kind of prahu for their use called a bangkong. Joining their forces with the Malays they were able to get together a formidable fleet of a hundred

THE PIRATES OF BORNEO

or more of these craft, with which they swept the seas of any ships that might come their way, laying waste the shores of Borneo and carrying off crews as captives into slavery just as had been done by the Moslem corsairs.

One of the chief characteristics of these Dyaks was their passion for collecting human heads. It is difficult for a civilised person to understand this propensity, but headhunting was not merely a sport, but the accumulation of heads was looked upon as the essential possessions of manhood. Now among all the romance which centres round the splendid work which has been done in far-off countries by Englishmen as rulers and governors, as administrators and reformers, few stories are more interesting than that of the late Sir James Brooke, first Rajah of Sarawak, in the island of Borneo. Under his rule and that of his successor, Sir Charles Brooke, this barbarous custom of head-hunting, as well as the persistent piracies, have been happily put down. And in the small space which is at my disposal I propose now to give some idea of the kind of evil which had to be tackled.

In the 'forties of the nineteenth century the English Navy was sent to act against the Malays and Dyaks of Sarebas, and it is to the interesting account written by Captain the Hon. Henry Keppel, R.N., that I am largely indebted for the following details. Although the Rajah of Sarawak had done much to banish piracy, yet he found that an intrigue was on foot to revive this crime. So in the year 1849 we find a strong force under Captain Arthur Farquhar, R.N., consisting of H.M. sloop *Royalist*, the honourable East India Company's armed steamship *Nemesis*, H.M. steam tender *Ranee*, together with a flotilla made up of the gig, pinnace and cutter of H.M.S. *Albatross*. These craft were fully armed and manned by 103 officers

THE PIRATES OF BORNEO

and men. The *Albatross* had been sent by the British Government from the China station, and while this was being done Sir James Brooke was making every preparation for the forthcoming expedition.

On the 24th of July the s.s. *Nemesis*, together with the *Royalist* and the *Ranee*, started inland. Owing to her size and draught, the *Albatross* was left behind at the entrance to the river Sarawak. Following astern of the other craft were towed three of the *Albatross*' boats, three from the *Nemesis* and the *Royalist*'s cutter. In addition to these there were also brought eighteen native craft, the Rajah being in his new prahu. A little later and this expedition was also joined by the Orang Kaya of Lundu with 300 men in prahus of various sizes: and presently, too, the Linga Dyaks and others, about 800 strong, came with their help, so that eventually there were altogether 2500 men ready and keen to meet the pirates.

The reader will wish to know, before we proceed further, some details concerning the prahu. She is one of the fastest vessels in the world propelled by sail. Measuring no less than 90 feet, with about 9 feet beam, pulling about eighty oars in two tiers, she was manned by 100 men. Over the oarsmen was a light, strong flat roof of thin strips of bamboo covered with matting to protect the ammunition and provisions from the rain and also to serve as a platform from which she could fire the rifles or hurl spears. The rowers used to sit cross-legged on a shelf, and they could get a wonderful speed on to their craft. Six swivel guns were mounted on either side and thirty rifles were also carried, so that one can quite easily imagine that such a craft, with a score more like her, could inflict almost any harm they liked on a trading ship becalmed. The Dyak bangkongs, which were very similar to these, drew very little

AN ATTACK ON MALAY PIRATE PRAHUS

The Malays were naturally sea-rovers by habit and instinct, and their native craft, the swift-flying prahu, was particularly suited for darting out from a snug lurking-place to harass the more cumbrous and slower merchant-ship.

THE PIRATES OF BORNEO

water, so were able to creep into shallow hiding-places. Propelled by their eighty paddles, these craft, with their overhanging bow and stern, were so noiseless in their approach and so stealthy in their movement, so easily capable of darting to and fro that no wonder they became a terror to all commercial shipping.

It was customary for these pirates when attacked to rush back up the river into the jungle rather than to stand out to sea. For they knew how to hide themselves in the thickets, and as to the prahu they could either conceal that by hauling her ashore or else destroy her. Very difficult, therefore, was the task of dealing with these artful fellows, and the wisdom of taking so many boats and craft similar to those of the enemy is quickly apparent. Sometimes the pirates would try to run out to sea when no other course was left, but this was rare. Very useful did the fast-pulling boats of the punitive expedition prove for keeping a look out and signalling the approach of the enemy. For now the expedition had arrived at the spot where they were to wait.

It was known that the pirates were coming along with 150 pranus and that they had the great chiefs of the Malays to help them. After capturing trading vessels loaded with sago and cotton goods they had come along the river with the strong flood-tide. Between them and the main body of the punitive expedition were the latter's scouts waiting anxiously in the darkness of the night to give the warning. Suddenly a rocket went hissing up into the sky and lit up the dark arc of heaven. This was the signal from the scouts that the enemy were approaching. They came on in two divisions, whilst the Rajah's fleet behind the scouts were guarding the breadth of the river. The hot tide was bringing the rival forces nearer and nearer, but as soon as the pirates, peering through the night, outlined the form of

THE PIRATES OF BORNEO

a steamer they began to be nervous, for here was a craft at last superior to their own. The first firing had taken place when they came in touch with the expedition's scouts in man-of-war's boats, and then the discharge of musketry became fiercer and fiercer, so that it was not long before the pirates, in spite of all their strength, were thrown utterly into confusion. During the fighting it was difficult to tell foe from friend, but the happy arrangement had been made of the expedition's boats burning blue lights. And what with these dotted about the dark river, what with the glare of the rockets, the cheers of the bluejackets, the discharge of musketry and the defiant yells of the pirate it was a most impressive night.

It was not long before the enemy realised that his chances were hopeless. No fewer than eighty bangkongs were run on shore, while some others tried to escape down the river and out to sea. Seventeen of the larger prahus, in avoiding a shoal, attempted to pass the steamer and so were destroyed forthwith. The pirates lost very heavily, whereas our casualties were but slight, though when bluejackets were humanely endeavouring to rescue pirates struggling in the water from drowning the rescuers were viciously attacked, as the half-drowned creatures could not comprehend this consideration for human life. When morning came there were found no fewer than sixty deserted prahus in addition to a quantity of débris on the beach. As many as 2500 of the enemy had hurriedly dashed their craft ashore and fled into the jungle. Our men had captured or destroyed 88 of this fleet, or over one-half of the 150 which had set out, and from 500 to 800 of the pirates had been killed. Our losses were nil and only a few men wounded in trying to prevent these men sinking with sword and shield still in their wicked hands. It had been a well-organised attack

THE PIRATES OF BORNEO

from our side and the spot just by the entrances of the rivers Kaluka and Sarebas had been well chosen. The enemy had been thoroughly terrified from first to last. As he had come up with the flood-tide and realised the strength of the expedition he had lost his senses completely and become obsessed with no other idea than to get out of it as quickly as he could.

So, having dealt piracy a very severe blow, the expedition spent a couple of days securing prisoners and destroying captured boats. Then on the 2nd of August the fleet proceeded up the Sarebas River and anchored near the entrance of the Paku branch. Here it became necessary, owing to the nature of the river, to leave the *Nemesis* and the heaviest prahus behind. But the lighter boats and the captured bangkongs continued the advance, the small steamer *Ranee* and the men-of-war's boats going on ahead. Astern came several hundred of the native boats all eager for plunder. But the rushing tide swept them all together in confusion, and meanwhile during this medley a tree branch overhanging the river got athwart the *Ranee* and swept away her funnel. Simultaneously she got aground forward, and her stern being free she was carried right across the river by the current.

Steam was let off in the usual manner, and this noise, so strange and awe-inspiring to the natives, caused them so much terror that some of them jumped into the water, others leapt into other boats, thus swamping them, while the remainder resigned themselves pathetically to their fate. It was a ludicrous sight, but comprehensible. As the enemy had felled so many trees into the water to bar the progress of the expedition it became necessary, before attempting further procedure, to send a party of Dyaks on land in order to clear away these obstacles. The rest of the

THE PIRATES OF BORNEO

journey was quite easy. The fleet anchored and took Paku, and having wooded the steamer with her necessary fuel, the expedition once more proceeded up the alligator-infested river till they came to the mouth of the Kanowit, up which no European had yet ascended.

It was now found impossible for the steamer to get farther, so only the lighter boats with their 2000 men now advanced, their instructions being to punish the guilty but to spare those who surrendered. Slow progress was made against a strong stream, and this had given the inhabitants time to realise that trouble was approaching. For it was presently discovered that they had hurriedly left, and before doing so had burnt down their farmhouses. But in the ruins of these were ample evidences of the amazing collections of human heads which these men had made. These Sakarrans had never expected that a big force of 2000 Malays and Dyaks, led by a European Rajah and a few English, would have penetrated a hundred miles into the interior. But as the expedition had taught them a salutary lesson it refrained from touching one of these natives, and presently the return journey was begun. Back this miscellaneous fleet went, with cotton fields, sugar-cane, and cocoa-nut trees growing on either hand, and with plenty of pigs and poultry in evidence.

Finally the expedition returned home in safety. It had been a great success and made a deep impression on the natives, not merely in respect of its display of strength but in its humane dealings with those who were alive. This latter characteristic caused especial surprise. The fines which were now levied were applied to reward the captors or prisoners who had been caught without being injured. Only a few years before this firm action no European merchant ship had ventured on the north-west coast of

THE PIRATES OF BORNEO

Borneo, and those which had previously risked coming had paid for their temerity. It was asserted by Lloyds that within a space of only a dozen years no fewer than thirty or forty square-rigged craft had been captured, plundered or in some way molested by these pirates, and the European crews murdered. But this successful expedition also had an indirect effect, for before long many piratical chiefs came to the Rajah and made a pledge that they would never engage in piracy again.

The admissions of these men sufficiently indicated the extent of the depredations. Within eight months, admitted one ex-pirate, three large fleets had sailed from the Sarebas on piratical cruises. Their object was to take plunder and heads on sea, and they made a point of attacking all they were likely to overcome. Chinese, Malay fishermen, merchants—it made no difference. These pirates, it was proved, did not engage in trade, but whenever they stood in need of money or slaves they went pirating. "We have no friends when at sea," remarked one of these corsairs on oath. They would attack towns and lay them waste simply for two motives—love of plunder and the desire to collect heads. As illustrative of their recognising no friends at sea, the following instance may here be cited. On a certain occasion a prahu was attacked off the coast by two other prahus. "Why are you attacking your friends?" inquired the first. The answer came quite candidly: "At home we make a distinction between friends and enemies, but at sea everybody we kill and plunder."

With such views on the subject and such deeply rooted bias towards piracy it was hardly to be expected that the neighbourhood would remain free from this nuisance for all time. By the year 1862 the pirates had become so daring that they attacked quite large craft. A Spanish

THE PIRATES OF BORNEO

steamer and gunboat had had some smart encounters, but they had sunk two prahus and their crews. They had also bombarded a pirate stronghold and rescued twenty-one Christian Indian natives as well as twelve Javanese Malays. And the Spanish steamer had run down fifteen more prahus, one after the other, on their way to Borneo.

And there is still preserved a copy of a letter written in that year by Rajah Brooke to say that on 27th May 1862, while lying at anchor in his steam yacht the *Rainbow*, a boat came alongside giving information that six large pirate craft were passing along the coast, having killed several people and taken many captives. Even this very boat which had brought the message had barely escaped. So the *Rainbow* and a gunboat were immediately prepared for action and steamed out over the bar, the Bishop of Labuan being on board at the time. At daylight one morning three of the enemy were discovered from the masthead seven or eight miles to seaward. Chase was now at once given and the prahus were seen to be crowded with men. It was now clearly their object to get ashore if possible before the *Rainbow* should get up with them. The leading craft actually did so succeed and ran herself on to the rocks at Kadwrong Point. The *Rainbow* stood as near inshore as she could, and while steaming in two fathoms the pirates fired on her from their muskets. This fire was now returned with interest, and after ten minutes' cannonade the survivors as usual disappeared into the jungle.

The *Rainbow* now attacked the other two boats, one of which she ran down. The other was captured and brought alongside full of men, women and children whom the pirates had taken as prisoners. These were brought on board and the wounded attended by the Bishop. From

THE PIRATES OF BORNEO

one boat alone there were taken one Spanish and five Dutch flags, which showed doubtless as many acts of piracy. Shortly after the remaining three pirate prahus were found at sea and eventually destroyed, though one of them made a most desperate fight, killing and wounding several of the *Rainbow's* complement, and they even continued to fight when in the water. The *Rainbow* took thirty on board, who were pinioned and placed in the hold. The poor captives were found to be nearly starved. The pirates had treated them most cruelly, having given them salt water to drink, and for the first few weeks had disabled them by beating their knees and elbow joints with bamboos.

Thus civilisation, good administration and a determination to oust these sea-robbers and murderers have to be thanked for doing a sound work not merely to individuals but to ships and commerce generally. If ever there were any men who may unquestionably be set down as universal enemies of the human race, certainly they are the brigands on shore and the pirates afloat.

CHAPTER XXVII

CRUISING AMONG CHINESE PIRATES

PERHAPS it will be a long time before the last of the Chinese pirates can assuredly be said to have gone. We know too well that if a liner ever happens to get ashore in this neighbourhood she stands grave risk of being looted and losing some of her people by murder. Things have indubitably altered for the better, but in the 'sixties and 'seventies the coasts of China were infested with pirates, especially to the southward. At that time when so many fine tea-clippers and other sailing ships were passing and repassing full of such valuable cargoes, just prior to the time when the steamship was altering matters and the Suez Canal was about to be opened, there was what we may rightly call the grand period of Chinese piracy, and the following incidents were taken part in by Captain H. C. St. John, R.N., who was sent to keep these pests in check at this time. I wish to acknowledge my indebtedness to this officer's notes of these events which were subsequently published.

One day, whilst at anchor in his gunboat in Hong-Kong harbour, there happened to be lying close by a fine, large opium junk. She was armed with no less than a dozen 12- to 18-pounders and carried forty-five men. During the afternoon a number of passengers went aboard her, and at dusk she got under way and cleared out. But as soon as

CRUISING AMONG CHINESE PIRATES

she had reached the outer roads of Hong-Kong it fell a flat calm, so that she was compelled to anchor about 9 p.m. About midnight another large junk ran quietly alongside, and some of her crew jumped on board the opium craft. In a short space of time the pirate's crew had seized both passengers and crew of the Hong-Kong craft and placed them below hatches. The pirate then got under way and steered for the south side of Hong-Kong. On the way thither, soon after daylight, the unfortunate prisoners were one by one brought on deck by the pirates, and first their hands were tied behind their backs, then their feet were fastened together and they were then thrown overboard. This treatment happened to all—eighty-three of them—with the exception of one, a boy twelve years old. Him the pirates spared, as he would be useful for making their tea and preparing their opium pipes.

The pirates had taken this cargo of opium, for they knew how valuable it was and how easily sold it could be. They then made for their harbour, near to Macao, where they divided their spoil. Seven of them then took the boy with them and proceeded to Macao, from where they went by steamer, bound for Hong-Kong, a little farther on. During this steamer trip the captain of the vessel noticed that the youngster was in great distress and questioned him. In a few minutes the captain realised that among his passengers were seven pirates, and determined to have them arrested. So, instead of taking his steamer as usual alongside the jetty at Hong-Kong, he anchored in midstream and hailed the police-boat to come out to him. The latter arrived, and then the hundred odd Chinese passengers were lined up and the boy was told to pick out the seven pirates. This he succeeded in doing, and the police took them ashore and locked them up.

CRUISING AMONG CHINESE PIRATES

Now it happened that the evening previous to this some one else had arrived in Hong-Kong and told a similar story. This was one of the eighty-three who had been thought dead. For this fellow, on finding himself in the water, had managed, with a desperate struggle, to release his hands by slipping through the lashing which bound them. And then when he came up to the surface of the water he succeeded in releasing his feet. He was thus able to swim to the nearest island, and from there made his way to Hong-Kong in a fishing-boat. It was a true but remarkable story, and the evidence of the boy coming on the top of this made the case against the seven pirates so clear that they were tried at Hong-Kong, found guilty and subsequently hanged.

On another occasion this British gunboat was cruising up the coast on the look out for pirates, when, on passing a small island, two fishermen paddled off in a sampan and pointed out a couple of small junks that were standing out to sea. Knowing that as the wind was absent there could be no escape, the gunboat steamed quietly on. Presently about a dozen other smaller junks put off and opened fire on the two junks which had first been seen. But the gunboat now running alongside the latter captured them, took their crews on board prisoners and then steamed in towards the town and let go anchor. The local mandarin now came off and expressed his thanks for having captured these two junks and twenty-one men. The incident had caused tremendous delight, as the craft had been giving a great deal of trouble recently and no local junks had dared to come out. But what was surprising was that seven had not dared to tackle two larger than themselves! And yet it is said that the Chinese are no cowards.

I mentioned just now that this was the time of the

CRUISING AMONG CHINESE PIRATES

famous tea-clippers which used to make such marvellously fast voyages from China to London. Now one day, whilst one of these clippers was on her way down the China Sea she was becalmed. Shortly after, apparently bringing a faint breeze with them, appeared fifteen junks with their large sails. They opened fire on the helpless clipper from just within range, and everything looked as if the junk fleet would soon capture the clipper. But, as every one knows, these clipper ships were famous for two things—the beauty of their hulls and the enormous mountain of canvas which they could set. Consequently the combination of a fine-lined hull with a light and lofty sailspread could be used in a light air to give an advantage over the heavy junk with her equally heavy sails. And as the breeze now strengthened a little, the clipper was able by the narrowest of margins to draw right away and escape.

Captain St. John was now sent to capture these junks. After steaming through a lovely starlit night the gunboat arrived with the dawn by the first of the islands which fringe the coast-line just to the west of the Canton River. It was then noticed that there was one junk well inshore and some miles ahead. The weather was quite calm and her bat-winged sails were flapping uselessly in the ocean swell. Presently there were signs of activity observed, and a boat was launched from the junk with a dozen men who pulled for the shore as quickly as human muscles could impel the craft. But they were useless against the steam gunboat, which managed to cut in and arrest both boat and junk. The latter was then taken in tow by the gunboat, with twenty-four pirates on board, who were soon handed over to the governor of the nearest province; so that put an end to their activities for the present. And a curious thing was noticed when the junk was being

CRUISING AMONG CHINESE PIRATES

examined. It was seen that the sails of the craft had holes in them, and the shape of these suggested that they had been made as the result of somebody's cannonade. Later on it was learned that this was not originally a pirate junk but a trader which had the bad luck to be captured by Chinese pirates three months previously after killing the crew. Those in the gunboat remembered as they were approaching this junk that the pirates were busily heaving bags of something overboard as fast as they could. You may imagine with what emotions they discovered later that these were bags of dollars. The sum of £4000 had been found on board the junk when the pirates took her, and although they had done their best to throw as much overboard as they could, rather than see it fall into the hands of the British ship, there still remained about £2000 of this amount when the gunboat took her in tow. The prisoners were sent on to Canton and executed for their piracy, though seven were allowed to escape before Canton was reached.

In the year 1875 an English brigantine was sailing to the northward, past the Chinese coast, when, about a hundred miles from Hong-Kong, they were attacked by pirates who promptly killed the captain and ship's boy. The rest of the crew went aloft and remained on the top until the pirates below had finished ransacking the ship. After a terrible suspense, wondering who was to die next, the crew watched the Chinamen leave the ship and return to their junk. So the Englishmen came down from their lofty perch to the deck, and without further excitement they navigated their craft into port and gave information against the pirates. But it was not always an easy matter to locate these cunning creatures, who were as artful as they were cruel. But the following incident shows how

CRUISING AMONG CHINESE PIRATES

cleverly the English Navy could grapple with a difficult problem. In some respects the story is a kind of nautical detective tale and is well worth relating.

It happened one day that while the gunboat was coaling, information was brought to Captain St. John that a large fishing-junk, belonging to Hong-Kong, with her owner and his Chinese family on board, had been attacked by pirates whilst the innocent vessel had been engaged in her lawful fishing at sea. The owner had been sent adrift in a sampan, his junk taken from him, together with his three daughters. He was ordered to make his way as best he could to the shore and there collect 500 dollars from his friends if he wished to obtain his daughters' release. He was advised not to be too long about it as otherwise the girls would be put to death. The harassed Chinaman had got to land and at length came aboard the British gunboat.

So, after the latter had finished coaling, she got under way at dusk and made good progress towards the cluster of islands about thirty miles away from Hong-Kong; and now began a series of interesting events based on deductive and inductive reasoning to outwit Oriental cunning. Arrived at this island cluster the commander well knew that he was in the very centre of the favourite resort of pirates. The channel ran between the islands, and on either side were numerous little coves where the junks could easily withdraw and yet as easily get away again. Having reached this district before dawn, just as the darkness was sweeping away there was seen a junk moving cautiously in the shadows of the cliff towards the farther entrance. This was certainly suspicious, so the gunboat stood in, bided her time and presently caught the junk, although the latter's crew had escaped to the shore. It

CRUISING AMONG CHINESE PIRATES

was a great piece of luck to have lighted upon this craft in such a manner, for the Chinaman, whom the gunboat had brought with her, immediately recognised her as the very junk which had run off with his daughters.

The gunboat's voyage was now becoming exciting, and a little farther on she was passing another cove when another junk hove in sight. The gunboat went in pursuit, but the Chinamen, nervous for their lives, ran the junk ashore and her crew of twelve made off into the bushes. After some little effort the junk was re-launched from her sandy bed and got afloat again, and you may judge of the joy of the Chinaman on the gunboat when he realised that this was his own junk in which he was fishing when the pirates had come to attack him. So she also was now taken in tow. So far, so good. Both junks had been found and taken in tow by the gunboat, but even if the pirates were not likely to be captured, yet the fisherman's daughters had still to be found. Even the guns which had been taken by the pirates from the fishing craft were found, after a little searching, buried in the sand quite close to the junk.

So the gunboat proceeded along till she arrived at the head of a bay, where lay a town almost concealed by a woody point, and here the British craft let go anchor whilst her commander played very cleverly the part of detective. He began by bluntly demanding the deliverance of the three girls. This was met with blank astonishment. The townspeople pretended, with typical Oriental manner, that they knew nothing about the girls. They were completely innocent of all knowledge concerning them. This fervent assurance might possibly have convinced some Europeans, but Captain St. John was far too experienced in the ways of the crafty Chinee to believe a word they said. He had every reason to suppose that the girls were

CRUISING AMONG CHINESE PIRATES

in this town, near which he had found the two junks, and he was determined to obtain the object of his mission.

Therefore, having been met with this protestation of innocence, he insisted on the three headmen of the village being sent on board the gunboat. They came in their silk robes and, accompanied by a couple of bluejackets, proceeded to the man-of-war. Preparations were now made on the gunboat's deck for hanging the three Chinamen. A good deal of ostentatious activity was spent in passing a rope from each masthead and tying knots, arranging nooses suitable for the heads of these three men. The intention of the commander was to frighten the Chinamen into submission, for he was convinced they were lying. For a time these efforts had not the desired effect, and one at least of these three Orientals even laughed satirically at the arrangements. But when the nooses of rope were put over the head of each the effect was magical. So soon as the rope touched their yellow skin their manner was altered and their memories suddenly awoke from their untruthful stupor. Yes: the Chinamen now recollected that the girls were indeed in the village, and if only the commander would spare the lives of these three headmen the girls should be returned in safety. So directions were sent to the village, and before long the girls appeared on the beach, escorted by crowds. The three headmen were then exchanged for the three girls, and the gunboat once more got under way. The ship's company made them as comfortable as possible, wrapping them up in a sail for the night and feeding them with all the tea and jam which their Oriental palates delighted in. To the great joy of their father they were brought safely back to Hong-Kong, and the incident, thanks to Captain

CRUISING AMONG CHINESE PIRATES

St. John's clever stratagem and determination, had been brought to a happy issue.

The part which the British Navy has played in Chinese waters alone in putting down piracy has been considerable. Sometimes the efforts have had to be made against superior numbers, and only British pluck and cleverness could have brought about the results which followed. Such an occasion occurred when this same gunboat once rounded a headland in these seas, and, after opening up the channel, found no fewer than fifteen junks drawn up in line in such a manner as to command the centre of the channel with their guns. The navigation hereabouts was tricky, especially for a vessel drawing as much water as the gunboat. But she was taken full speed through the soft mud on to the north side, so that she kept all the junks end on and not broadside. This somewhat surprised the junks, who were still more amazed when the gunboat, with her guns out and ready loaded, dashed into the middle of them before ever a shot had been fired by either side. Indeed, so terrified were these Chinamen that they jumped overboard and swam from their craft to the shore, where they presently manned their land-batteries. But, before they had fired, the gunboat had come to anchor and sent a shot against them. This had the salutary effect of clearing the Chinamen from their new stronghold.

Then the English officer followed this up by landing the whole of his men, with the exception of three, plus the Chinese portion of his crew. He came ashore with his men some little distance below the position the Chinese pirates had taken up, as the ground was less unsuitable. His force consisted only of twenty bluejackets and marines all told. The enemy amounted to 300 or 500. Forming in single file, the English advanced towards the pirates, but a minute

CRUISING AMONG CHINESE PIRATES

later the enemy hesitated and then fled for their lives. Although the difference in the strength of the two forces was so great, yet the result of the encounter was instant and unmistakable. All that the English had now to do was to walk into the battery from behind and burn the village. This, together with the blowing up of three junks, was readily accomplished.

So the Englishmen returned aboard their gunboat, and just then they espied a whole fleet of junks steering into the creek. The gunboat's Chinese interpreter assured himself that these were pirates, so another engagement was imminent. But in a short time it was found that they were the opposite of pirates: in fact, these junks belonged to a certain mandarin who assured the gunboat's commander that he would not have dared to have come into the channel had he not seen the British gunboat there lying. For the mandarin had been living in terror of these corsairs. However, the gunboat was in a hurry, and had no more time to waste over these pirates, so, handing over the junks to the mandarin and leaving the devastated town in the latter's charge, the man-of-war got up her anchor and made for Macao.

After leaving Macao the gunboat steamed some miles to the west and then turned sharply to the right, thus approaching the mainland, which was separated from the chain of islands by a dozen miles of shallow, muddy water. As she was proceeding, the gunboat grounded, the time being about low-water, and no further advance could be made. Heavy clouds were coming up, and presently dirty weather set in. The water became lashed into a nasty short sea, and the wind increased in violence. At this moment, from amidst the heavy, driving rain, there emerged a junk tearing before the breeze with her great sails boomed out.

CRUISING AMONG CHINESE PIRATES

Here was a stroke of ill-luck, to have this pirate coming out just as the gunboat was immovable and unable to work her guns freely. However, the best had to be made of a bad job. So a big shot was pitched across the bows of the hurrying junk, which she ignored. In another minute the big gun would not be able to bear on her, and she would have dashed past and would have been able to rake with her guns the helpless gunboat stranded in the mud. It was now or never, and the order to fire into her had just been given, but before the trigger had been pulled, down came the great sail of the junk, and in a very few minutes she had rounded-to and anchored close to the man-of-war. Just then, too, the tide had risen a little, so that the gunboat was able to float off and dropped astern into deeper water. The junk was then boarded and found to contain forty-three men. These, in small parties, were now sent aboard the gunboat and secured for the night. The next day the gunboat and her junk arrived at the nearest mandarin station, where both junk and crew were handed over. She was found to be a pirate very heavily armed, and was the identical craft against which the gunboat had been sent out. With her eight big cannon she was capable of doing any damage she liked against a merchant ship. In fact, she was so big a craft that she made the gunboat look quite small when alongside her.

The 'sixties and 'seventies, which have been selected for our narrative to afford characteristic episodes of Chinese piracy, were the very climax of the sea-robberies by which those waters became so notorious. Hong-Kong itself was a veritable hotbed of piracy. Here resided the headmen of the pirate gangs, and in this selfsame harbour pirate junks had the audacity and impudence to anchor even close to a British gunboat whose mission it was to exterminate

CRUISING AMONG CHINESE PIRATES

this class of nuisance. A favourite practice was for a pirate to wait in harbour till he saw another merchant junk getting under way bound for a coasting voyage. The pirate would then get his anchor up also and follow the other junk round the first headland, when he would attack her, board her and rob her, with or without murder, as suited his convenience. But this evil practice was largely overcome by the introduction of a system of compulsory registration, which caused the junks to be numbered. And, additional to this, the Chinamen were prevented from entering Hong-Kong without a passport.

And let us now close this story of pirates with the narrative of an incident which showed yet again that the white man was more than a match for the cunning and often cowardly Mongolian. Information had been received from some fishermen that three large junks were anchored in a snug bay six miles away. The gunboat's commander was well aware that the pirates scented his coming, and they did not fail to realise that the exceedingly narrow and shallow entrance was quite unsuitable for the gunboat. However, there were other means for attaining the same object, and this is what happened. The man-of-war was taken as near as she could safely float to the rocky shore. Then Captain St. John, with seven men, quietly left his ship and rowed ashore, the gunboat having orders now to steam on and appear off the entrance to the bay as close as practicable, and to send another boat to the assistance of the eight when the gunboat should reach her position.

Captain St. John and his seven men had barely three hundred yards of bushes and grass to traverse before the low ridge overlooking the bay was reached. Then it was found that they were within a hundred yards of the spot where the junks lay below them. These craft were clearly

CRUISING AMONG CHINESE PIRATES

aground in the middle of the bay and broadside on to the entrance. Two of them were very fine vessels, mounting ten guns, though the third was smaller. There were about twenty men in each, and, at any rate, the enemy numbered about ten to one of the naval men. The Chinese had expected that the English would row round the point, and so the wily Orientals had trained their guns, ready loaded, straight for the entrance, and it had never occurred to them that their enemy would make an overland attack.

Now, lying hauled out of water on the beach in front of the houses was a sampan, and when the party of seven got down to the beach, three of them launched this sampan and pushed off to the junks, while the rest were on the beach. These tactics so surprised the Chinamen that they jumped and tumbled into their boats alongside the junks and some of them fell spluttering into the water. One of the boats from the gunboat now came on to assist, and the pirate craft were quickly taken possession of. The junks were destroyed, some of the pirates were killed, while the rest of them fled into the bushes. Thus, with a little force and much sound judgment and daring, another nest of pirates had been got rid of to the further benefit of mankind.

And so we bring our story of the rise and growth of piracy to an end. Within the number of pages here afforded it has been impossible to do more than indicate both the historic outline of the subject and to illustrate this with real-actual events of the most interesting character. A complete history of piracy will never be written. Such a task would be impossible, for the reason that all records of many of the most notorious pirates perished with themselves. In the lives of even those of whom we have certain knowledge there are gaps about

CRUISING AMONG CHINESE PIRATES

which history is silent. Perhaps those were the periods when they were enjoying their ill-gotten gains on land: perhaps in those times they were engaged in still more daring sorts of piracy. We cannot tell. But one thing I believe to be certain, and in this any reader who has perused this volume will, I trust, agree with me. However charming and romantic a story the novelist may weave for us concerning these bold sea-robbers and pillagers, yet it is not necessary to overstep the limits of actual occurrence in order to demonstrate at once the daring, the ingenuity and the undoubtedly clever seamanship of these lawless wanderers and enemies of the human race.

FINIS

Printed by MORRISON & GIBB LIMITED, *Edinburgh*

INDEX

----, Antonio 166-167 Black
  Beard 155-161 Old Treky
  113 Seraphina 249 264-267
  275 279
ACKERMANN, Karen 23
ADMIRALTY, First Lord of The
  164
ALGIERS, Governor of 60
  Sultan of 62-63 66
ALLEN, Thomas 108
ALVES, Peter 39
ANTONIUS, M 24
AP, Fen Hugh 35
ARMSTRONG, 193-194
ATWELL, 213
AUSTRIA, John of 74-75
AVERY, 175-182 Capt 174
BARBAROSSA, 56-60 62-63 65-
  68 71 75 151
BARBAZAN, 285-286 288
BARBE, Nicholas 43
BASHA, Ali 72 74-76
BEACH, Capt 218
BELL, Mayor 39
BELLOMON, Earl of 163
BELLOMONT, 164 166 169
  Lord 163
BEME, Francis 47
BERE, Sulivan 85
BERMUDAS, Governor of 157
  160
BLAKE, 106-107
BODENHAM, 88 Roger 87

BOLTON, 169-170
BONNET, Major 152 154
BOWEN, 40
BRODELY, Capt 147
BROOKE, Charles 295 James
  295-296 Rajah 302
BROWN, Admiral 212
BROWNE, John 133
BUJEYA, Corsair of 58 King of
  56
BURDON, Capt 201
BURGESS, Lt 220 Mr 220
BURGHLEY, Lord 86
CAESAR, 26 Julius 24 27
CALLES, 85-86 John 84
CALLFATER, Admiral 116
CALLIS, John 84
CAREW, Peter 79
CARRUTHERS, Lt 226
CAT, Gervase 34
CHADERTON, John 45
CHANCELLOR, Lord 164
CHANDLER, Henry 119-120
  133
CHARLES II, King of England
  114 149
CHARLES V, 54 63 223
  Emperor 64-67 71 74
CHURCH, 213
CICERO, 26 30
CLARKE, Richard 133
CLINTON, 84
COHEN, Hyman 279

COOK, George 133
COOKE, 270 Capt 272
CORBET, 82-83
CORK, Mayor of 39
CORNELYS, 44
COWPER, 241-242 244 Capt 238
CROMWELL, 45 47 106
DANSKER, 102 113
DAVIES, 120-121
DAVIS, 132 183-184
DAVY, 44 Henry 43 45
DAWES, 213-215
DEIGLE, 83 Richard 82
DELIZUFF, 62
DEMELTON, 38
DESOTO, 282-283 285-291 Benito 281
DOREA, 72
DORIA, Andrea 57 62 64-68 70-71 74-75 223 John Andrea 74
DOVER, Mayor of 81
DRAGUT, 70-72 74-75
DRAKE, 101 122 137
DROMYOWE, Peter 41
DULAERQUERAC John 40-41
DUQUESNE, 115 218 Adm 217
DUDLEY, 43 John 41-42 Thomas 41-42
DUNTON, 136
EASTON, 102
EDWARD, 36
EDWARD II, King of England 31
ELIZABETH, Queen of England 20 54 78-84 87 101 103-104 135 281
ENGLAND, Chancellor of 32 King of 163
ESPINOSA, Alonso Del Campo Y 144-146 149
EXMOUTH, Lord 21 219-223
FARQUHAR, Arthur 295
FERDINAND, King of Spain 27 52 57

FILLIE, David 105
FITZMORRIS, James 85
FLEMING, 84
FOSTER, Thomas 105
FOXE, 93 95 97-100 John 90 92 94
FRANCE, King of 85
FRANCIS I, King of France 37 63
GENNINGS, 102
GIBBS, 212 214 Charles 210-211 213 215
GIBSON, 176-177 182 Capt 175
GILLARD, Hayman 43
GODEKINS, 34
GOODALE, 120-121 John 118 133
GOWLLYS, Richard 39
GRAHAM, Lt 229
GRAND, Turk 54
GRENEBURY, 44
GROVE, 90
HAKLUYT, 100
HALL, Lt 231
HANDS, Israel 156 161
HAQUINUS, King of Norway 31
HARMAN, 111-112
HARRIS, 102
HASSAN, Muley 65 72
HAVANNAH, Governor of 274
HAWKYNS, 281
HAYES, Capt 279
HEARN, Capt 272
HEIDON, 83 Capt 82
HENRY III King of England 31
HENRY IV, King of England 32 35
HENRY VIII, King of England 37-38 41 45-46
HERBART, Walter 45
HERBERT, Admiral 115 Capt 109
HITCHINS, Robert 82-83
HORNOGOLD, Benjamin 152

HORUSE, Richard 33
HYLL, Rowland 45
IBRAHIM, Ameer 231-232
ISABELLA, Queen of Spain 27 52
JAMAICA, Governor-General of 139 Lt-Gov 149
JAMES I, King of England 102 127
JONES, 199 201 Paul 196-197 200 202 205 207-209
JULIUS, Ii Pope 55
KELLWANTON, 38
KEPPEL, Henry 295
KHEYR-ED-DIN, 54 57 60-62 68 70-71 74
KIDD, 162-165 167-170 Capt 171
KNIGHT, Sophia 279
LABUAN, Bishop of 302
LAUGHTON, John 137
LAWRENCE, Capt 210-211
LEVERET, 45
LISLE, Viscount 38
LIVINGSTONE, Robert 164
LLOYDS, 301
LOCK, Mr 45
LOUIS, King of France 217
LUMSDEN, 236-242 244-247 263-264 268 274 278 Mr 243
LUSINGHAM, 83
LYLLYK, 44-45
MACDONELL, Miss 219 Mrs 219
MANSELL, Robert 118
MANSFIELD, 140 Edward 139
MARTINIQUE, Governor of 188
MAY, Lt 155
MAYNARD, 158-161 Lt 157
MIDDLE, Barbary Sultan of 58
MILNE, David 219 Rear-Admiral 222
MODYFORD, 140 142 149 Thomas 139

MOLLONER, Capt 85
MOORE, 168 170
MORGAN, 140-150 Edward 138 Henry 136-139 183
NARBOROUGH, John 115
NELSON, 97
NORTH CAROLINA, Governor of 154
O'SULLIVAN, Lord 83
ODENBURG, Grave of 47
PAINE, 278
PARKER, 166-167
PAUL, John 196-197
PEARSON, 203 Capt 202 207 R 206
PHELIPP, William 39
PHILIP, King of Spain 79-80 82
PIERCE, Lt 112
PIERCY, 207 Capt 206 Thos 203
PIN, Lt 112
POOLE, Stanley Lane 55
PRUSSIA, King of 32 Master-General of 32
PURSSER, 84
RAWLINS, 117-118 120-121 126-131 133-136 John 116 122 125 132
READHEAD, Philip 82
RICHARD II, King of England 32
RICHARDS, 153
RIGWEYS, Robert 35
RISE, Rammetham 119-121 Villa 116-118 121 133
ROBERTS, 184-195 Bartholomew 183
ROE, 120 132
ROGERS, Capt 187
ROREBEK, 33
RUSSIA, Empress of 208
SAINT CHRYOGON, Hadrian Cardinal 48
SAINT JOHN, Capt 307 309-312 315 H C 304

SALTER, Mr 226
SANDERS, Thomas 103
SARAWAK, Rajah of 295
SCARLET, 45 William 44
SELKIRK, Lady 199-200 209
    Lord 196 199-200
SHASTER, Roger 82
SHOVELL, Cloudesly 115
SMITH, 101-102 235 237-238
    240-243 246-247 249 251-
    257 259-263 265-278 Aaron
    236 248 250 279 John 84 279
SOLIMAN, The Magnificent 66
SOLYMAN, The Magnificent 62
SPAIN, King of 99
SPRAGGE, 109 111-113 Edward
    108
STANHOPE, Michael 207
STERTEBEKER, 34
STEVENSON, Robert Louis 235
STROMEDA, 264-265 268
STURGES, Capt 85
TALBOT, James 214
TEACH, 152-157 159-160 Blackbeard 151 Edward 151
TERRY, William 33
THOMPSON, 102
THORNBY, Capt 215 William
    212
TORRINGTON, Earl of 109
TRIPOLI, Sultan of 103
TUNIS, Sultan of 55 72
TURKEY, Sultan of 62 71-72 74

UNTICARO, 94-95 Peter 93
URUJ, 54-56 70 Red-beard 151
VANCAPPILLEN, Admiral 219
VANMEGHLYN, Hans 47
VAUGHAN, 47
VIRGINIA, Governor of 155
WALSYNGHAM, 84-85
WANSLEY, 215-216
WARD, 102
WARYN, Ralph 45
WHITEMAN, Lt 207
WILLIAM, The Conqueror 29
WILLIAMS, Capt 277-278
WINTER, William 133
WOLSEY, 48
WRIGHT, 168
WYNTER, John 40
YORK, Joseph 207
YORKE, Joseph 206

www.ingramcontent.com/pod-product-compliance
Lightning Source LLC
Chambersburg PA
CBHW060551230426
43670CB00011B/1783